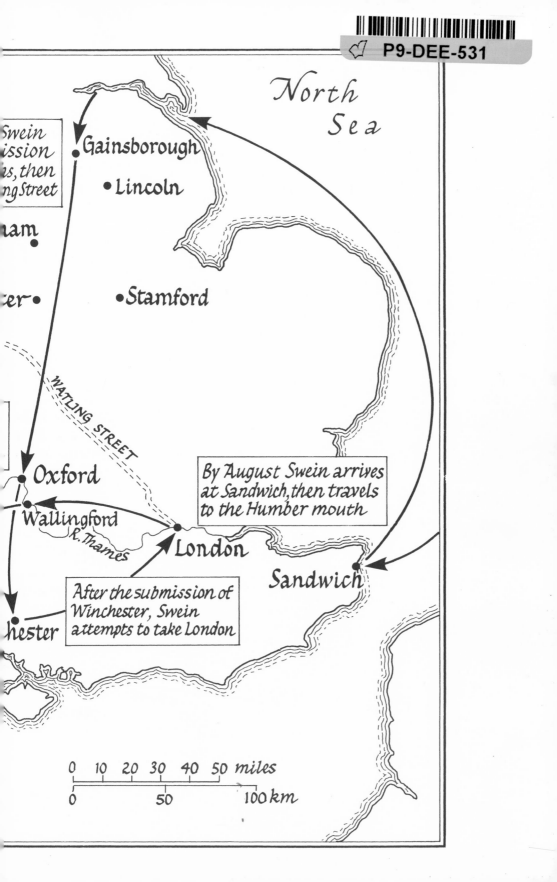

North Sea

● Gainsborough

● Lincoln

● Stamford

WATLING STREET

● Oxford

● Wallingford
R. Thames

● London

By August Swein arrives at Sandwich, then travels to the Humber mouth

Sandwich

After the submission of Winchester, Swein attempts to take London

...hester

Swein ...ission ...s, then ...g Street

...am ●

...er ●

0   10   20   30   40   50 *miles*

0   50   *100 km*

QUEEN EMMA
AND THE VIKINGS

QUEEN EMMA AND THE VIKINGS

A History of Power, Love and Greed in Eleventh-Century England

HARRIET O'BRIEN

BLOOMSBURY

To my sister, Sally

Published by Bloomsbury Publishing, New York and London
Distributed to the trade by Holtzbrinck Publishers

All papers used by Bloomsbury Publishing are natural, recyclable
products made from wood grown in well-managed forests.
The manufacturing processes conform to the environmental
regulations of the country of origin.

Cataloging-in-Publication Data
is available from the Library of Congress.

ISBN 1 58234 596 1
ISBN 13 978 1 58234 596 3

First U.S. Edition 2005

1 3 5 7 9 10 8 6 4 2

Typeset by Palimpsest Book Production Limited, Polmont, Stirlingshire, Scotland

Printed in the United States of America by Quebecor World Fairfield

CONTENTS

Family Trees
EMMA AND HER NORMAN FAMILY

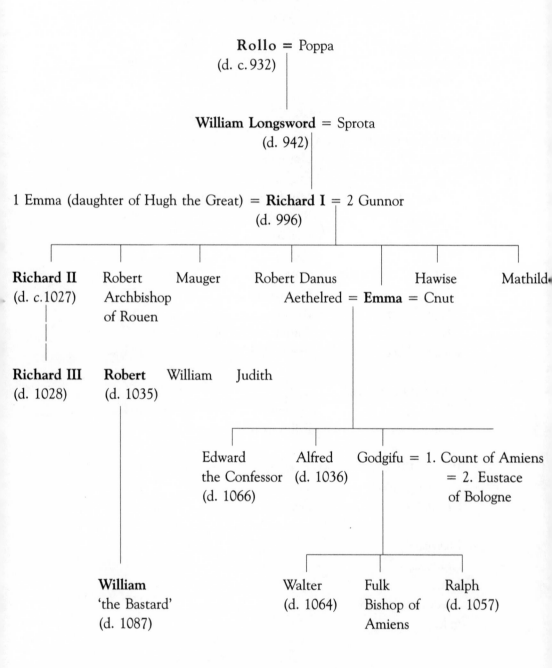

Rollo = Poppa
(d. c.932)

William Longsword = Sprota
(d. 942)

1 Emma (daughter of Hugh the Great) = **Richard I** = 2 Gunnor
(d. 996)

Richard II   Robert   Mauger   Robert Danus   Hawise   Mathild
(d. c.1027)   Archbishop   Aethelred = **Emma** = Cnut
         of Rouen

Richard III   **Robert**   William   Judith
(d. 1028)   (d. 1035)

Edward   Alfred   Godgifu = 1. Count of Amiens
the Confessor   (d. 1036)   = 2. Eustace
(d. 1066)   of Bologne

William   Walter   Fulk   Ralph
'the Bastard'   (d. 1064)   Bishop of   (d. 1057)
(d. 1087)   Amiens

EMMA AND THE ANGLO-SAXON ROYALS
(from the West Saxon line of Cerdic, Alfred the Great to Edward the Confessor)

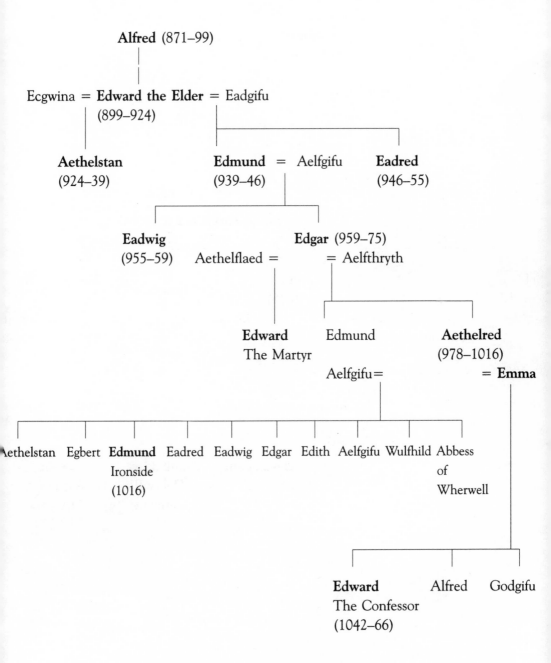

Alfred (871–99)

Ecgwina = **Edward the Elder** = Eadgifu
              (899–924)

Aethelstan   **Edmund** = Aelfgifu   **Eadred**
(924–39)   (939–46)   (946–55)

Eadwig   **Edgar** (959–75)
(955–59) Aethelflaed =   = Aelfthryth

Edward   Edmund   **Aethelred**
The Martyr   (978–1016)
             Aelfgifu=   = **Emma**

Aethelstan Egbert **Edmund** Eadred Eadwig Edgar Edith Aelfgifu Wulfhild Abbess
                   Ironside   of
                   (1016)   Wherwell

Edward   Alfred   Godgifu
The Confessor
(1042–66)

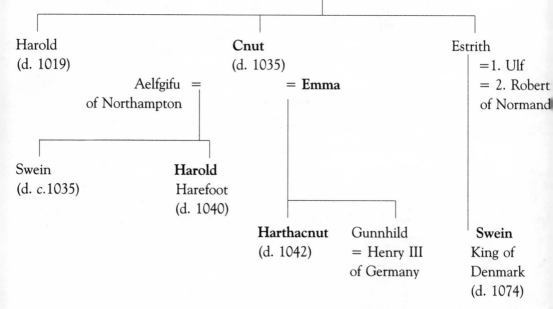

Gorm the Old = Thyri
(d. 959)

Harold Blue Tooth (d. 988)

Swein Forkbeard (d. 1014)

Harold
(d. 1019)

Aelfgifu =
of Northampton

Cnut
(d. 1035)

= Emma

Estrith
=1. Ulf
= 2. Robert
of Normand

Swein
(d. *c.*1035)

Harold
Harefoot
(d. 1040)

Harthacnut
(d. 1042)

Gunnhild
= Henry III
of Germany

Swein
King of
Denmark
(d. 1074)

Dramatis Personae

NORMANS

Emma

Daughter of Richard I of Normandy and his Danish mistress Gunnor. She married Aethelred II of England in 1002, was widowed in 1016 and subsequently married the Viking invader of England, Cnut, in 1017. With Aethelred she had three children: Edward, who became King of England in 1042, Alfred, who was murdered in 1036, and Godgifu. She had two further children with Cnut: Harthacnut, King of England 1040–2, and Gunnhild.

Gunnor

Emma's mother. Most, if not all, of Gunnor's children were born while she was the mistress of Richard I of Normandy; however, the couple later married so that their offspring could become the legitimate heirs to the principality. Gunnor is known to have been an important figure at the court of her son Richard II and is celebrated in the satirical poem *Moriuht* by Warner of Rouen.

Richard I

Emma's father. Richard I was the chieftain of Normandy from 942 until his death in 996. He aided and abetted the Vikings who were ravaging England in the 980s and 990s and despite the attempts of Pope John XV to broker a peace treaty between the Norman and English rulers he continued to support the Scandinavian pirates.

Richard II

Brother of Emma. Richard II was Count, or Duke, of Normandy from 996–c.1027. Through the marriage of his sister Emma, he formed an alliance with King Aethelred II of England but was quick to offer support to the Danish Viking Swein Forkbeard when he invaded the Anglo-Saxon kingdom in 1013. At the same time, however, Richard provided sanctuary for the exiled English king. He later gave refuge to Emma's children by Aethelred – Edward, Alfred and Godgifu – when they fled England during Cnut's attacks.

Richard III

Nephew of Emma. The son of Richard II was not a popular man: he was Count, or Duke, of Normandy for about a year before being poisoned.

Robert I (The Magnificent)

Nephew of Emma. Robert became Duke of Normandy on the death of his brother, Richard III. It was probably at Emma's instigation that he married Cnut's sister Estrith, whom he then swiftly divorced. He continued to provide refuge for his English cousins, Emma's sons Edward and Alfred, and in 1033 is thought to have attempted to invade England on their behalf. He died in 1035 on pilgrimage to Jerusalem, having named his young and illegitimate son William as his heir.

Robert, Archbishop of Rouen

Brother of Emma. He may have been close to his sister: the chronicler Orderic Vitalis records that from England Emma sent Robert a large and lavishly decorated psalter. A surviving book believed to have belonged to him contains two satirical poems – Moriuht, in which his mother Gunnor is represented, and Semiramis, which castigates Emma's marriage to Cnut.

Rollo

Emma's great-grandfather. Rollo the Viking left Denmark in the 870s and having plundered England and Holland landed in northern France.

By 911 the French king Charles the Simple ceded him land there as a means of keeping him under control. The territory of the North men was subsequently known as Normandy.

William Longsword

Emma's grandfather. The son of Rollo, William inherited his father's province and in 942 came to a premature end when he was murdered by Arnulf of Flanders.

William ('The Bastard')

Emma's great-nephew. William may have met his great-aunt on a visit to England in 1051. He famously conquered the Anglo-Saxon kingdom in 1066.

ANGLO-SAXONS

Aelfgifu

Emma's predecessor as wife of Aethelred 'The Unready'. Other than the fact that she was the daughter of a nobleman very little is known about her. She is thought to have died before Aethelred married Emma, but he may simply have divorced her. Aelfgifu is believed to have been the mother of at least ten children with Aethelred although it is possible that some of these offspring were produced by yet another wife.

Aelfgifu of Northampton

Emma's great rival. Aelfgifu was the first wife of Cnut – who did not divorce her when he later married Emma. In the 1030s Cnut appointed Aelfgifu regent of Norway with their son Swein but by 1035 she was ousted from the country by Magnus the Good. She returned to England where she outmanoeuvred Emma with her schemes to ensure that her second son, Harold Harefoot, became king.

Aelfheah

Archbishop of Canterbury 1006–12. He was captured by Vikings in 1011, held prisoner at Southwark and executed during a drunken feast on 19 April 1012. He subsequently became a saint. Until at least the mid-thirteenth century his tomb at Canterbury was one of the country's biggest pilgrimage sites.

Aelfhelm

Ealdorman of southern Northumbria and father of Cnut's first wife, Aelfgifu of Northampton. Aelfhelm was one of the most trusted advisers of Aethelred The Unready but he fell victim to court intrigues and in 1006 was murdered. His death gave rise to the rapid promotion of the nefarious nobleman, Eadric Streona.

Aelfric

Archbishop of Canterbury 995–1005. He presided over the wedding of Emma and Aethelred.

Aelfthryth

Mother of Aethelred The Unready. Allegedly, Aelfthryth plotted the murder of her young stepson King Edward (The Martyr) so that her own child, Aethelred, could claim the throne. She was an extremely forceful figure at court in the early years of his reign.

Aethelnoth

Archbishop of Canterbury 1020–38. Aethelnoth was appointed to this senior office in a sort of double act by Emma and Cnut. After Cnut's death he showed some support for Emma by refusing to crown Harold Harefoot, son of her rival Aelfgifu of Northampton.

Aethelred

Emma's first husband and King of England 978–1016. Later nicknamed *Unraed* (bad counsel) which became transliterated into 'Unready', Aethelred acquired a reputation for disastrous incompetence. The thirty-eight years of his reign were dominated by Viking attacks: unable to defend the country, he levied high taxes in order to pay off the marauders. In 1013 he was driven into exile by the Danish chieftain Swein Forkbeard. However, the following year he was invited back as monarch of England. He died less than two years later, his kingdom once again under Viking invasion.

Eadric Streona

Ealdorman of Mercia. Nicknamed *Streona*, or 'the acquisitor', because of his purported appropriation of church land, Eadric came to power under Aethelred. He became notorious for his double dealings between the Anglo-Saxon nobles and the invading Danes. When Cnut became King of England he initially reconfirmed Eadric's position but then ordered his execution.

Edgar

Grandson of Edmund Ironside. He was born as an exile at the royal Hungarian court and as a young boy invited back to England with the rest of his family by Edward the Confessor. There he was evidently treated as the monarch's potential heir, but he did not become king when Edward died. After the Battle of Hastings in 1066 he fled to Scotland.

Edith (or Eadgyth)

Daughter of Earl Godwine and wife of Edward the Confessor. Educated at the convent of Wilton, Edith could both read and write – probably unlike her future husband. She married Edward, about fifteen years her senior, three years after he became King of England. The marriage did not produce any children, a factor that was later ascribed to Edward's godliness. After her husband's death she commissioned a book, *The Life of King Edward* (Vitae Aedwardi), which helped to establish Edward's reputation as a saintly figure.

Edmund Ironside

Son of Aethelred The Unready and (probably) his first wife Aelfgifu. He valiantly defended England from the Vikings, for which he appears to have been much admired by Cnut. In 1016 he agreed to divide England with Cnut but was murdered that year, probably on the orders of Eadric Streona.

Edward

Son of Edmund Ironside. An infant when Cnut became King of England, Edward was spirited out of the country and given refuge at the court of Hungary. There he married and produced three children. In 1057 he returned to England on the invitation of Edward the Confessor, but died on arrival.

Edward (The Confessor)

Son of Emma and Aethelred The Unready and King of England 1042–66. During Cnut's invasion of England, Edward fled to his relatives in Normandy. He remained an adjunct at the court there until he was well into his thirties. In 1042 he was invited back to England by his half-brother, Harthacnut, who died later that year. Edward then became king – and stripped his mother of her wealth and power.

Edward (The Martyr)

Half-brother of Aethelred The Unready and King of England 975–8. The Viking attacks at the end of the tenth century were regarded by many Anglo-Saxons as divine retribution for the murder of their boy king on 18 March 978. More than twenty years later King Aethelred formally pronounced his half-brother a saint. Edward's tomb at Shaftesbury remained a significant pilgrimage site until at least the fifteenth century.

Godgifu

Daughter of Emma and Aethelred The Unready. Godgifu spent much of her childhood as an exile at the court of her uncle Richard II of Normandy. From there she married the Count of Amiens, with whom she produced three sons. At least one of them, Ralf, was to be favoured by his uncle King Edward the Confessor. By 1036 Godgifu had been widowed and remarried. Her second husband was Eustace of Boulogne.

Godgifu

Wife of Earl Leofric. A powerful and wealthy woman, Godgifu is said to have lobbied her husband over high taxes demanded of the people of Coventry. This gave rise to the legend of Lady 'Godiva', in which Godgifu rides naked through the town on the understanding that the tolls will then be rescinded. She outlived her husband by a number of years and is thought to have died in at least her sixties, after the Norman Conquest.

Godwine

Earl of Wessex and one of Cnut's most trusted courtiers. He was married to Cnut's sister-in-law, Gytha, with whom he produced at least nine children. Among them were Edith, who married Edward the Confessor, and Harold, who became King of England. Godwine was probably Cnut's most significant adviser and after his death continued to exercise enormous power. He allegedly masterminded the murder of Emma's son Alfred but retained a very prominent position at court under both King Harthacnut and King Edward The Confessor. Although Edward banished Godwine and his family in 1051, the Earl was reinstated within twelve months. He died the following year.

Harold Godwineson

Son of Earl Godwine, brother-in-law of Edward The Confessor and King of England in 1066. Although banished by King Edward in 1051, Harold later became quasi-regent of England – and amassed a fortune. On Edward's deathbed he was declared king but his reign lasted less than a year: he was killed during the Battle of Hastings.

Leofric

Earl of Mercia and one of Cnut's most trusted courtiers. He came to power under Cnut and on his death supported Harold Harefoot rather than Emma's son Harthacnut in the rival bids for the throne of England. However, he retained a prominent position at court when Harthacnut finally became king and continued to exercise great influence after Edward the Confessor's coronation. He died in 1057.

Lyfing

Archbishop of Canterbury 1013–20. In 1017 he probably presided over the coronation of Cnut. Charter evidence suggests that Emma and Cnut were anxious to win his approval and support.

Ordulf

Uncle of Aethelred The Unready and a prominent adviser to the King. His retirement before 1006 is thought to have precipitated a spiral of decline in Aethelred's reign.

Siward

Earl of Northumbria and one of Cnut's most trusted advisers. He continued to wield a great deal of power at the courts of Harold Harefoot, Harthacnut and Edward the Confessor.

Stigand

Emma's priest, later Archbishop of Canterbury. Emma was probably behind Stigand's promotion to Bishop of Elmham in 1043. However, the same year both she and her former priest were stripped of their respective positions by Edward The Confessor. Both, though, were subsequently reinstated. Stigand then became ever more powerful: he was appointed Bishop of Winchester in 1047 and in 1052 was made Archbishop of Canterbury (while still holding his Winchester see). He was deposed, after the Norman Conquest, in 1070. It is as Archbishop that he is depicted in the Bayeux Tapestry.

Uhtred

Ealdorman of Northumbria. Although his third wife was Aelfgifu, daughter of Aethelred The Unready, Uhtred showed wavering support for the King and in 1013 submitted to the Danish invader Swein Forkbeard. He appears subsequently to have backed the cause of Aethelred's son, Edmund Ironside, but in 1016 was forced to surrender to Cnut. However, just before his formal submission he was ambushed and killed, prompting a bloodfeud that lasted sixty years.

Wulfstan

Archbishop of York 1002–16. Moralist and statesman, Wulfstan exercised enormous influence over both Aethelred and Cnut, and wrote the law codes of these two kings.

SCANDINAVIANS

Cnut

Emma's second husband and King of England 1016–35. He accompanied his father, the Danish chieftain Swein Forkbeard, when he invaded and conquered England in 1013. After Swein's death the following year Cnut returned to Denmark, mustered a strong force and attacked England again. During 1016 most of the Anglo-Saxon nobility surrendered to him, and he agreed to split the country with Edmund Ironside. Aged nineteen, Cnut became full King of England later that year when Edmund was murdered. He then demanded Emma as his wife – a type of Scandinavian marriage by seizure. Emma, though, guided Cnut into presenting himself as a model Christian king: he was a great patron of the Church and in 1027 he visited Rome. For Cnut, England was the base of a Scandinavian empire: on his brother Harold's death in 1019 he became King of Denmark; and in 1028 King of Norway as well. He died suddenly in 1035 without naming his successor and in the ensuing confusion his empire crumbled.

Eric of Hlathir

Chieftain of Norway and Viking supporter of Swein Forkbeard and Cnut. He is said to have accompanied Swein during his final invasion of England and he later fought alongside Cnut. For this he was rewarded with the earldom of Northumbria in 1016. He disappears from English court records after 1023 – according to Norse sources he died from loss of blood following an operation.

Estrith

Cnut's sister. She was the wife of Ulf, whom Cnut appointed regent of Denmark after 1019 and with whom she had one son, Swein. When Ulf was murdered on the orders of Cnut she was married on to Emma's nephew, Duke Robert I of Normandy – who rapidly divorced her.

Gorm the Old

Cnut's great-grandfather. He is credited with being the founder of Denmark as a nation, probably in the 930s.

Gunnhild

Daughter of Cnut and Emma. It was probably during Cnut's visit to Rome in 1027 that he betrothed Gunnhild to Henry, son of the German emperor Conrad II. The wedding took place, after Cnut's death, in 1036. However, Gunnhild's marriage to Henry III did not last and she is thought to have retreated to a convent.

Gunnhild

Sister of Swein Forkbeard and wife of the Viking commander, Pallig. Gunnhild evidently accompanied her husband during his raids on England in the 990s. In 1001 she and Pallig were captured by the Anglo-Saxons and held hostage. They were both executed a year later during the Massacre of the Danes, prompting ferocious retaliation from Swein Forkbeard.

Hakon

Son of Eric of Hlathir and one of Cnut's foremost Scandinavian commanders. When Cnut took over Norway in 1028, Hakon was appointed regent of the country. However, he drowned a year later on a visit to England.

Harold

Cnut's brother. On Swein Forkbeard's death in 1014, Harold became King of Denmark. He refused to divide the kingdom with Cnut but supplied him with troops to reconquer England. He died childless in 1019 whereupon Cnut claimed the Danish throne.

Harold Blue Tooth

Cnut's grandfather and King of Denmark c.935–85. The inscription on a runestone Harold erected for his father, Gorm, at Jelling claims that he 'made the Danes Christian'. He died having been wounded in battle against his son, Swein Forkbeard.

Harold Hardrada

Uncle of Magnus the Good and King of Norway 1047–66. In 1066

Harold, accompanied by Harold Godwineson's brother Tostig, invaded England but died during the Battle of Stamford Bridge.

Harold Harefoot

Son of Cnut and Aelfgifu of Northampton and King of England 1037–40. Emma was forced into exile a second time when, amid much scheming, Harold Harefoot succeeded his father Cnut as king. Very little is known about the three years of his reign.

Harthacnut

Son of Cnut and Emma, King of Denmark 1035–42 and King of England 1040–2. As a young boy he was sent from England to Denmark, where he became regent. Detained by warfare with Magnus the Good of Norway, Harthacnut did not return to England on the death of Cnut in 1035, an oversight that resulted in the English crown passing to his half-brother Harold Harefoot. Visiting his exiled mother, Emma, in Bruges, he planned an invasion of England but this was pre-empted by Harold's death, when he was invited to become the next king. However, due to high taxation, he was not a popular monarch. He died in his early twenties while drinking at the wedding feast of an Anglo-Danish aristocrat, Tofi the Proud.

Magnus the Good

King of Norway c.1035–47. The son of Olaf Haroldson, Magnus became the focus of nationalist Norwegian feeling when his father was declared a saint. Before Cnut died in 1035, he had succeeded in driving out the empire-builder's regents, Swein and Aelfgifu of Northampton. He remained extremely aggressive to Cnut's heirs and is also thought to have planned an invasion of England during the reign of Edward the Confessor.

Olaf Haroldson (or Olaf The Stout)

King of Norway 1015–28. As a mercenary Viking leader, Olaf served Aethelred The Unready and in 1014 helped him return to England from exile in Normandy. Olaf subsequently went back to his native

Norway, where he was accepted as king. When Cnut became the monarch of Denmark as well as England, Olaf refused to accept him as overlord. Cnut, though, enticed the Norwegians to rebel against their king and Olaf was driven out in 1028. Two years later he attempted to return to Norway but was killed by his own people. It was largely because of the unpopularity of Cnut's regents in Norway (his son Swein and first wife Aelfgifu of Northampton) that Olaf was later declared a saint.

Olaf Tryggvason

Viking leader. A Norwegian warrior, Olaf Tryggvason attacked Aethelred's England during the early 990s. However, in 994 he came to an understanding with the Anglo-Saxon king, converted to Christianity and swore to leave England in peace. He returned to Norway, where he became king and was killed in battle some five years later.

Pallig

Viking leader and brother-in-law of Swein Forkbeard. Pallig was among the many Vikings who looted Aethelred's England. Captured by the Anglo-Saxons, he and his wife Gunnhild were executed in 1002 during the Massacre of the Danes.

Swein

Son of Cnut and Aelfgifu of Northampton. After Cnut was accepted as King of Norway in 1028 he appointed Swein and his mother as regents there. They made themselves extremely unpopular and were ousted by Magnus the Good. Swein is thought to have died in Denmark in 1035.

Swein Estrithson

Son of Cnut's sister Estrith and King of Denmark 1047–74. When Emma's son, Harthacnut, died in 1042 many regarded Swein as his cousin's natural heir to the thrones of both Denmark and England. Having battled with Magnus the Good, he was accepted as the Danish king five years later, but in the meantime the crown of England was accorded to another of Emma's sons, Edward The Confessor.

Swein Forkbeard

Cnut's father. King of Denmark, Swein Forkbeard conquered England in 1013, forcing Aethelred The Unready and Emma into exile in Normandy. He was murdered the following year – according to some Anglo-Saxon chroniclers, he met his death at the hand of St Edmund.

Thorkell the Tall

Viking leader. A ferocious warlord, Thorkell served Swein Forkbeard and attacked England in the early 1000s. But on the execution of Aelfheah, Archbishop of Canterbury, in 1012 he defected to King Aethelred The Unready and later accompanied him into exile in Normandy. After Swein's death he switched sides again and fought for Cnut when he invaded – and conquered – England in 1016. Thorkell was rewarded for his efforts with the earldom of East Anglia. However, Cnut banished him from England in 1021. By 1023 he appears to have reached a *rapprochement* with Cnut and to have been appointed co-regent of Denmark, but he soon disappears from surviving records.

Ulf

Cnut's brother-in-law. When Cnut became King of Denmark in 1019, Ulf was appointed regent and also guardian of the heir apparent, Emma's son Harthacnut. After the Danes were defeated by the Swedes and Norwegians at the Battle of Holy River in 1023, Ulf was murdered in the church at Roskilde by order of Cnut.

Prologue

She looks a little peevish, although this would not have been the intention of the artist. Doubtless he was trying to emphasise the solemnity of the occasion – and the commanding nature of his patron. He shows her centre-stage, dominating the scene that she shares with three other figures who lurk subserviently to her left. The artist's patron is depicted wearing a large crown that has been decorated with laurel leaves – more than a hint of classical grandeur. She is seated on a bench-like throne, but an ambitious attempt at perspective gives the impression that the royal seat is a background building with a sloping roof and as a result the lady sits in mid-air, as if levitating a foot or so off the ground. In her hands she holds up an open book that she has turned outwards so as to invite the onlooker to wonder at its contents. Kneeling at her feet is a monk, a tiny tonsure at the crown of his head. Above him, peering around the pillar of an arch that frames the scene, are two young men with fuzzy little beards. They are also crowned. All three men look up deferentially at the seated lady. But she seems impervious to their presence: her eyes are firmly on the book.

The lady in this eleventh-century picture is a remarkable woman called Emma. The drawing depicts her receiving for the first time a book that she has commissioned. The monk is the scribe who wrote it. The young men are two of her sons. Emma lived at the tail end of a period that dismissively became known as the Dark Ages, because it was considered a benighted time of warfare, with a corresponding lack of learning and cultural activity. The paucity of surviving documentary records contributed to this image. In England, conventional history has ignored the era. Yet the so-called Dark Ages was a vast period roughly spanning the departure of the Romans in about 410 to the arrival of the Norman conquerors in 1066. Between these two momentous events were others of equal, if not greater, significance: the migration of the Saxons to England; their conversion to Christianity; the invasions of the Vikings. It was the era of the Anglo-Saxon kings under whom England gradually became a united entity.

Recently, 'Dark Ages' has become an unfashionable term and much of the period has been relabelled 'Early Medieval'. The rehabilitation has much justification. That bulging lump of 650-odd years swept untidily under the carpet is the root of Englishness, the Anglo-Saxon stock. And Queen Emma, at the end of the era, was the formidable catalyst for the country's immutable change into a Norman state.

By birth Emma herself was Norman. But she effectively became the wife, mother and aunt of England. She married, and outlived, two English kings, saw two of her sons crowned and enthroned and was the great-aunt of William the Conqueror. And in 1066, fourteen years after Emma died, this blood connection gave the Norman invader a greater right to the throne of England than the incumbent Harold.

Essentially Emma was at the centre of a triangle of Anglo-Saxons, Vikings and Normans variously jostling for control of the kingdom. (They were respectively victims, very successful chancers, and upstarts.) From political pawn Emma became an unscrupulous manipulator for power, and along the way was diversely regarded by her contemporaries as a generous Christian patron, the admired co-regent of a prosperous nation, and a callous and treacherous mother. She was, above all, a survivor, her life marked by dramatic reversals of fortune, all of which she overcame.

It was after one such fall and rise that Emma appointed a monk to write her book. The book is entirely unusual for the time. It is a political tract – a work of spin – written essentially to support her sons' rights to the crown of England. In itself, it is palpable evidence of Emma's power and cunning. And for all its artful bias, it also gives an enormously valuable account of the world and dramatic times in which she lived. Indeed it is one of the very few records that remain from this period.

The initial manuscript no longer exists. It would have been something of a rough draft from which other, neater versions were made. We do not know how many were produced, but just one survives. This may well have been the presentation manuscript that became Emma's own copy for it carries the picture of the queen with her book, crown, throne, monk and sons as the frontispiece.

Sometime after Emma's death this book became the property of St Augustine's monastery at Canterbury. Records show that it remained there until at least the fifteenth century. It is not known where it was kept during the Reformation or how it survived this period when so many church-held manuscripts were destroyed. Perhaps it was dextrously hidden, or was simply overlooked by the henchmen of Henry VIII. Its provenance remains unknown until the early-nineteenth century when it was bought or given to the tenth Duke of Hamilton. In 1882 the Hamilton library was sold to the Royal Library in Berlin, Emma's book among the stock. But five years later all these works were acquired by the British Museum. Today the book is housed in the British Library.

It is a phenomenal sensation to hold the book that she probably held more than 950 years ago; to turn the pages that she turned; to feel the faint oiliness of the vellum on which the text is written – human skin against animal skin. It is a relatively small and slim volume, about seven inches long and five inches wide, its sixty-seven leaves written on each side in Latin in a brownish ink (a further page is missing). There were clearly two different scribes at work, for there are two distinct characters of handwriting and there is a change in the number of lines per page.

The book's embellishments, along with the picture of Emma, were probably the work of other craftsmen, some more talented than others. S, the very first letter, is a decorated capital six lines deep. It is skilfully drawn as a twist of two serpent-like creatures: the top one sports tiny ears and is being devoured by the lower one, which has little legs. By contrast, F, the drop capital at the start of the next section of the book, is far less refined and looks like a hurried, somewhat botched job. However, R, at the opening of the main body of the text is a wonderful concoction of tracery, swirling foliage and dog-like beasts.

But more intriguing than the ornamentations are the marks in the margins, which show the book's living history. The text appears to have been closely studied during the fifteenth and sixteenth centuries when annotators whose writing is identifiable to these periods[1] added their comments – also in Latin. As well as notes and corrections they have included small pictures, images that are so cartoon-like they look as if they were added with a sense of fun: there are elegantly drawn hands with long index fingers pointing to passages that were considered partic-ularly significant; there is a crowned head beside the section where Emma's second husband becomes king of England; and there is black humour, for next to a description of how one of Emma's sons was blinded, a pair of eyes peers out from the margin.

The covers of the book are of an even later date: they are leather, probably an early-nineteenth-century contribution. Originally the pages would have been bound on to wooden boards that may have been covered with sheepskin and then decorated with metalwork. It does seem astonishing, though, that for all the changes in production and materials the very form of a book has not altered at all since at least the eighth century. A book is and was a series of written (and often illustrated) rectangular pages that were and are folded, then stitched together (or now more often glued) and finally enclosed in protective covers.

Other aspects of the England Emma married into a thousand years ago are also surprisingly familiar. The climate, for example: it is gener-ally accepted that summer temperatures were as high[2], if not higher, than they are now, for all the more recent global warming. Scientific research on the Greenland icecap provides evidence of wide fluctu-ations in European weather patterns (hot summers, very cold winters) between about 950 and 1300. In addition, *Domesday Book*, the great survey of England conducted in 1086, mentions a number of vine-yards – in Somerset, Wiltshire, Berkshire, Hertfordshire and Norfolk[3] –

indicating that there must have been hot, fruit-producing seasons.

The people who enjoyed the results were probably no smaller in stature than much of the population today. Whereas in the later medieval period height was to diminish markedly[4], archaeological finds suggest that in Emma's time the average Anglo-Saxon man was roughly 5ft 8in, the average woman slightly more than 5ft 4in.

The population was less than a fortieth of what it is now. However, the existing names of almost every town and village in the country can be traced back to the Anglo-Saxon period and a good quantity has been retained almost verbatim: Swindon or pig hill (swin – pig, dun – hill); Sandwich or settlement on the sand (the ending – wic being a frequently used compound meaning dwelling, settlement or village); Kirkby or settlement with a church (showing the influence of northern settlers – the name is derived from Scandinavian kirkja plus -by for settlement).

The individuals who inhabited late Anglo-Saxon England were for the most part illiterate and had almost no concept of science and mathematics (indeed Arabic numerals had yet to be introduced to the country). They were profoundly Christian and they spoke a highly inflected language, Old English, which would sound practically foreign now. Indeed, many of their names look dauntingly obscure – such as Aelfric and Aethelred, the first A and E originally a diphthong but separated here for greater accessibility. Some names, though, have survived in a transmuted from – Alfred from Aelfred, Edith from Eadgyth – and in this text the modern versions are used wherever possible. Yet despite impediments over names and language, the human spirit of the Anglo-Saxons, their imagination, their love of food and drink strike a chord today. They drank a form of lager as well as *beor*, strong alcohol made from fermented fruit, which was avidly consumed. They entertained each other with witty verse about frost, ice, onions, dough. Those rich enough enjoyed fine clothes of linen and even imported silk.

Emma's world seems in some instances almost tangible, but at other times wholly alien. Her story is one of power, politics, love, greed and scandal. By tracing that story the England that became her home emerges. It was an England that Emma's Norman family was shortly to conquer and change radically, and her story also tells us why that happened.

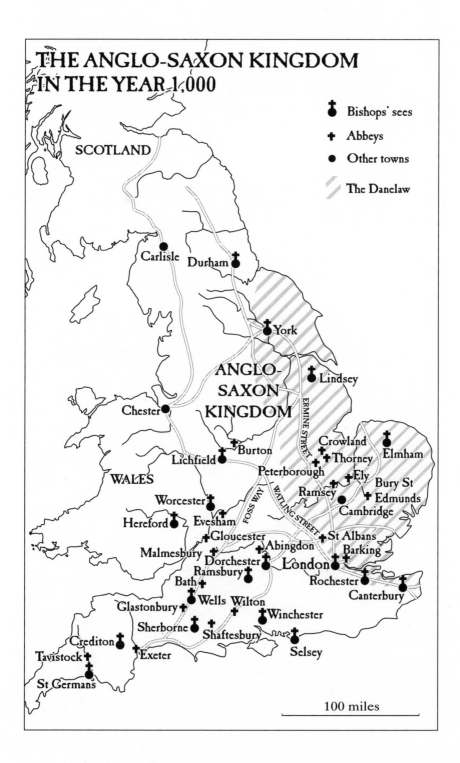

THE ANGLO-SAXON KINGDOM
IN THE YEAR 1,000

SCOTLAND

Bishops' sees
Abbeys
Other towns
The Danelaw

Carlisle

Durham

York

ANGLO-
SAXON
KINGDOM

Lindsey

Chester

ERMINE STREET

Burton
Crowland
Thorney   Elmham
Lichfield
Peterborough   Ely
WATLING STREET
WALES   Ramsey   Bury St
Worcester   Edmunds
FOSS WAY
Hereford   Evesham   Cambridge
Gloucester   St Albans
Malmesbury   Abingdon   Barking
Dorchester   London
Ramsbury
Bath   Rochester
Wells Wilton   Canterbury
Glastonbury   Winchester
Sherborne   Shaftesbury
Crediton   Selsey
Tavistock   Exeter
St Germans

100 miles

PART I

PEACEWEAVER

CHAPTER ONE

Normandy

Imagine a flotilla of longships, brilliantly painted and splendidly gilded. The largest features a giant sea monster, a great figurehead that towers up from the prow as if raring not just to ride the waves but to take on the might of the fiercest ocean. For this journey, only the best, most ornate of vessels will do. Loaded with generous provisions of bread, salted meat and wine, as well as chests containing fine linens, silks, brooches, coins and cups of gold and silver, the ships are launched into shallow water. Then a retinue of courtiers wades out to the vessels through the chilly sea, their tunics tucked up into their belts. One of them carefully carries a girl who clutches her cloak tightly around her and stares back at the shore. She is lifted gently into the master ship where she joins several attendant ladies who have already embarked, some under rather wetter circumstances. The crew is anxious to catch the right combination of wind and tide: commands are shouted, a few expletives yelled, and as 150 or so oarsmen swing into action, sails of ochre hues are released, catching a light breeze that sends the ships dancing over the waves. And so Emma sets off from Normandy to marry the King of England.[1]

She has been told that even with the most advantageous south-westerly wind it will take at least three days to reach the coast of Kent. She is prepared for that. But she is apprehensive at seeing the shores of home receding. Losing sight of land emphasises the aching distance between her own country and the alien territory where she must make her future.

Emma is the sister of Richard II of Normandy, a princeling subordinate to the King of West Francia. The man she is to marry is Aethelred II, the uneasy ruler of a country struggling to repel a relentless stream of Scandinavian raiders, or 'Vikings' – not so much an ethnic designation as a contemporary job description for pirates. It is the spring of 1002 and she is barely into her teens. Her future husband is about twenty years her senior, is already the father of at least ten children and has a record of dismally bad relations with her family. That she has only a limited understanding of his language at least serves to shield her from the full extent of his troubles. The outlook seems hardly promising from a personal perspective, but such considerations are irrelevant. Emma has little, if any, choice in the matter: she has been raised to make just such a political match.

She is a 'peaceweaver', the creator of a fragile fabric of friendship between hostile families. Her sisters have been similarly betrothed, but to less immediately aggressive neighbours: Matilde to the Count of Chartres; Hawise to the Count of Rennes. These matches are less glamorous, too. Granted the King of England does not have the kudos of the Germanic emperor Henry II, but Aethelred has significant status in the perceived pecking order of European rulers and, unlike Emma's brother and the other counts in Francia, he bends his knee to no overlord.

Given past relations between the English and Norman courts, it has been explained to the young girl that her situation in England may be uncomfortable, and that life will undoubtedly be tense for the Norman retinue who will, for the time being, remain with her. She has been instructed that it will be expedient for her to produce a child with her ageing husband as a way of clinching the pact with the Anglo-Saxon king. And she has been made aware of the motives for the marriage deal: her brother – and Normandy – will gain greater strength through the alliance with their powerful neighbour; the English monarch, meanwhile, wants to stop the Normans from supporting his Viking enemies. But for Emma, it seems puzzling to be siding with the Anglo-Saxons against the sea-warriors from Scandinavia: she and the Norman people are, after all, of Viking blood.

*　　*　　*

The above is fact interspersed with plausible conjecture. The early western European histories of a thousand or so years ago are no less speculative. Written records of events that had passed into collective memory through oral tradition, they are part observation and eyewitness accounts, part hearsay, part folk tale and part embellishment by the monks who penned them. These monks generally knew how to tell a good tale, injecting much spice and intrigue into their Latin texts. Alongside surviving court annals, these provide the basis of what we know about the period, with accepted facts corroborated by legal documents – land charters, law codes and the like – as well as archaeological evidence. Through them glimpses of Emma emerge, increasing as she gains prominence.

She was born into a mainland Europe that had splintered into feuding states controlled by warrior kings. Charlemagne's enormous empire – extending over modern-day France, Switzerland, Austria, Belgium, The Netherlands, much of Germany, some of Spain and part of Italy – had dissolved after his death in 814. Viking raids played no small part in the fragmentation, which was also caused by civil war as well as attacks from the Magyars of Hungary and the Saracens of North Africa. In 843 the once-great dominion had been formally divided into three: East Francia, effectively Germany; West Francia, essentially modern-day France; and a thin strip (more or less what is now Alsace and Lorraine) between these two kingdoms that remained the cause of bitter dispute into the twentieth century. The supreme kings of these regions sporadi-cally attempted to broker peace between the warring chieftains who were obliged to pay homage to them. But marriage between the fami-lies of regional rulers was a more effective way of reaching a truce, even if it was often short-lived. Such was the manner of Emma's match to Aethelred of England.

Until she became a high-profile pawn in the wrangles between the Normans and the Anglo-Saxons, reference to Emma in contemporary documents is almost non-existent. We can only guess at the contri-buting factors in her childhood that gave her the courage, if not bloody-mindedness, to rise above her circumstances. It was not unusual for aristocratic women of her time to exercise some power, and many owned vast estates, but Emma was to be exceptional, taking centre-stage and becoming the most notoriously determined, manipulative and forceful female in western Europe.

She was one of seven children born to Richard I of Normandy and Gunnor, his mistress of Danish descent. There may have been other progeny who did not survive childhood. The couple later married so that Gunnor's offspring could become Richard's legitimate heirs, with the result that they were probably considered superior to the children of his other concubines. Such a two-tier system could have given Emma more than a touch of wilful arrogance as well as an innate expectation of privilege.

The exact date of her birth is not known, such information being unrecorded for almost any individual of the period. However, since she was to produce her first child by 1005 and her last in about 1021, it would be reasonable to assume that she was born in the late 980s. She may have been the eldest of Gunnor's three daughters, although such speculation is thinly based on the fact that she made a more prestigious match than her two sisters, whose own marriages were either in the same year or just a shade after Emma's. It is possible, on the other hand, that her brother Richard, who had inherited his father's title in 996, chose Emma for the most illustrious and difficult match because she was considered best able to cope with the challenge. She was undoubtedly younger than Richard, and was also probably born after her next brother, Robert. She is known to have had two more full brothers: Mauger, who became the Count of Corbeil; and Robert Danus, who died as a young man. Emma's sister Matilde also died early, possibly in childbirth, a couple of years after her marriage – prompting an ugly fracas as Richard II demanded her dowry back.

During the first few years of her life Emma would have had little contact with her mother, being raised instead by a wet nurse within the courtly household. Thereafter she would have become the responsibility of an attendant designated to her and her sisters and moving with them as the Norman court oscillated around the province, chiefly between Rouen, Fécamp and Bayeux. She almost certainly would not have been sent away to foster parents: such aristocratic practice was more common for boys, who were often farmed out as part of their education – and also as an attempt to keep them safe from hostage-taking or assassination during periods of political turmoil. Her own 'education' must have been extremely limited. She would have learnt the art of fine needlework – no idle occupation since the embroidered wallhangings created by aristocratic ladies had a very necessary purpose as draught excluders in houses and halls where glass had as yet to become a common feature for windows. However, she would not have demeaned herself with weaving, which was the work of less noble women. She would have been schooled in the refinements of court diplomacy: meeting, greeting and serving wine at feast days were important accomplishments given that she was almost inevitably to be married off as part of an alliance with another noble family. It was also a useful way of gleaning what was being discussed at court. She would have been illiterate – her sisters and most of her brothers, too. Reading and writing were not secular attainments and Emma would hardly have considered it within her sphere of possibilities to acquire skills that were taught only to those entering monasteries and convents.

She would have spoken a form of Old French, a Gallic development from Latin influenced by the Germanic tongues of the Franks and the Scandinavians. She would also have been fluent in Old Scandinavian, which was the language of the Vikings and was not entirely dissimilar to the Old English spoken by the Anglo-Saxons. Whether Emma would have regarded Old French or Old Scandinavian as her mother tongue is a pertinent consideration.

In origin the Normans were not French at all but 'north men', Vikings who had been ceded territory around the Seine in the early 900s. The exact derivation of the word 'viking' is a slight puzzle. It may be a development from Viken, the name of an area around the Oslo Fjord, the term gradually being applied to all men of the fjords. It may have originated in the Old Scandinavian word 'vik', which meant creek or bay: a 'viking' essentially being a trader or raider who kept his ship in a bay or estuary. From the ninth century onwards the word had become synonymous with the northern pirates who were plundering from the coastlines of much of western Europe and indeed as far afield as Russia and north Africa. In many areas they eventually settled, particularly

Ireland, Scotland, eastern England and northern France. Emma herself was from the third generation of such colonists, and by the turn of the first millennium the territory of these particular 'north men' had extended to cover roughly the same area as Normandy does today: from just south of Alençon to the Channel coast in the north and from Mont Saint-Michel in the west to several miles east of Dieppe. And it seems that at this stage the Normans were attempting to improve their image and status among other European states.

At the time of Emma's departure to England, a Frankish ecclesiastic from the monastery of St Quentin near Laon was at court compiling a history of the Normans. Dudo had originally been commissioned by Emma's father, who had orchestrated the project as a means of building up the credibility and grandeur of the renegade rulers of the Viking province. After the death of Richard I, Dudo continued the task for Emma's brother for whom he worked until about 1015. A type of vanity publishing, tinged with requisite flourishes of godliness, Dudo's history became the basic material for subsequent Norman chroniclers writing around the time of the Norman Conquest and also in the mid-twelfth century. They revised and abbreviated his work, while also updating it and contributing their own additions drawn from other sources now lost. Together these surviving histories provide a thoroughly biased and consistently colourful story of the makings of Emma's Normandy, emphasising, probably inadvertently, how strongly Viking her family had remained.

The principality of Normandy had been founded by her great-grandfather, the Scandinavian warrior Rollo. The Norse saga-writers of the late-twelfth century claim that he was the son of the west Norwegian chieftain Rognvald of More, whose descendants famously became the earls of Orkney. However, the Norman chroniclers trace Rollo back to Denmark. They record that he and his bellicose followers were driven out of the 'island' of Scania (presumably Skane, on the southern tip of what is now mainland Sweden) by other Viking groups, an expulsion that would have taken place sometime during the 870s. After ten years ravaging the coasts of England and Holland, Rollo and his men moved on to the territory of the King of West Francia – and here questionable myth starts to merge with proven fact.

When Rollo arrived in what is now northern France, there were already a number of Scandinavian settlements around the Cotentin peninsula and the Seine. As a sea-faring plunderer, the Viking newcomer would not have been entirely welcome with those who had made homes in the area. In the 880s he sailed up the Seine, captured Rouen and made it his strategic base. From there he joined other Viking plunderers in besieging Paris, and he petulantly ravaged the country-side when he considered he was not being paid enough to leave the city in peace.

His activities must have been particularly menacing, for eventually Charles the Simple of West Francia struck a deal with Rollo. A ruler more shrewd than his nickname suggests, Charles demanded terms to keep the Viking very much under his control: in return for land, Rollo was obliged to convert to Christianity, marry Charles's daughter Gisla and become a vassal of the King. The unfortunate, peaceweaving, Gisla did not survive long. She died childless whereupon Rollo reinstalled his companion Poppa, to whom he was 'bound according to the Danish custom'.[2]

This presumably refers to pagan Scandinavian marriage practice. Northern marriage traditionally took place by seizure: the prospective bride would be forcibly carried off and the union formally recognised once her abductor had paid a 'bride-price' to her relatives. If the wife subsequently committed adultery she would be severely punished – in some regions she risked being killed. No such limits were imposed on Scandinavian men. They were openly promiscuous and would often keep one or more concubine whose children they might choose to recognise, or not. From a Scandinavian man's perspective, sex was unlicensed and marriage existed principally for making alliances. And for the newly Christian Viking leaders, the recognition of two separate marriage practices, Christian and pagan – and two convenient possibilities of making alliances this way – was an open door to flagrant bigamy. As Emma was later to find out to her cost.

Rollo named Poppa's son, William 'Longsword', as his heir. William expanded the territory of the 'north men', gained credibility through patronage of the Church, flirted with the idea of becoming a monk –

and came to a premature and bloody end on 17 December 942 when
he was murdered by the Count of Flanders.

Emma's father, Richard I, succeeded while still a minor. He was the
offspring of William's Danish-style union to the 'noble maiden' Sprota.
However, like Rollo, William too had another wife. His Christian
marriage to Leyarda, daughter of the Count of Vermandois, did not
produce children and on William's death she was married on to the
Count of Blois and Chartres. Richard, if the Norman chroniclers are
to be believed, was the uncontested heir from birth and at the express
wish of his father was brought up variously at Fécamp, the large Norman
settlement on the coast, and at Bayeux. Both were places where he
could learn Scandinavian ways and the Scandinavian language, Rouen
being considered too French.

However, his childhood was to have some strongly French influence
of a turbulent nature. According to the early Norman writers, shortly
after his father's death, Richard was snatched by Louis IV of West
Francia and held hostage at his court at Laon. Among the European
nobility it was an established practice for young boys to be taken away
or exchanged as an act of surety against potentially aggressive neighbours. They were generally treated honourably and accepted into court
life, where they enjoyed those essential aristocratic pleasures of feasting
and hunting. Louis at first claimed he was taking Richard to his court
in order to educate him, no doubt a slur on his Scandinavian upbringing.
In reality the French king had other objectives, for he swiftly tried to
make his hostage renounce his claims to Normandy on the grounds of
his purported illegitimacy. When the young Richard refused, he
became a heavily guarded captive. Yet his loyal and resourceful
Norman regents managed to mastermind his escape and even briefly
took Louis himself prisoner when he retaliated by ravaging Richard's
territory. Richard subsequently looked for friends in more powerful
places and later married the daughter of Louis's arch enemy Hugh
the Great, a magnate whose vast estates gave him authority over huge
swathes of France and whose son Hugh Capet was subsequently elected
king in 987.

Although he avoided having two wives simultaneously, Richard's marital arrangements were quite as complex as those of his father and grandfather before him. Like them he had no children by his high-status wife. But he kept a number of concubines with whom he variously produced two sons and two daughters – the boys later becoming counts, the girls being usefully married to neighbouring war leaders. He also had a 'mistress', Gunnor. With the benefit of hindsight, the Norman chroniclers infer that there was a big distinction between her and the mere concubines. Dudo maintains that it was on the death of Richard's French wife that he started 'an alliance of forbidden union' with Gunnor, although this may be putting a semi-reputable spin on the chronology of their relationship. She was, he says, from the 'noblest house of the Danes'[3] and as such a very suitable partner. And he relates how it was at the insistence of the Norman nobles that Richard and Gunnor were later married according to 'matrimonial' (and Christian) law so as to establish a clear line of succession.

Richard I was the chieftain of Normandy for a little over forty-four years, emerging as a strong leader who broadened the 'north men's' territory still further and plundered much of the rest of northern France while aiding, and trading with, the Vikings who were attacking Aethelred's England. The Norman chroniclers depict him as a near-perfect specimen: tall, well built, handsome; he had a long beard; he was a devout patron of the Church; he was compassionate to widows and orphans; and he had a healthy sense of fair play, generously buying back Norman captives who had been taken during his skirmishes. He died at Fécamp on 20 November 996 whereupon the shrieking and wailing of the grieving Normans was such as 'would touch the summit of heaven'[4] – a very Viking-style lamentation.

Gunnor survived her husband by a good twenty years. Although no records remain that reflect her involvement in his reign, later evidence shows that she was a significant political figure. She was certainly involved in the court of her son, where she was active until well into the 1020s – a redoubtable dowager duchess. Documents recording grants of land provide a *Who's Who* of court life through the list of witnesses asked to attest the proceedings. These invent-ories detail the chosen court council and what their status was – the higher up the list the better. Not that the witnesses actually signed any charters or grants they had been asked to testify: most of the nobility would not have known how to do so. Instead a monk, seconded to the task of scribe, would write down the names of those gathered. On her son's charters Gunnor's name consistently appears at the top, after Richard's and sometimes after that of her second son Robert, but always before her daughter-in-law, her grandsons and other courtiers and churchmen.

However grand she became, Emma's mother did not have quite the pedigree that the Norman chroniclers claim for her. What little has been established about Gunnor's background points to the probability that her parents were first-generation settlers with modest lands in the Cotentin[5]. One of her sisters certainly appears to have been fairly humbly married. Sainsfrida was the wife of a forester in northern Normandy and it was apparently through her that Richard met Gunnor. One story[6] relates that while on a hunting expedition Richard stayed at the forester's house, where he became much enamoured of Sainsfrida. Wanting to retain her virtue while not insulting the Count, she neatly sent her sister to his bed – and they all lived happily ever after, give or take a few mistresses and Richard's unproductive first marriage.

Through Gunnor Emma would have learnt the value of church patronage: giving was not simply an expression of piety, it was also very much a means of establishing credibility and status. Gunnor donated land to the monastery of Mont Saint-Michel and gave generously to the churches at Chartres, where her son Robert Danus was buried, her daughter Matilde died, and her brother Herfast later became a monk. She was also evidently well aware of the importance of the written word and its power as a political tool, working with Dudo as he wrote his history at court: she was 'well versed in the talents of feminine artistry', Dudo commented lavishly, and 'profusely endowed with the treasure of a capacious memory and power of recollection'.

In a contemporary poem Gunnor is celebrated not just as the first lady of land, but as the controlling regent. The work is composed in Latin and dedicated to Gunnor and to her second son Robert, who by then had become the Archbishop of Rouen. The author, Warner, was a monk from Rouen who despite his religious background clearly had no difficulty in composing lewd passages. His puzzling poem tells the story of a degenerate Irishman, Moriuht, a cleric with a strong, even depraved, sex drive. In Warner's tale, Moriuht arrives in Rouen after many adventures with nuns, widows and young boys. He is, however, looking for his wife, who has been captured by Vikings and sold as a slave. He comes to court seeking the help of the widowed countess, who is described as being the effective ruler of the realm since her husband's death – and as such has a less than veiled similarity to Gunnor, herself a widow and a figure of great power at her son's court. The abject flattery, however, does not continue. In the poem, Moriuht is hardly dressed for the audience he is granted with the noble countess: 'In front of his buttocks he wore a black covering of a goat . . . and his genitals were visible in their entirety and the black hairs of his arse and groin. In addition, his anus . . . constantly gaped so openly when he bent his head and looked down on the ground, that a cat could enter into it and rest (there) for an entire year.'[7] Veiled and seated on a throne, the countess is unperturbed by his appearance. She graciously receives Moriuht, agrees to help, and wryly makes suggestive and flir-tatious overtures at which her courtiers double up in mirth. Ultimately Moriuht finds and rescues his wife, and the countess compassionately pays the ransom of his daughter who suddenly pops up out of nowhere, also as a slave. The poem then ends with ribald mockery of Moriuht and his libido. It is difficult to understand the purpose of this bizarre and brazen tale – which seems to avoid any Christian message of virtue and godly devotion. But it must reflect something of the bawdy nuances in the early Norman court, one in which the countess, the Gunnor clone, emerges as a powerful patron with an earthy and humorous take on life.

The poem was composed some years after Emma left Normandy, and after she had started to appear in English records as a commanding figure in her own right. However, the contemporary chroniclers in England were muted in their initial reactions to the arrival of their king's foreign bride, noting only that in the spring of 1002 'Richard's daughter came here to the land'.[8] There is no amplification to this curt little reference, no mention of a royal wedding, and no indication that this involvement with the Normans was of any great significance. How wrong they were: within a year 'Richard's daughter' was to have a significant impact on the country. But far from being a figure of peace she was to be seen as the cause of increased Viking aggression.

CHAPTER TWO

England

On an early April morning in 1002, Emma and her attendants arrive in Canterbury. They are escorted in slow and stately procession by the King and his vast retinue, who have been with the foreign party since they reached the shores of Kent several days ago. It is at Canterbury, the stronghold of the Cantware or Kentish people, that the Norman girl is to marry the ageing English monarch – and to be consecrated as queen.

For centuries Cantwaraburh has been a busy centre for both Church and trade. Horses, oxcarts, travellers on foot, farmers carrying live pigs suspended on poles – a constant flow of traffic squelches through the sturdy gates. A large cattle market just outside the walls adds a fetid odour of urine and dung to the mud road leading into the eastern part of town. Inside the walls, long, thin plots growing leeks, onions and other vegetables lie adjacent to huddled, single-storey houses. Back in the mid-800s the properties became so densely packed here that a local by-law was passed stipulating that at least two feet should be left between them to allow for eavesdrip.[1] In such crowded quarters fires become a major hazard: the timber and thatch buildings frequently go up in flames, and are speedily reconstructed using wood from the big forest of Blean a few miles north of the town.

Built largely of stone, the great religious centres of Canterbury are less susceptible to fire.[2] The monastery of St Peter and St Paul just outside the eastern walls, and Christ Church within the fortifications were both established many hundreds of years ago by St Augustine shortly after he arrived from Rome to convert the pagan people of Kent.

The town has grown up around Christ Church, although the original building has been thoroughly remodelled. By 1002 it has become an imposing, basilican-style cathedral. With its huge central tower looming over the little houses of the town it seems a miracle of elevation and solidity. Within the cathedral there is still a flurry of excitement over the arrival, a year or so ago, of a radical book from the Continent. Produced at Hautvilliers near Rheims,[3] it is a psalter, a basic work of monastic choral song, which has been startlingly illustrated: each one of its 150 psalms and sixteen canticles has been dramatically brought to life with drawings that are graphically emotional. No one here has seen anything like them before, and the monks at the scriptorium are copying the style with a sense of profound amazement.

However, such work has recently been interrupted for the clerical and ecclesiastical duties required over the King's marriage ceremony to the Count of Normandy's daughter. It is to be a large and lavish event. Quite apart from the King's own entourage, other members of the nobility and the Church have been arriving from across the south of the country and even further afield. They have been crowding into the town with a sense of some relief: the wedding festivities make a very welcome diversion from recent preoccupations over Viking attacks. Meanwhile, for the young bride it is both intoxicating and bewildering to be the focus of so much attention among so many strangers.

* * *

The country that Emma married into stretched over roughly the same area as it still does a millennium later, although at the start of the eleventh century the borders with Wales and Scotland were blurred, permeable demarcations. Despite immigration issues in the east, where a sprawling region had been colonised by Scandinavian settlers, in 1002 the people of England ostensibly recognised the authority of one king. It was, however, a relatively new sense of unity for which Viking attacks, somewhat tangentially, had been largely responsible. Indeed, long-term Viking aggression had effectively shaped the power structure not only of England but also of her immediate neighbours.

Emma's new territory was, above all, a kingdom of Germanic people. Traditionally known as Angles, Saxons and Jutes, the ancestors of these family groups had migrated to England from areas such as Jutland and Saxony across the North Sea, arriving after the Romans left in the early-fifth century. These pirates and invaders gradually absorbed, expelled or annihilated the existing population (the precise fate of the Celtic Britons is hazy) and established a myriad of small, aggressive kingdoms. Over a period of about 400 years, they fought each other backwards and forwards, gaining or losing territory in the turmoil. Some were wiped out, some made sporadic peace through marriage, a few became ever more powerful. At the start of the ninth century four kingdoms were dominant: Northumbria, East Anglia, Mercia (roughly from the Thames to the Humber), and Wessex, in the south. However, by this juncture Scandinavian raiders had begun attacking the coastline and in the 860s and 870s they essentially defeated the first three of these kingdoms. Only Wessex, under King Alfred the Great, held out. His successors managed to drive the Viking leaders from the rest of the country, a process perversely termed the 'reconquest of England' as it was, in fact, the creation of a greater Wessex. When Emma arrived to marry Aethelred in 1002, England, the land of the Angles, had been unified under the wavering control of rulers from the Wessex royal family for about two generations. But, after an interval of roughly thirty years, Vikings were once again attacking the land.

Meanwhile, other Scandinavian raiders and invaders had encountered little unified resistance from the patchwork of Celtic kingdoms that was Ireland. And they thrived there, particularly around Dublin. Yet some-time after 960 Brian Boru of Munster (founder of the O'Brien clan) defeated several of their leaders who were allied with local chieftains. During the year that Emma and Aethelred were married he was declared the first high king of all Ireland. But the flimsy unity was to be fairly short-lived. Although Brian Boru effectively saw off the last of the Viking aggressors in the Battle of Clontarf in 1014, he died in the effort and thereafter Ireland splintered again into belligerent factions.

With fewer rich religious centres to plunder, Wales was not as much of a target for the Vikings. Nevertheless, they often disrupted life for the many competing chieftains there. A degree of tribal cohesiveness was introduced by Howell the Good of Dyfed in the mid-tenth century, but on his death the area reverted to a state of warring disunity. And there were also frequent clashes with the Anglo-Saxons to the east – on both sides of Offa's Dyke. This prodigious man-made boundary is so called because it is believed to have been the creation of King Offa of Mercia in about 785, built to deter attacks from marauding Welsh tribes and to control trade. However, it was evidently not an unassailable obstacle. Raids and land-grabbing incursions from both sides frequently took place during Emma's lifetime.

England's relations with Scotland were just as aggressive. There, as in the land of the Anglo-Saxons, Viking attacks ultimately resulted in a greater sense of unity, with one warring faction becoming increasingly dominant. Before 800, Scotland was divided into four ethnic groups: Picts in the northern and eastern Highlands; Scots (who originated from Ireland) in the area of the western Highlands known as Dalriada; Britons in Strathclyde; and Northumbrian Anglo-Saxons whose territory extended into the Lothians. Scandinavian raids and invasions affected all these groups, but the Scots emerged as the strongest survivors – and they took over the entire area. Between the 840s and the 970s they defeated the Picts (who they appear to have wiped out) and the Britons and laid claim to the Lothians. Their warrior kings were chosen by the people and several ruling families vied with each other for control. Yet quite apart from these internal power struggles was the problem of a very flimsy border with Northumbria. During Emma's life this region remained extremely unstable.

Yet the northern frontier was not such a pressing concern to the King of England – it was a far greater issue for Northumbria's governing ealdorman. Royal interests lay principally with the regal estates, most of which were in the south. And it was on the south-eastern coast that Emma first arrived in the country.

Emma was to become queen of a country with a population of one-and-a-half million at the very most. With such small numbers it had not yet become common practice for each clan to be identified by a family name: most individuals had just one personal name, usually consisting of two elements – such as Aethelstan or 'noble stone'; Godgifu, 'good gift' or 'good grace'.

Some men, though, retained part of an ancestor's name in their own, while the newer settlers in the east of the country occasionally adopted a Scandinavian custom of appending their personal name with that of their father – as in Olaf Haroldson or Olaf son of Harold. Meanwhile, nicknames were fairly frequently given; some laudatory – Edith the Fairhair, Edgar the Bold; others sardonic: Eadric the Acquisitor; Godwine the Slobberer.

A wry response to life was also displayed in the riddles that were passed down orally from generation to generation. One of the more risqué is a description of a churn.[4] It starts:

> *This knave came in where he knew she'd be,*
> *Standing in a corner. He stepped across to her*
> *With the briskness of youth, and, yanking up his own*
> *Robe with his hands, rammed something stiff*
> *Under her girdle as she stood there . . .*

Other riddles show a deep affinity with the natural world, and a poignant sense of awe. Ice is the solution to the short verse:[5]

> *The wave, over wave, a weird thing I saw,*
> *Thorough-wrought, and wonderfully ornate:*
> *A wonder on the wave – water became bone*

The rhythms of nature marked the passage of time far more than the labels of months and dates. The people of Emma's England were profoundly rural folk whose year was measured by agricultural seasons – ploughing and seeding, harvest, winter. But recently these essential tasks had frequently been disrupted by Viking attacks. Defence had become a pressing concern – and timber was a vital resource.

In addition to wide expanses of downland and forest where wild boar, deer, hare,[6] bear and even beaver roamed, England contained large stretches of managed woodland. Oak, ash, hawthorn, hazel, lime and maple (but no conifers except the occasional yew) provided the timber required in building ships and ramparts quite apart from the substantial amount needed for domestic use in houses, bridges, carts and cowsheds. Coppicing produced materials to weave into wattle fencing for flimsy lines of security as well as for animal enclosures. Brushwood, the basic fuel for cooking and warmth, was lit in beacons warning of attacks. And wood was also the basis of essential weaponry: spears were the principal implements for fending off Viking raiders, bows and arrows were less widely employed (while swords of iron and steel, usually soldered with precious metals, were treasured riches of the nobility).

Elsewhere this very rural England was fairly heavily farmed, many areas of dense trees and thicket having long since been grubbed out to create narrow, rectangular fields where crops of grains and pulses were cultivated. Livestock was kept close to scattered settlements and small but growing villages: bristly, leggy pigs with long snouts; goats, valued more for their milk than their meat; small cattle, strong enough to pull a plough when not foraging in fields left fallow for grazing; skinny little sheep, tended by shepherds whose big dogs guarded against wolves. These predators were not the only hazard to foodstock: blight and resulting famine were far from unknown. Nevertheless, England was a land of some agricultural prosperity. Such urban communities as existed had grown up largely because a surplus of food produce had generated an increase in trade and a need for market places.

The towns were tiny. Some, such as Bath, Cirencester, Canterbury and London, had been built on, and with, the remains of Roman sites whose ancient walls provided useful fortifications. Others – Oxford, Wallingford, Wareham, Cricklade, for example – were enclosed by ditches and earthworks. Defences became vital during the 800s when Scandinavian raiders started attacking, and sacking, the country. About fifty[7] years before Emma arrived in England this first wave of intruders was eventually driven off, leaving the large number of settlers in the east – in Lincolnshire, Leicestershire, East Anglia and Yorkshire – where they were allowed to retain their own laws and customs. By 1008 the diffuse area these Scandinavian colonisers occupied was known as the Danelaw.[8]

But the loyalties of these settlers must have been acutely challenged. Although by 1002 many Scandinavians had married into local families, it would have been tempting, not to say expedient, to show some allegiance to the more brutal of the pirates arriving from the North. From the 980s this second wave of Vikings rampaged around England, and King Aethelred's attempts to stop them were painfully inadequate. The Battle of Maldon in Essex, when almost an entire English army was wiped out in 991, became the most famous of the tragic defeats largely through the survival of the poem of the same name. The court annals of the *Anglo-Saxon Chronicles* record that after this wretched loss the first of many payments was made to Vikings – effectively bribes to get the raiders to go away, although this rarely worked for long: in 991, 10,000 pounds bought a brief truce, a figure that was to spiral alarmingly.

One court chronicler wrote that in 999[9] Aethelred and his army attempted to confront the Scandinavian invaders in a pincer movement by land and sea. But the ships were not ready in time, 'And always whenever matters should have been advanced, the slower it was from one hour to the next, and they always let their enemies' strength increase . . . And in the end they achieved nothing, except the people's labour and wasting money, and the emboldening of their enemies', he noted despondently.

There was no trained, standing army. The Anglo-Saxon rulers never had such a formal military tradition; it was simply every man's duty to be called up in arms for the King. There was also no nerve centre, no military or even civil headquarters. England did not yet have a recognisable capital, instead Aethelred's court moved from one royal residence to the next. This mobility not only offered a degree of control over the land and the people, it was also a convenient way of sustaining the King's vast entourage. Aethelred and his ensemble lived on food rents, or feorm, levied from his subjects and delivered to his palaces and estates. The court literally ate its way around the country. London, Bath, Gloucester, Cheddar, Winchester: Aethelred's draughty mansions and manors were scattered across the south of the kingdom (and probably further afield, but there is no surviving evidence to show that he

ever journeyed very far north). He travelled with a cast if not of hundreds
then a good eighty or ninety retainers at the very least. As well as his
immediate family (and, after all, Aethelred already had ten or more
children who might all be with him at any one time) he was frequently
accompanied by a host of legal and spiritual advisers. This coterie of
bishops and other churchmen was augmented by ealdormen, the
regional, aristocratic governors who were effectively the forerunners of
earls. In turn, the travelling nobility brought their own household
servants. And in addition was an elaborate caravan composed of the
King's personal bodyguards, his diplomatic hostages and assorted foster
sons from noble families, his minstrels, and his battalion of outdoor staff
from grooms and stablehands to blacksmiths, falconers with their hawks,
and huntsmen attending the pack of royal hunting dogs.

In the spring of 1002, this band of courtiers and servants would have
been awaiting the arrival of their future queen and preparing for the
royal wedding. There are no records to clarify when precisely this took
place, or where. But by tracing Aethelred's movements at the time we
can hazard a good guess. A series of land charters he issued indicates
that he was in Kent in January and April 1002[10] and it would be logical
to assume that he was making arrangements for his wedding there. This
would almost undoubtedly have taken place in the great religious centre
of Canterbury, where, coincidentally, the extraordinary book of psalms
had fairly recently arrived. It still exists, a medieval masterpiece that
had enormous influence on the evolution of expressive art in Europe.
The book remained in England for centuries and was saved from destruction during the Dissolution of the Monasteries when a large amount of
manuscripts went up in smoke. Subsequently it fell into private hands
and in the seventeenth century was bequeathed to the University of
Utrecht where it acquired its current name, the *Utrecht Psalter*. It is
conceivable that the monks used this book during Emma's marriage
ceremony.

Records of Emma's wedding to Aethelred have not survived.
However, an account of a royal marriage, albeit idealised and made in
heaven, is given in an early *Life of St Dunstan*, written at about the
time of Emma's arrival in England. This wedding is formally witnessed

by the King's most eminent and trusted advisers and is performed to
the accompanying chant of hymns and praises from attendant monks.
Emma's own ceremony would have been similar, with the monks of
Canterbury singing psalms that they would have known by heart. But
in keeping with the grandeur of the occasion their much-prized psalter
may have been on show.

The Archbishop of Canterbury, Aelfric, would have presided over
the splendid occasion of the King of England's wedding. He probably
included in the ceremony a statutory marriage blessing that focused
entirely on the bride and her conduct: 'May she be bashful and grave,
reverential and modest, well instructed in heavenly doctrine. May she
be fruitful in childbearing, innocent and of good report . . .'[11] No injunctions at all would have been made to the bridegroom: the responsibility
for the welfare (and chastity) of a marriage rested principally with the
woman. Such thinking would not have been regarded as blatant sexism
on the part of the Church: it is implicit in the very language of the
Anglo-Saxons. There was no distinction between the words for wife
and woman – 'wif' meant both. To be a wife was the defining role of
a female.

At the start of the eleventh century, England was a God-fearing nation
in that the clergy literally induced a terror of the Almighty into their
congregations. In part they did so as an attempt to stamp out hints of
lurking paganism. Christianity had been introduced to the Anglo-
Saxons in 597[12] and by the time Emma married Aethelred about four
centuries later it was firmly established across the country. But not
entirely to the exclusion of older beliefs, and in particular there remained
a fine line between ancient and accepted lores of healing and the darker
aspects of magic and witchcraft. Around the time that Emma arrived
in England, one of the greatest scholars of the era, Aelfric of Cerne
Abbas (later first abbot of Eynsham abbey), reflected such concerns in
a series of homilies. Upholding Christianity as the rational faith, he
wrote that some people were 'so blinded that they bring their offerings
to an earth-fast stone, and eke to trees, and to well springs, even as
witches teach and will not understand how foolishly they act, or how

the dead stone or the dumb tree can help them, or give them health'.[13]

The practice of witchcraft, meanwhile, appears not to have been tolerated by the state. A surviving charter from the mid-tenth century[14] describes how the estate of one widow was forfeited to the king because she was found to have driven nails into a doll representing her victim. The charter goes on to state that the widow was taken away and drowned at London's bridge.

There was little difference, though, between the rulings of the state and the Church. The king had a symbiotic relationship with the clergy: they needed his patronage, while through them he could claim divine associations and so add to his credibility. On a more practical level, he was also reliant on the clergy for literacy – and, indeed, his laws were drafted by the chief churchmen of the day. This left room for manoeuvre when it came to the king's own conduct. Technically there might have been some question as to whether Aethelred was entitled to marry Emma in a church since it was forbidden for the clergy to provide such services for second weddings, whether the previous marriage had ended through divorce or through death.

Emma was Aethelred's second, if not third, wife. There is no evidence as to what happened to her predecessor: she may have recently died or she may possibly have been divorced on the convenient grounds that the marriage was discovered to have contravened the laws of the land. Surviving details about her are confused, but she was undoubtedly the daughter of a *thegn*, or nobleman, and she appears to have been called Aelfgifu ('noble gift' or 'noble grace'), which was a conventional and widely given name of the time. If she was even distantly related to Aethelred this could plausibly have breached the latest rulings against consanguineous marriage. A period of church reform which had started in the reign of Aethelred's father saw a tightening of definitions of incest: marriage between individuals as widely related as fourth cousins was ostensibly prohibited, as were unions between spiritual relatives – godmother to godson and so on.

It was not, however, necessary to be married in a church or indeed by a priest. Only gradually did the medieval church assert its authority in this area. While some rites of passage were recognised as important

Christian issues – particularly death and ensuing supplications for a merciful afterlife for the deceased – marriage was principally a secular, business arrangement. It was above all a type of contract between a man and his bride's family.

A betrothal tract, *Be Wifmannes Bedweddunge*, written in the vernacular, survives from this period, outlining what financial agreements should be reached and showing some concern that a woman should not be forced into marriage against her will. 'If a man wishes to betroth a maiden or a widow, and it so pleases her and her kinsmen,' it instructs, 'then it is right that the bridegroom, according to God's law and proper secular custom, should first promise and pledge to those who are her advocates that he desires her in such a way that he will maintain her according to God's law as a man should maintain his wife; and his friends are to stand surety for it'.[15] The tract goes on to stipulate that the groom should pay a fee in remuneration for the bride's upbringing (to whom is unclear – possibly to the woman herself) and that he should also grant her a marriage settlement of her own as well as announcing what property she will be left in her own right should he predecease her.

These agreements would have been witnessed by the groom's chosen friends and by the bride's family, but in the overwhelming majority of cases not written down: in this period of sparse literacy such verbal promise was ostensibly binding. The tract concludes with a warning that the prospective couple should not be closely related and a suggestion, only, that the marriage be blessed by a mass-priest, an ordained member of the clergy able to celebrate Holy Communion.

Emma and Aethelred, however, would have been married in church and would have received a blessing regardless of whether this contravened the law codes. The King needed to make clear to his new brother-in-law and to Emma's Norman retinue that his marriage was fully legitimate. The religious formality was performed not only to endorse the union with a godly stamp of approval: it was not uncommon for a man, particularly a person of rank, to ignore his marriage vows if a better alliance with another family came his way – Emma's own family history was, after all, littered with such untidy arrangements – and

Aethelred needed to be convincing about his honourable intentions. There was also the matter of inheritance. If the wife was cast off, where would that leave her children, who might find themselves disinherited and replaced by the offspring of the new marriage? A church service made it far more difficult for a man subsequently to wriggle out of his responsibilities.

Dispossession of the children of a first marriage was, of course, a possible outcome after all second weddings, regardless of whether the former spouse had been divorced or had died – and this was a good reason for the Church to be cautious about lending any credence to the proceedings. In the case of Emma's marriage, the Norman nobility may have tried to stipulate that her children should become the principal heirs to the English throne irrespective of the claims of Aethelred's existing offspring. Emma would have been roughly the same age as her husband's eldest sons, Aethelstan, Egbert and possibly Edmund, who very probably regarded their father's new wife as a significant threat.

Emma's wedding must have taken place against a backdrop of much courtly intrigue and suspicion. And much fanfare. She was the first foreign bride to marry an English king for more than seventy years and the event would have been staged with a great deal of splendour. For the old groom this was undoubtedly a major public-relations exercise in which he aimed to persuade his subjects that he was in fact a fine king – and that this was a turning point in his beleaguered reign. He badly needed such a show, having acquired an appalling reputation, and later a joke name. Subsequent chroniclers scathingly depict Aethelred II as a foolishly incompetent ruler, so ill-judged in his choice of tactical advisers for the nation's defence that he earned the epithet *Unraed*, meaning 'bad counsel'. Since the name Aethelred literally translates as 'noble counsel', Aethelred Unraed was a neat pun. But it was not to stand the test of time: long after Aethelred's death, and after the Norman Conquest, Anglo-Saxon ceased to be fully understood and *Unraed* was transliterated into 'Unready'. The slip was not entirely inapposite.

'Aethelred the Unready' was clearly badly prepared for many of the attacks of the Scandinavian armies, who for more than thirty years of his reign ravaged their way around his country. However, it was his practice of paying off the Vikings, who would disappear for a while only to come back for more booty, that was most criticised by near-contemporary chroniclers. Shortly before Emma arrived in England, 24,000 pounds was paid to one Viking army alone 'on condition they should leave off from their evil deeds'.[16] There is, though, a mitigating view that to produce such a hefty sum, largely in the form of silver coins, reflects not only the inherent wealth of the country but also Anglo-Saxon England's efficient coinage system and its administrative wherewithal to raise taxes for the national treasury. The government of the kingdom apparently functioned fairly efficiently despite the attacks and was evidently able to pay the substantial amounts that the Scandinavian raiders demanded from it.

In spite of his troubles Aethelred remained a rich man, and he would have been obliged to make a large marriage settlement. Emma's brother Richard II was no doubt keen to extract generous terms, not only in his sister's interests but also to reflect his own dignity and the import-ance of the alliance. There was a significant difference in status between Aethelred and Richard, but the Norman count was in a good bargaining position.

While the Vikings had attacked the Anglo-Saxons, the Normans had blithely continued to trade with the looters and, worse, to provide them with safe harbours across the Channel. Norman support for the Scandinavian raiding armies had, understandably, enraged the English. By the early 990s Aethelred's resulting clashes with Emma's father had become so aggressive that Pope John XV had seen fit to intervene between his 'spiritual sons'. In a letter[17] to 'all the faithful', he had reported on the mission of his envoy, the Bishop of Trevi, who had arrived at Aethelred's court hot-foot from the Continent, clutching papal missives to bring about 'a most firm peace'. But the truce clearly had little long-term effect in curbing Norman involvement with the Vikings. By the turn of the millennium Scandinavian armies had once again found sanctuary in the principality and their raiding ships had been plaguing England – at Folkestone, Sandwich and Ipswich, up the mouth of the Humber and up the Thames estuary to London.

The death of Emma's father provided Aethelred with fresh opportunities to negotiate. In addition, his mother died in 1001. A staggeringly domineering individual, Aelfthryth had been far more powerful than the wife (or wives) of her son. She had been anointed and crowned Queen of England during her husband's coronation of 973, and after his demise she may adamantly have refused to allow another woman to ascend to that position during her lifetime. There is no indication that Emma's predecessor was ever crowned and her name does not appear as a witness on any documents recording court business, although there is clear evidence that Aethelred's mother was a major player at court for a number of years during her son's reign. The death of the dowager queen must have been timely for Aethelred.

Full recognition of his sister as queen, crowned with due splendour, was undoubtedly part of the package that Richard insisted on. He would probably have granted some Norman land for her dowry, and he would have expected bequests of land for Emma from Aethelred – estates that would be inherited by her children or revert to her husband's family should she die without issue. The dower agreements would also have included a traditional 'morning gift', or *morgengifu*, to be received by the bride on consummation of the marriage. This would become her personal property, and in Emma's case may have consisted of sizeable landholdings. As a whole, Emma's dower is believed to have included Rutland; part, at least, of Winchester; some of Rockingham Forest in Northamptonshire; and Exeter.[18] It may also have comprised Amesbury and Wantage, which are known to have belonged to previous queens and are both recorded as still being in royal hands in *Domesday Book*.

Although no account remains of the anointing and crowning of Emma as Queen of England, a small but vital shred of evidence that this ceremony took place survives in a charter of 1004 in which she is described as having been 'consecrated to the royal couch'.[19] The service would probably have been held in Canterbury Cathedral either as part of her wedding proceedings or very shortly afterwards. According to the coronation rites of the time, bishops would have anointed the young girl with oil and blessed her. She would then have been presented with a ring, symbolic not only of her union with the King but also with his country. Finally, amid prayers and much glory, she would have been crowned.

All of which would have been a daunting experience for any teenager, let alone a newly arrived foreigner. The coronation of this mere girl was more a recognition and blessing of the Queen as royal bedfellow and producer of heirs to the throne than a conferment of great authority. But it clearly elevated Emma way above her husband's subjects and offered healthy scope for developing a role of enormous power. Even with only a small understanding of English, and probably little grasp of the Latin in which the service took place, Emma would have been acutely aware of that. Aethelred's courtiers attending the event would, too, have been conscious of the potential for political dynamite. They were no doubt mindful of the machinations of the last crowned Queen of England. Aethelred's mother had enjoyed significant power at her husband's court and after his death had notoriously schemed against his son by a former marriage to ensure that her own child became king – and that she retained much of her glory.

A near-contemporary account of the festivities following the cor-onation of Aethelred's parents provides a clue as to what Emma might have worn on the occasion of her own consecration. In his *Life of St Oswald*, Byrhtferth, a monk from Ramsey, describes Queen Aelfthryth as being sumptuously dressed in gowns of finely woven linen, her outer robe adorned with embroidery into which precious stones were sewn.

Generally, there is disappointingly little pictorial evidence as to what Anglo-Saxon women wore – they are very rarely featured in surviving illustrations. Men, however, are well represented in the Julius Calendar of the early-eleventh century and in illuminated manuscripts (and, slightly later, in the Bayeux Tapestry). Their everyday clothes consisted of long-sleeved, knee-length tunics – baggy frock-like garb tied at the waist with a belt or cord and worn over undershirts made of wool or, in the case of the rich, linen. On their legs men wore woollen or linen bindings, and on their feet a rudimentary form of leather shoe. Over their tunics noblemen (but not, apparently, the lower classes) would often sport cloaks secured at the shoulder or just above the chest with a brooch, buttons as yet being unknown. On grander occasions aristo-crats replaced their tunics with long, foot-length gowns. Aethelred was probably dressed like this for his marriage to Emma.

Two images of Emma herself provide almost the only visual references we have as to what women wore. Both pictures were made in
her later life and both show her in completely figure-concealing
garments – no hint of a bosom or even a waist – while her hair and
neckline are covered by hood-like headdresses. In the drawing that
forms the frontispiece of the book she commissioned she is depicted in
a wrist-length, ankle-length robe that is decorated down the front and
along the edges of the sleeves with jewel-encrusted braids, the stiffness
contrasting with the soft folds of the rest of the material, which was
probably a type of fine linen. In the frontispiece of another book, this
time a religious work that belonged to the New Minster church in
Winchester, she is less formally clad but her gown is equally as voluminous and in this image her right-hand sleeve is slightly pulled back,
revealing an undergarment that reaches the wrist.

Surviving texts offer other evidence as to female dress. Among the
bequests itemised in the will of a wealthy noblewoman[20] (dating from
about 950) are a cloak and a filigreed cloak pin. A rather more tangential, if eccentric, source is an intriguing document detailing monks' sign
language.[21] Monasteries were Benedictine institutions whose inmates
were supposed to uphold vows of at least partial silence. How far these
were strictly enforced is not known, but a type of handbook for an alternative means of communication was found amongst manuscripts from
Christ Church in Canterbury. It offers a lateral insight into Anglo-Saxon
life. There are hand signs for a variety of foods as well as living essen-
tials: honey, for example, is indicated by placing a finger on the tongue,
a candle by blowing on your index finger and then holding up your
thumb. And there are signs for different types of women. The gestures
relate entirely to what they wore on their heads. A nun is indicated by
a sign for a veil. A laywoman is defined by running a finger across the
forehead, a gesticulation representing a headband – which presumably
was ubiquitous. The king's wife is accorded her own, slightly baffling,
sign: a circle is made around the head and then the hand is placed on
the top of the head. This may be indicative of a headdress and crown,
or it could translate as a headband that holds a veil in place. But why,
in any case, would silent monks be discussing the queen?

Perhaps they simply needed to gossip. There would have been a number of monks as well as nuns present at Emma's wedding and the celebrations afterwards. And there would have been strict demarcations of church hierarchy. In the *Life of St Oswald* Byrhtferth writes that during the celebratory feast after Queen Aelfthryth's wedding the bride sat with abbesses and abbots while her husband kept company with more eminent bishops as well as his senior courtiers.[22]

The celebrations for Emma's own wedding and coronation may have continued for as long as three days, which was not uncommon for such high-profile occasions – and could have been awkward for some of the guests since it was deemed rude to leave before the end of the festivities. The Anglo-Saxons were enthusiastic and joyous feasters, and a royal banquet was a particularly lavish event. Feasts were usually held in a great hall, furnished with benches and long trestle tables perhaps covered with cloths, the walls decorated with large, finely worked textiles that blotted out the worst of the draughts. On arrival guests were admitted by doorkeepers, effectively eleventh-century bouncers, who had the serious task of removing weaponry and keeping out gatecrashers and would-be assassins.

Those who were allowed in were often required to wash their hands before being ushered to the part of the hall appropriate for their rank. Only guests of sufficient status were served the rarest food such as curlew, crane and heron, caught by the royal hunting hawks.[23] All tables were supplied with copious quantities of roasted meats – beef, great hunks of venison, sides of pork and wild boar – as well as bread and possibly platters of fish such as eel, herring and salmon.[24] At Emma's wedding feast near the coast, oysters may have been consumed. Porpoise, too, which was considered a delicacy. All of this was eaten with knife, spoon and hand.

However much the Anglo-Saxons relished their food, the poetry and illustrations of the period show an overwhelming preoccupation with the consumption of alcohol on feast days. Wine was the most prestigious and expensive drink because of its limited supply. Some of it was produced in England although most of it was imported in flagons from the Rhineland and also from the French principalities, no doubt via the big trading centre of Rouen.[25] *Beor*, made from fermented fruit, and ale (less sweet and brewed from malted grains) were evidently knocked back. Mead, an alcoholic form of crushed honeycomb, was also popular. Would Emma have imbibed such intoxicating drinks after her wedding? Quite probably, for there appears to have been little option. No evidence survives to suggest that fruit juices and herbal infusions were widely drunk, while water seems to have been something of a last resort of deprivation – largely, no doubt, because of impurities through lack of sanitation.

In the poems featuring Anglo-Saxon feasting, women are noble servers of mead and ale but they do not join the carousing that was clearly a large element of such occasions. At her wedding feast Emma and other female guests may have eaten separately or could have retired early to another room so as to avoid the worst of the debauchery. As the assembled revellers became progressively merry, minstrels performed. The *hearpe* was frequently played, often by a *scop*, a lyricist who sang praises about the bravery of the lord or king (even Aethelred was extolled by the Icelandic poet Gunnlaug in 1001[26] – and gave the *scop* a scarlet cloak for the honour). At larger banquets the music of flutes, pipes, horns and even a form of bagpipe swelled above the noise of conviviality. Poetry was part of the proceedings, too. The singing of lays is certainly an intrinsic element in that great Anglo-Saxon epic *Beowulf*:

> *They sang then and played to please the hero,*
> *Words and music for their warrior prince,*
> *Harp tunes and tales of adventure:*
> *There were high times on the hall benches*
> *And the king's poet performed his part . . .*[27]

It is conceivable that *Beowulf* itself might have been part of the in-hall entertainment at Emma's marriage feast. Although the poem is thought to have been composed around the late-eighth century, the only surviving manuscript is believed to date from the late-tenth or early-eleventh centuries – so the epic was evidently not unfamiliar during Aethelred's reign. The tale of the man-eating monster, Grendel, and the warrior hero who overcomes it and is ultimately killed by a dragon, contains two poignant references to noble women in Emma's situation of peaceweaving bride. These reflect a great deal of scepticism about the value of any truce arranged in this fashion.[28] Many of Aethelred's courtiers were probably just as doubtful about their king's marriage to the foreign girl: could it really establish a lasting alliance with the Normans, and in any case would this actually bring an end to the Viking attacks?

CHAPTER THREE

Murder and Massacre

A big fireplace, billowing smoke, offers a show of warmth in the great hall. Much of the heat, though, is rapidly dispersed through the room's open doorway and windows, ineffectively draped with large swathes of cloth whose embroidered details are blurred in the haze. Daylight pierces the gloom of the interior through the gaps around these hangings, making it possible for the new queen to discern the faces of those courtiers who are positioned closest to her.

Emma is seated in a chair beside her husband. In front of them is a hefty table around which are clustered the most senior of the King's assembled advisers – his uncle Ordulf; his kinsman Aethelmaer; Wulfstan, the Archbishop of York, among them. Behind these aristocrats and clergymen others of less apparent importance have crowded into the room, anxious to have their presence noted at this meeting of the king's council.

Next to King Aethelred is a scribe, his robes and tonsured head reflecting his ecclesiastic status. He jealously guards a candle which provides him with just about enough light to see what he is writing. He takes his cue from the King and from the most vocal of the churchmen, the Archbishop of York. They dictate the wording he should use to record the decisions being made, and they call out the names of those who are formally invited to ratify the proceedings. The scribe then notes down these names in strict order of precedence: it is a mark of great honour and importance to be included as witness.

Just a few weeks after her wedding, Emma feels a distinct sense of pride in attending this meeting of the king's council or *witan*, literally

meaning wise men in the Anglo-Saxon tongue. She cannot fully compre-
hend the language of her new realm but despite her inability to follow
what is being discussed she is called upon to act as a prominent witness
and is given high status. She knows that as yet this is a purely ceremonial position but she appreciates that she has a potentially powerful
role. And she has ascertained with some satisfaction that her husband's
previous wife had no such involvement in state matters.

However, she does not immediately recognise when she is called
upon to act as a witness, for she has been made to change her name.
An English name for her new, English life was given to her on her
coronation – 'Emma' is deemed too foreign-sounding for Anglo-Saxon
royalty. Officially she is to be known as Aelfgifu, although she is mostly
to be referred to as the Lady.[1] It rankles that Aethelred's previous
wife was also called Aelfgifu, but Emma has been assured this is purely
a coincidence.[2] The name has been conferred on her in memory of
the king's late grandmother, a queen reputedly so compassionate and
godly that a great many sick people praying beside her tomb at the
convent in Shaftesbury have been healed. Almost thirty years have
passed since this revered woman was declared a saint, her feast day
celebrated every year on 18 May. And the miracles keep occurring.
Emma has been firmly told that to be connected with St Aelfgifu is
a great distinction.

She has also been told that she needs to rethink her appreciation of
her Scandinavian ancestry. She has been left in no doubt that the
Northmen are the hated scourge of England. Indeed the meetings of
the king's council are dominated by debates as to how best to cope with
the Vikings, and much time is spent thrashing out a consensus as to
what humiliating tribute money needs to be paid to buy peace from the
pirates.

Many of the Scandinavian raiders are on friendly terms with Emma's
brother. The names of their more prominent leaders are well known
to the new queen of England: Swein Forkbeard of the Danes; his
brother-in-law Pallig; Olaf Tryggvason of the Norwegians. Emma has
learnt that Aethelred and the English nobles have had some limited
success in playing on the animosities between Viking groups, winning

– and buying – round some of their leaders who then fight with the
English king against other Scandinavian armies. Pallig and his men
were for a while in Aethelred's service, but in 1001 they deserted and
joined Swein Forkbeard's troops in attacking Devon. Pallig and some
of his cohorts have since been captured and are now held hostage. But
not before these Scandinavians left a smouldering trail of burnt-down
estates and manors. Aethelred had better results with Olaf Tryggvason.
After the brutal series of raids in 994, 16,000 pounds bought peace
and an understanding with the Norwegian pirate. Olaf became a
confirmed Christian, vowed never again to darken the coastline of
England and, loaded with gold and silver, disappeared northwards to
win himself the crown of Norway. However, according to recent news
from northern messengers, Olaf has been killed in battle with his
Norwegian enemy Earl Eric.

In the midst of this confusion of deals, double-deals, and tenuous
loyalties there is much concern that the new queen harbours a sense
of fellowship with the Scandinavians. Is she aware of how barbarous
they are, and does she understand quite what terror they have spread?
Since arriving in England Emma has been told horrific stories about
the misery inflicted on the English by the Vikings. She hears of women
raped by as many as fifteen men while their husbands are forced to
watch; of children forced back into homes that have been set alight;
of bodies mutilated beyond recognition; of men, women and children
roped together and dragged on to trading vessels to be sold as slaves.
The degree of cruelty and brutality described to her is inhuman.

She starts from her dark reverie. Her English name is being called.
'Yes, I, Aelfgifu, royal bedfellow, am a favourable witness,' she responds
formally. And one day soon, she hopes, she will actually be able to
understand what it is that she is witnessing.

*   *   *

As the anointed queen, Emma started to participate in court business
almost immediately. She is listed as a witness to documents dated
1002 and even though at that stage she would not have been able to
contribute much to the royal proceedings, she would at least have
been in a good position to glean who were the most frequent and

influential advisers in the king's council. This was by no means a
parliament. It was a fluid group of the country's elite and was composed
of foremost churchmen as well as prominent members of the nobility.
The king was the supreme ruler of England but he was not a complete
autocrat and was dependent on the cooperation of the country's
regional governors and spiritual leaders. As he made his way around
the kingdom meetings of the council were periodically held. These
formal gatherings were huge, often involving several hundred people
and mainly taking place on the monarch's rural estates where there
was room to accommodate the crowds. On these occasions, the large
ensemble travelling with the king was swelled by other members of
the nobility and by archbishops, bishops, abbots and their more junior
ecclesiastics. Many of them made journeys lasting several days in order
to join the assembly. Numerous tents were erected to house their
servants and often even themselves since there were rarely enough
permanent, wooden buildings. The meetings were held in a great hall
where clerks joined the high-ranking delegates in order to write down
the charters that were agreed.

While the enforcement of law and order and the collection of taxes
were duties at a lower, local level, matters of state importance were
discussed and ratified at these great court gatherings: the sanctioning
of grants of land; the endorsement of new legal codes; the settlement
of major disputes; the agreements over when and how to pay the
latest demands for tribute money to the Scandinavian raiders. The
Viking issue was the overwhelming preoccupation of Aethelred's
council.

Among the nobility who regularly attended the council, Aethelred
clearly relied a great deal on his old uncle, Ordulf, brother of the late
dowager queen, and on his kinsman Aethelmaer, the new ealdorman,
or governor, of western Wessex. Beyond the family circle, Aelfhelm, the
ealdorman of southern Northumbria, was also significant, as was his son
Wulfheah.[3] But, of course, not all the nobility could be trusted, and
outbreaks of violence between courtiers frequently needed to be
checked.

Shortly before Emma's wedding the ealdorman of Essex negotiated a substantial deal to pay off one Viking army: matters progressed fairly smoothly until the ealdorman fell into an argument about the proceedings with the king's high-reeve and in a fit of rage killed him. The disgraced aristocrat was swiftly banished from the kingdom.

Relations with the Church were also marked by bouts of some tension. While the king could, to a large extent, control the rise and fall of aristocrats, he needed to proceed with greater caution in his dealings with churchmen. In England, as in Normandy, the ruler gained credibility through the backing of the men of God. Technically the Pope, as head of the Church, chose who should be elevated to the senior positions of archbishop and bishop. In practice this was a matter for the ruler and his council. However, on their appointment these most eminent churchmen often make the long trip to Rome to receive the Pope's blessing as well as a pallium, a finely worked band of cloth worn across the shoulders as a type of badge of office.

In 1002 Wulfstan, former Bishop of London, became Archbishop of York as well as Bishop of Worcester.[4] This formidable man was renowned for his enormous learning: his sermons and homilies, written under the Latin pen name of Lupus, were widely circulated and read out loud. As were the works of Aelfric, a monk of Cerne Abbas in Dorset, who remained an ecclesiastic rather than a statesman. For both these literary giants moral degeneracy had become widespread in England and was a matter of deep concern.

As well as Wulfstan, Aethelred's prominent church advisers included senior ecclesiastics from Winchester. The ancient Roman town was revived back in the seventh century and further redeveloped in the ninth century by King Alfred, since when it had become a significant royal base. Its importance was reflected in the two major churches there: the New Minster, built in the 800s, and almost next door the much earlier Old Minster, which contained the relics of Saint Swithun. In 1002 substantial work on this building had recently been completed. It had been reconstructed on a huge scale – and contained an amazing feat of engineering and harmony: a stupendous organ with twenty-six bellows supplying wind to 400 pipes and requiring seventy strong men to work it in relays. The final stages of the Old Minster's rebuilding

had been overseen by Aelfheah, Bishop of Winchester and in 1002 a
rising power in ecclesiastic and court circles.

Much of court life, though, was dominated by the monarch's own large
family. And for Emma, Aethelred's many offspring must have been an
intimidating tribe. His six sons, Aethelstan, Egbert, Edmund, Eadred,
Eadwig and Edgar, had all been christened after former kings, their
names neatly sharing an alliterative element, as was the custom of the
ruling dynasty. They were no doubt stony-faced in her presence.
Aethelred's daughters may have been slightly less hostile: they did not
have so much to lose should Emma produce a new family for the King.
One daughter was destined for a life devoted to the Church; the others,
Edith, Wulfhild and another Aelfgifu, were soon to be betrothed. In
1002 several of the nobility would have been angling for the honour –
mindful of the power resulting from the royal connection.

At intervals Emma's eldest stepsons would have been absent from
their father's itinerant court, cantering around the country on hunting
and hawking expeditions, making time to visit the great religious centres
en route and wherever possible involving themselves in local strategies
against Viking attacks – in tune with their aristocratic status as fighting
men.

According to contemporary records, during the decade before Emma's
marriage to Aethelred significant damage had been wreaked by the
Scandinavian raiders; in 993 the defences of Bamburgh on the
Northumbrian seaboard were destroyed and 'much war-booty taken';[5]
1994 saw London attacked and successfully defended – the Vikings
moved on, burning, raiding and slaughtering in Essex, Kent, Sussex and
Hampshire; in 997 large areas of Devon and Cornwall were looted and
set alight; 998 saw the Vikings ravaging Dorset and then resting up in
the Isle of Wight; in 999 they invaded Kent and defeated the local army
there, raiding the countryside and demanding big sums of money; in
1001 a large English army confronted the Vikings at Pinhoe in Devon,
where they were roundly defeated and the area sacked.

Accounts of the Viking raids of tenth- and early-eleventh-century
England are provided by the *Anglo-Saxon Chronicles*. These remarkable

manuscripts are year-by-year records of significant events – wars, famines, cattle disease, the crowning of kings, the appointment of bishops. They were compiled over several centuries, fizzling out in the 1150s. Mostly written in Old English rather than Latin, the international language of learning, they offer the first continuous history of England recorded in the vernacular. It was at the court of King Alfred in the early 890s that the initial compilation started, with scribes drawing on earlier material to cover retrospective events: the migration of the Saxons to England; the conversion to Christianity; the clashes between the Saxon kings; the arrival of the first Scandinavian pirates. From about 892 the entries become reasonably contemporary with the matters being reported, although it is not necessarily the case that the annals were then written concurrently with the years on record. The original chronicle has been lost or destroyed; however, copies were made and circulated with many resulting regional additions, omissions and embellishments. Seven of the copies, and fragments of an eighth, remain.

In the surviving chronicles, entries for the years of Aethelred's troubled reign are particularly copious. Most of these were not directly contemporary and are believed to have been written towards the end of the King's life, or even shortly afterwards. They were composed with the benefit of hindsight, weighted with a heavy sense of failure – and their accuracy is suspect. It is possible that the numbers of Vikings arriving and the extent of the damage they caused are exaggerated, while Aethelred's responses are probably presented as being unduly bumbling. What the chronicles do indicate, however, is that the nature and the intent of the attacks altered over a thirty-year period. In 980 Scandinavian opportunists began looting the coastal communities of England. By the 990s larger numbers were arriving, moving further inland, and starting to demand serious sums of money either for their complicity in seeing off other raiders or simply to call a truce, however short-lived. At this stage, too, significant Viking leaders were involved. Although the powerful Norwegian pirate Olaf Tryggvason was successfully bought off, by the turn of the millennium Swein Forkbeard, the warlord who controlled Denmark, was becoming increasingly aggressive. During the early years of the new millennium there must have been a sickening realisation that his ambitions were developing beyond the mere acquisition of treasures and silver coins. Overlordship of England itself was soon to become his objective.

How brutal he and his men actually were is open to question. Without doubt, the Vikings were extremely effective warriors and exceptionally skilled boat-builders. In the aftermath of battle they did rape and pillage and they did capture slaves – a practice that had very lucrative business potential. But they may not have been entirely deserving of their reputation for widespread and unmitigated savagery. It is possible that the English, frequently defeated and humiliated by Viking raiders, made much of the ferocity of the Scandinavians in order to preserve a shred of pride.

Conversely, however, some recent makeovers depict the Vikings simply as intrepid if rough traders who have been much maligned in the course of history. Such theories seem more than overly anodyne. Yet these are not as eccentric as the misrepresentation conceived in the nineteenth century. Finds of Bronze Age headgear with antler-like protuberances, probably used in religious ceremonies, inspired Richard Wagner and the Romantic exponents to portray the Vikings sporting helmets with horns welded to each side. The image stuck although in reality such curious garb would have been extremely impractical in battle: how could a sword or spear be wielded with any degree of ease if the assailant was encumbered by cow-horn headgear? Archaeological evidence shows that the Vikings wore conventional conical helmets made of metal or leather in a style common in Europe at the time.

While Viking dress was not notably very different from that of the Anglo-Saxons, the men from the North seem to have had much higher standards of hygiene. Indeed life for the average Anglo-Saxon was squalid. Archaeological finds, for example, show that in towns and villages open latrines were situated close to the back entrances of houses – whose thatched roofs would have been infested with insects. In monasteries there was generally a better grasp of basic sanitation: latrines were often carefully positioned, in some cases over running water well away from sources for domestic use, and residents were sometimes urged to wash themselves as frequently as five or six times a year. Cleanliness, though, had some appeal for Anglo-Saxon women. According to the chronicler John of Wallingford[6] Scandinavian men had great success with local girls because of their salutary, if not foppish, appearance. He writes that the Viking settlers had a bizarre reputation for bathing on Saturdays, that they changed their woollens with amazing frequency and that they combed their hair regularly.

For the Viking raiders, the Anglo-Saxon state was a wealthy country offering very rich pickings. There were great churches to plunder for precious metals, an efficient network of mints to loot for hoards of silver, affluent manors and estates to pilfer or hold to ransom (and burn down should payment be unforthcoming). Initially England was a soft target, too. This was not only because of its extensive coastline: when the first attacks against Aethelred's kingdom took place defences were weak. The nation was recovering from a period of internal turmoil and a child ruler had just been enthroned. Meanwhile for the English, the Vikings were a terrifying threat, stories of the last Scandinavian invasions still being part of living memory. In England it was widely believed that the people had brought such misery on themselves. The Viking raids were seen as the scourge of God, divine retribution for moral waywardness and particularly for the nation's heinous crime: the killing of a king.

When Emma first arrived in England she may not have been aware of the lingering suspicions over Aethelred's involvement in the assassination of his brother. This crime had taken place more than two decades before, but many of Aethelred's subjects would still have believed that the murder of King Edward lay at the root of their problems, and that the royal family was largely to blame.

In 975 the death of Aethelred's father, King Edgar the Peaceful, prompted an ugly scrummage over the issue of succession. In Anglo-Saxon England there was no cut-and-dried tradition of regal primogeniture. The first-born son might be selected to inherit his father's position, but one of his uncles, brothers or even cousins could be considered more worthy of the throne. The very word king derives from the Anglo-Saxon *cyning*, or descendant (*ing*) of the kin (*cyn*). The monarch was chosen from close relatives of the previous king who, importantly by the tenth-century, could clearly trace their line back to Cerdic, founder of the governing dynasty. The last king might have named his heir but failing that, after his death, the *witan* would select the strongest (or possibly in this case the most malleable) male member of the ruling family. Not an ideal situation if there were any division of opinion.

Edgar had probably married three times. By wife number one, he produced Edward, who was a young teenager when his father died. This first wife disappears from any surviving records fairly swiftly.[7] Edgar's following liaison with his putative second wife may never have been formalised. It too produced one child, Edith, later to join the burgeoning list of royal Anglo-Saxon saints. She was raised at Wilton convent, where she pursued the whole of her short and blameless life. And it was here that her mother retired sometime after Edith's birth. Whether this was a chosen path of righteous retreat is debatable; she may have been forced into it as a convenient way of allowing scope for Edgar's next marriage. His match to Aelfthryth, the widow of his foster brother, was controversial. The relationship was close enough to cause shock waves and there may also have been a matter of suspected adultery and murder. Later, twelfth-century accounts claim that Edgar and Aelfthryth were so enamoured of each other they actually plotted the death of Edgar's foster brother so that they would be free to marry[8] – a heady accusation given the lack of love matches during this period.

They had two sons: Edmund and Aethelred. Edmund appears to have been Edgar's chosen heir (in the refoundation charter of the New Minster, Winchester, of 966 he is named as *legitimus clito*, legitimate heir to the throne). However, he died four years before his father, and subsequently succession seems to have been up for grabs between Edgar's eldest son, Edward, and Aethelred, his surviving son by Aelfthryth. On Edgar's death, sparring noble families backed each claimant. Edward won and was duly consecrated to the throne against a backdrop of what appears to have been near civil war. Two-and-a-half years later the boy king was killed. Aethelred, little more than ten years old, was then crowned and his mother became a prominent regent. So much is gleaned from near-contemporary accounts by Byrhtferth of Ramsey.

He describes Edward as an odious young man who 'inspired in all not only fear but even terror for he scourged them not only with words but truly with blows'.[9] He maintains that the young king's murderers were a group of *thegns*, or aristocrats, in the faction supporting Aethelred. Yet later chroniclers in the twelfth and thirteenth centuries point the finger of blame firmly at the wicked stepmother, Aelfthryth, who would evidently let nothing impede her intentions to see her own son on the throne. She, they variously claim, personally stabbed Edward as she beguilingly offered him a drink, or, at the very least, issued the orders for her men to butcher him.[10] In an extravagant, eleventh-century account of the crime,[11] Aethelred himself is portrayed as a somewhat witless bystander of his mother's machinations: on hearing of the death of his half-brother, so the story goes, Aethelred burst into tears, enraging his mother so much that she beat him with a set of candlesticks, the first object to come to hand. The experience left him with an unfortunate phobia – for the rest of his life he would never allow lit candles in his presence, quite some disadvantage in the long, dark winters when there was little alternative light.

Aethelred was not to escape some implication in his brother's murder. Whatever the murky truth of Edward's death, the fact remains that it took place on 18 March 978 at Corfe in Dorset, where the young king was a guest at the estate of his stepmother and half-brother. The body was hurriedly disposed of in nearby swamps. But it became the subject of increasing angst and nearly a year later the grave was purportedly revealed to locals who saw a great pillar of fire stretching down from the heavens to a damp and desolate spot. Edward's remains were duly exhumed and taken to St Mary's abbey at Wareham, where they were buried on 13 February 979 and where it was subsequently reported that blind people had miraculously regained their sight after bathing their eyes in a spring of clear water that had suddenly bubbled up beside the grave. It was at the insistence of a number of powerful churchmen and women that Edward's body was exhumed again and transported to Shaftesbury convent, which was deemed a more fitting resting place for a king (while the nunnery could profit from another pilgrimage trail alongside that of Edward's sainted grandmother, Aelfgifu). Here his remains were ceremoniously buried in the churchyard – while a couple of cripples were reputedly cured en route. Two years later, after more graveside miracles had been reported (some ostensibly witnessed by Aelfric, the Archbishop of Canterbury who was shortly to conduct Emma's wedding), Edward was dug up yet again and transferred with due honour to the sanctuary of the abbey church where he was declared a saint.

It was no coincidence that this was some months after Aelfthryth had died and also during the height of Viking invasions. Meanwhile Aethelred's late half-sister, Edith, had also been elevated to sainthood. Creating royal saints was a convenient way of demonstrating the spiritual success of the ruling family at a time when their earthly power was clearly faltering.

Aethelred, though, was doomed almost at the very outset of his life – according to one of the most remarkable of the chroniclers writing just after the Norman Conquest. William was a learned monk from Malmesbury who, scholarly as he was, knew how to entertain as well as inform and was particularly gifted at injecting juicy anecdotes into his text. It is unlikely that these were entirely fabrications and they must, to some extent, have been based on stories passed down through oral traditions or recorded in documents that were subsequently lost. Aethelred's worthlessness, writes William of Malmesbury, was foretold at his christening. This was conducted by the Archbishop of Canterbury, Dunstan, considered the greatest man of his time and later also elevated to sainthood. As Aethelred was being plunged into the font, William confides, the infant prince 'interrupted the sacrament by opening his bowels, at which Dunstan was much concerned – "By God and His Mother," he said, "he will be a wastrel when he is a man".' The Archbishop later presided at Aethelred's coronation. When Dunstan placed the crown on the child's head William notes that he 'could not restrain himself, and poured out in a loud voice the spirit of the prophecy with which his own heart was full. "Inasmuch," he said, "as you aimed at the throne through the death of your own brother, now hear the word of the Lord. Thus saith the Lord God: the sin of your shameful mother and the sin of the men who shared in her wicked plot shall not be blotted out except by the shedding of much blood of your miserable subjects, and there shall come upon the people of England such evils as they have not suffered from the time when they came to England until then".' Sure enough, writes William with an edge of told-you-so satisfaction, in the third year of Aethelred's reign 'there came to Southampton, a harbour near Winchester, seven ships full of pirates . . .'

The *Anglo-Saxon Chronicles*[12] actually maintain that this raid took place just a year after Aethelred's coronation at Kingston. And that not only was Southampton attacked by northern raiders (and most of the town dwellers killed or taken prisoner) but that Thanet in Kent was also ravaged, and Cheshire, too. So began the troubles that were to continue for the entire duration of Aethelred's reign and that along the way led him to start an Anglo-Norman affiliation.

By the autumn of 1002 Aethelred must have been considerably buoyed up by his marriage and by his new alliance with Emma's brother Richard. He evidently felt sufficiently confident to take action that was guaranteed to taunt and enrage his Scandinavian enemies. Towards the end of that year the *Anglo-Saxon Chronicles* record, staggeringly, that 'the king ordered all the Danish men who were among the English race to be killed'.[13] The deed was done on St Brice's Day, 13 November, and thereafter in England the feast day of the fifth-century Bishop of Tours was to be associated with this singularly bloody event.

It beggars belief that Aethelred really intended every single Scandinavian living in England to be annihilated – 'Dane' frequently being employed as a blanket term for all people from the embryonic states of Norway and Sweden as well as Denmark. Statistics for the period are impossible to adduce with any degree of accuracy but it is clear that at this date Scandinavians formed a substantial proportion of the population in the east of the country, having settled there around the turn of the tenth century in the first wave of Viking attacks on England. It seems likely that Aethelred was in reality targeting those 'north men' who were more newly arrived and were living in areas outside the region where Scandinavian customs and law prevailed.

The *Anglo-Saxon Chronicles* claim that the King was acting to subvert a 'Danish' assassination attempt on him and his councillors. A later charter referring to the event makes no such mention but does assert that Aethelred was operating very much on the agreement of the *witan*. 'A decree was sent out by me with the counsel of my leading men and magnates, to the effect that all the Danes who had sprung up in this island, sprouting like cockle amongst the wheat, were to be destroyed by a most just extermination'[14] Aethelred's scribe wrote on his behalf, alluding to the Bible (Matthew 13, verses 24–30) with the reference to cockle and wheat. The very reason for this document's existence attests to an enthusiastic local response to the orders for the Scandinavian bloodbath. Dated 1004, the charter is a renewal of a grant of lands to the monastery of St Frideswide, Oxford, whose original records had been lost in the mayhem of the massacre. It describes the circumstances under which these manuscripts, and the church itself, were destroyed. On 13 November 1002, some wretched Scandinavians living in Oxford had tried to seek sanctuary in the church at St Frideswide, probably the site of what is now Christ Church cathedral.[15] In their desperation to escape what seems to have been a baying mob they broke down the doors of the building and barricaded themselves in. But the townsfolk, and indeed people from further afield who had joined the Dane-hunt, determined to kill the immigrants, and set fire to the church. It went up in smoke – and all its precious books and manuscripts too, notes the charter, which fails to confirm the fate of the victims. Presumably they were either incinerated too or were butchered as they fled the burning building.

The evidence of surviving charters such as this one is considerably complicated by the fact that many of them are forgeries. Not that the good monks who wrote these counterfeit documents were necessarily making completely false claims so as to expand the landholdings of their monasteries. In the aftermath of the Norman Conquest, when the new king was rewarding his commanders with great gifts of land, it became imperative to justify claims to estates held before the invasion. If legitimate records were not readily available they had to be created. In some instances the fakes are fairly easily identifiable in that they contain hopeless anachronisms where the devious monks mistakenly included in the lists of witnesses the names of people who had actually died some time before the document was purportedly drawn up. Others are more cleverly devised – and make the genuine articles difficult to authenticate. The 'Frideswide' charter in which Aethelred recompenses the people of Oxford for their losses during the St Brice's Day massacres, does, however, appear to be legitimate – with the possible exception of a subsection relating to lands in Headington. The list of witnesses is certainly very plausible. The top names read:

> Aelfric, archbishop of the church of Canterbury, have corroborated it [the charter] under pain of anathema
> Wulfstan, archbishop of the city of York, have confirmed
> Aelfgifu, consecrated to the royal couch, have promoted this donation
> Athelstan, first-born of the king's sons, with my brothers was present as a favourable witness
> Aelfheah, bishop of Winchester, have joined in signing[16]

Emma, under her court name Aelfgifu, is clearly ranked below archbishops but above bishops and, significantly, above her stepsons.

As a foreigner, and one of Scandinavian descent, who had newly arrived in England, would she really have concurred with the tenor of the charter's contents? Two years on from the massacre, Aethelred still sounds vitriolic about the 'Danes' and by quoting from the Bible implies that there was some Christian justification in this act of ethnic cleansing. Whether Emma's family in Normandy was impressed by Aethelred's petulant display of power is, unsurprisingly, not recorded. The event, however, was later to be used by Norman chroniclers as a useful piece of propaganda to show how barbarous the English monarchy was. William of Jumièges, writing in the 1050s (with many revisions made after 1066), comments that Aethelred defiled his kingdom 'with such a dreadful crime that in his own reign even the heathens judged it as a detestable, shocking deed. For in a single day he murdered, in a sudden fury and without charging them with any crime, the Danes who lived peacefully and quite harmoniously throughout the kingdom and who did not at all fear for their lives. He ordered women to be buried up to the waists and the nipples to be torn from their breasts by ferocious mastiffs set upon them. He also gave orders to crunch little children against doorposts.'

And the Viking response? The ferocity of their retaliation would not have been entirely unexpected – although Emma herself was to be caught in the middle of the recriminations.

CHAPTER FOUR

Revenge

Exeter has been raided by Swein Forkbeard and his army, and Emma is held largely to blame. Much of the town has been reduced to a mass of smouldering buildings. The remaining folk there are struggling to bury their dead and grieving over other relatives who have been rounded up by the Vikings and taken away to be sold as slaves. Several of Exeter's twenty or so churches have been completely rased to the ground, the treasures of gold and silver plundered; the town's potteries have been smashed up, the kilns ruined; its mints have been looted for hoards of silver and gold coins; many of its houses as well as weavers' workshops have been utterly destroyed by fires whose flames have spread rapidly across the grid of narrow streets – a neat urban plan dating back to the late 800s. With a population of some 2,000, Exeter has been one of southern England's most prosperous trading centres, and a significant target. But until this atrocity it was considered unassailable.

Fortified by old Roman walls that were strengthened with more recent stonework, the town had one of the best defence systems in the country. So how on earth did the Vikings get through? It is widely believed that the Scandinavian raiders can only have penetrated Exeter's gates and huge ramparts through an act of treachery from within. The town is the property of the new queen – it was given to her less than a year ago as part of her dower on her marriage to the King – and she had installed Hugh, one of her own Norman courtiers, as her manager and agent there. He has fled, as many others did in the face of the ferocious onslaught, and accusations are rife that he was the contemptible quisling[1] who provided the Danish army with vital defence information. Why did the queen employ this Viking-loving Norman, who quite clearly was not to be trusted? The court mood is unforgiving, and the strained situation puts other members of the Queen's Norman entourage in jeopardy.

From where, in any case, did the Vikings launch their onslaught? The last big attack by Scandinavian raiders was about a year ago, and in the interval Swein may have returned to his homeland to recruit additional men and requisition more ships. Could he have made his assault directly from Denmark, or did he shelter first on the Isle of Wight, as Vikings have done in the past? There are many, however, who are willing to believe that he was allowed safe harbour in Brittany, or even in Normandy despite the new alliance between Emma's brother and the English king. Yet suspicions of connivance on the part of the Norman ruler seem, for once, far-fetched. The raid has been deliberately aimed at the Queen's property, and by extension at the recently created bond between the Norman count and King Aethelred. Swein Forkbeard has evidently been enraged by the affiliation.

But quite beyond that, undoubtedly the attack has also been an act of revenge. The Massacre of the Danes a few months ago has, of course, given general cause for Viking retaliation. There is, though, a more personal dimension to Swein Forkbeard's ferocious measures of retribution. His sister Gunnhild was among the Scandinavians who were butchered under orders of the King. She was the wife of Pallig, the Viking leader who had been bought into Aethelred's service only to double-cross the English king. And she had been with her husband on many of his exploits, having travelled from Denmark with him and his pirate crew. Along with Pallig, she had been captured after the raids of 1001 and had become a political hostage in England. It is rumoured that Eadric, a rising court favourite of Aethelred, issued the orders for her decapitation.[2] Pallig, too, was killed. Gunnhild was apparently forced to watch the proceedings shortly before her own execution.

The exacerbation of England's most aggressive Viking enemy clearly has not been a wise move, and Swein Forkbeard's onslaught has not been confined to Exeter. Reports have arrived that after ransacking this town he and his army travelled on to Wilton, where houses and churches have been torched – although news is not yet forthcoming about the fate of the convent there, which contains the relics of Aethelred's sainted sister Edith. With Wilton burning, Swein's troops then attacked Salisbury before returning to their ships and sailing away in these stallions of the waves.[3]

*   *   *

Swein Forkbeard's retaliation, grim as it was, would not have come as a complete shock to the people of England. This was a society whose very ethos was based on revenge and feud. From time immemorial it had been the paramount duty of a person's family group to take vengeance or extract compensation if he or she were to be murdered. This ingrained obligation was the foundation by which order was maintained in earliest Anglo-Saxon society: fear of retaliation being a strong deterrent to the taking of a life. Of course, such a system did not always work. Homicide and subsequent revenge killing often resulted in feuds – many of which lasted decades and left great trails of corpses. The king, as the patron of social peace, regulated revenge proceedings and attempted to limit the violence. From the reign of King Alfred of Wessex in the late-ninth century, the later monarchs of Anglo-Saxon England took greater steps to curb the possibilities for bloody vendettas – not least by noting in many of their law codes that a person's family members were not to be held answerable for their relative's crimes.

However, there was an alternative to revenge: financial compensation for the bereaved family. This was a clear option, dating from at least the first written laws of the Anglo-Saxon period – those of King Ethelbert of Kent in the very early-seventh century. The amount deemed appropriate was a recognised legal value: a fixed sum for murdered members of each level of society, except that of slaves.

Every free man knew what he or she was worth. Their *wergild*, literally meaning 'man-price', was an early version of life insurance. The Scandinavians also had such a code of compensation, an age-old tradition common to Germanic peoples. A document surviving from Aethelred's reign enumerates the sliding scale of *wergilds* in one part of the Danelaw – although tariffs outside the Danish-dominated region of England would almost certainly have been different. The amounts are given in thrymsa, which are thought to have been composed of three silver pennies. The King himself is valued at 30,000 thrymsas; his sons 15,000; archbishops are worth that amount, too; bishops and ealdormen are also equal, at 8,000 thrymsas; mass-priests and noblemen have a *wergild* of 2,000; while peasants are priced at just 266.[4] There is no mention of women in this or similar documents in the Anglo-Saxon period. The lack of such information has been taken to indicate that females had a *wergild* equivalent to that of men of their social status. Emma's worth as queen, however, is difficult to gauge: it would have been somewhere below that of the King but above, or at least on a par with, his sons' value. When pregnant her indemnity rate would have risen sharply. There is evidence that an expectant mother had increased value: that of her own rank plus half of her husband's *wergild*.

Revenge by death or the payment of compensation were the only legal penalties in the case of murder: in the Anglo-Saxon period there were no prisons. For many other crimes, a convicted person was subject to corporal punishment, often by mutilation, and/or fined. The compensation rate was the basis on which many of the charges were levied. *Wergild* was payable for social offences as wide-ranging as adultery, incest, theft and indoor fighting. Whether the amount related to the value of the culprit or that of the victim is sometimes unclear from the various laws enumerating such misconducts. Meanwhile, who was to receive the money seems in certain instances vague. Aethelred's laws of 1008, drawn up by Archbishop Wulfstan but clearly with the approval of the King, include a clause asserting that in the case of ambush or open resistance to the law the offender was to pay *wergild,* or a suitable fine (a caveat that would, presumably, allow scope to raise the charge which in the case of a peasant's *wergild* would be fairly negligible). To whom this would be paid is unspecified. If the perpetrator were to resist arrest and be killed in the ensuing violence, it stipulates that his own *wergild* would be cancelled – in other words that his family would receive no compensation.

Fines that related to an individual's *wergild*, rather than directly to the nature of the crime, were in general a sensible way of ensuring that amount was affordable, and that there was a reasonable chance it would be paid in full. The pricing system is clearly redolent of an extremely firm class structure. Towards the end of the ninth century King Alfred had famously summed up the essential components of English society as *gebedmen, fyrdmen* and *weorcmen:*[5] those who pray, the churchmen, who in turn had their own hierarchical system; those who fight, the noblemen or *thegns*; and those who work, the peasants or *ceorls* (later to be transmuted into the disparaging word 'churl'). Slaves may also have been considered part of this labour force. Women, meanwhile, were apparently left out of at least part of the equation: the term *fyrdmen*, fighting men, for the nobility is a misnomer since the female half of the group rarely, if ever, took up arms.

Give or take this glaring omission, Alfred's delineation was still apposite during Aethelred's reign about a century later. The *thegns* had large landholdings (women as well as men), and according to the poetry of the period they spent vast amounts of time entertaining themselves by laying on great feasts, the menfolk hunting and hawking for outdoor amusement. But theirs was by no means an indolent, work-free life. The males of this rank had serious obligations: attending local and even royal assemblies; keeping order on their estates and in their extended households; and appearing for their social inferiors in any lawsuits brought to the regional assizes. These courts were related to administrative divisions of land: shires, and below that hundreds (known in the Danelaw as *wapentakes*) which were, notionally at any rate, made up of a hundred hides, a hide in turn being the basic plot capable of supporting a peasant family. Shire courts were held twice a year, those of the hundreds once a month. They were run by officials of the *thegn* class. However, quite above and beyond his legal and peace-keeping duties, the male *thegn* was, of course, a man of the sword. He belonged to the warrior class and in times of war was expected to show his prowess as a fighter and military commander.

His untrained soldiers were peasant stock: *ceorls* who worked the land or earned their living as craftsmen, and who were called to battle by their superiors. There were a great many minor categories to the peasant class. Some *ceorls* owned a modest amount of land, many had no such property but paid rent or rendered services in kind for a smallholding on a big estate, others were simply hired labourers. By the eleventh century a degree of social mobility had become possible: a *ceorl* could be promoted to the rank of *thegn* if he owned five hides of land, a bell-house and castle-gate as well as having a seat and special office in the king's hall. Quite what constituted a bell-house and castle-gate has not been clearly established, but these features may well have been cited as practical indications of the smallholder's ability to defend his land or raise the alarm if intruders approached.

But if a *ceorl* could rise, he could also fall: in times of famine and great hardship it was not unknown for the poorest of peasants to sell themselves or their families into slavery rather than starve. The unfree were a largely unpaid, and mainly agricultural, workforce. They were the commodities of their owners, to be bought and sold at will – the price being roughly equivalent to that of eight cattle.[6] A person was born into this unenviable position or became a slave either as a punishment for certain crimes or through refusal to pay fines he or she had incurred. In addition, captives of war were frequently enslaved – although the much deplored Viking practice of rounding up English men, women and children as items to be traded was extreme. These victims would subsequently be sold elsewhere in Europe, often at the great slave markets of Dublin and Rouen.

In England, relegation to the realms of the unfree was not necessarily terminal. In some cases it was possible to buy oneself, or be bought, out of slavery. It was also considered an act of Christian charity to redeem slaves. Surviving wills from the late-tenth century give detailed instructions as to the manumission, or setting free, of a number of men and women: in a document dating from about 950, one Wynflaed stipulates that on her death those who have been her property are to be released – Wulfwaru, Wulfflaed, Gerburg, Pifus, Eadhelm, Sprow and his wife among many other individuals. Evidently a very wealthy woman, Wynflaed includes in her will a request that 'for her soul's sake' her children are to set free any more of her penally enslaved people she has forgotten to mention.

Apart from personal pride, was there very much difference between a slave and the lowest grade of *ceorl*? Probably not in terms of the meagre standard of living – the most basic shelter, a much patched set of clothes, and barely enough sustenance on which to live being the pretty miserable lot of a great many people. But a slave had few rights and was simply the responsibility of his or her owner. All free men had a 'lord' they chose. In addition to family ties, lordship was a safety valve. It was a legal requirement, too, and it was a fundamental and mutually beneficial bond. Absolute loyalty and services, largely of a military and agricultural nature, were rewarded with protection and patronage – and in very aristocratic circles, treasures and gifts of land. Although in the lower echelons of society the tie was often between wealthy estate owner and tenant farmer, it was essentially a personal relationship rather than one relating to landholdings. In this respect it was subtly different from the 'feudal' system that developed after the Norman Conquest when land, rather than loyalty, became the primary focus of the bond between labourer and lord.

A boy's first oath of allegiance to his lord was effectively his initiation to manhood. Girls do not appear to have had a similar system of sponsorship beyond their families. Women were either minors, married or devoted to God. As a child, a girl was protected by her father. If she became a nun she removed herself from the hurly-burly of life when she committed herself to the Church – and was protected by it. If she married she and her children became the responsibility of her husband, although her brothers and other members of her kin continued to guard her own interests. So where would that have left Emma? Protection from her Norman family was to prove invaluable both to her and to Aethelred; meanwhile her husband was her guardian and lord.

As king, Aethelred was the supreme lord of the entire nation. It was a significant bond with his subjects. There was precious little to stop the most domineering *thegns* from raising their own private armies, but what deterred them from challenging the ruler of the country was the pragmatic knowledge that the monarch was more powerful, as well as the innate recognition that allegiance to him, theoretically at any rate, overrode the ties of men to their immediate lord. The king required all men to uphold his authority and to defend the land. This principally devolved into three duties: the strengthening of fortresses; the repair of bridges (a vital means of communication); and military service, which included the building of ships. In return the king was the ultimate

patron of his people. Aethelred's laws reflect a Christian sense of pater-
nalism: 'It is the decree of our lord and his councillors' wrote his law-
maker, Archbishop Wulfstan, 'that Christian men are not to be
condemned to death for all too small offences . . . But otherwise life-
sparing punishments are to be devised.' Meanwhile, along with 'deceitful
deeds and hateful abuses', over-eating and over-drinking were, in the
words of the law, 'to be shunned'.[7]

Not that there was much opportunity for over-indulgence in 1005.
'Here in this year there was the [sic] great famine throughout the English
race, such that no one ever remembered one so grim before',[8] the *Anglo-
Saxon Chronicles* record. Crop failure, or destruction, would have been
the principal cause of such calamity. For the ordinary Anglo-Saxon
person, meat was a feast-day rarity, while cereals – wheat, barley, oats
and rye – were the basis of their diet. Bread, preferably made from wheat,
was the staple of most households. Very labour-intensive it was to
produce, too: commercial mills had yet to become an established feature
of life and in the vast majority of homes grinding grain for flour was an
extremely arduous and time-consuming task undertaken by women. The
standard meal appears to have been bread and an accompaniment –
possibly broth made of peas, beans or other pulses, or of vegetables such
as leeks, onions, beet, parsnips and white and purple carrots (the orange
variety was a seventeenth-century development). Occasionally fish such
as eels or fresh or dried meat would have uplifted everyday meals. But
in very poor households this would have been almost unheard of, and
here even bread would have been infrequently consumed – for the most
part it was substituted by porridge-like cereal stews.

In 1005, the desultory lack of food was at least partly a result of the
Viking attacks. Since sacking Salisbury, the Scandinavian raiders had
set upon East Anglia, which was bravely defended by the magnate
Ulfketel Snilling, who married Aethelred's daughter Wulfhild around
this time.[9] The Viking onslaughts in the south and east would have had
a cumulative effect on farming capabilities: on the one hand, many
crops would have been set alight or otherwise destroyed; on the other,
local labourers would have been called up to defend the area, leaving
their fields untended at important times in the agricultural year.

Still, the famine was to have one beneficial effect: with little food available to be requisitioned or plundered the Vikings departed – for the time being. Meanwhile Emma's reputation was recovering from the setback of associations with their attack on Exeter. What happened to her Norman retainers after the raids of 1003 remains unknown – some of them may have been allowed to remain with the new queen in England. Thankfully, the convent at Wilton, where her sanctified sister-in-law lay buried, seems to have escaped the worst of the ensuing onslaught (a devout, and profitable, pilgrimage trail there continued). So Emma was spared long-term reproach. In any case, the birth of her first child, a son, gave her enough honour and prestige to rise above any mutterings at court.

Edward, named after his newly sainted and long-since murdered uncle, was born at Islip near Oxford. There is no information as to when exactly this was, but clearly he was at court in 1005. A charter of that year records Edward's name in the list of witnesses,[10] babe in arms though he may have been. The document formalises the founda-tion of Eynsham Abbey and a grant of fairly extensive lands. The gath-ering for this occasion must have been quite a crush: eighty-six people attested the proceedings, including all six of Edward's half-brothers. His own name appears eighth in the list: after Aethelred's and those of the older princes, and just before his mother's. In this hierarchy, it is almost as if the King was deliberately demonstrating that his new family did not take precedence over the children of his first marriage.

But even if Emma had somewhat low status in the King's immediate household, she clearly had powers in her own right for she granted Edward land at Islip to celebrate his birth. Perhaps this was also in thanks for her survival. Childbirth was, of course, a risky business and a big killer. Excavations of the cemetery at the late Anglo-Saxon church at Raunds in Northamptonshire show that of the women buried there nearly half died in their major childbearing years, before the age of twenty-five.[11]

In England at the turn of the first millennium there were midwives and there were physicians. There were no hospitals as such, but from at least the tenth century medical texts had existed in both Latin and Old

English. Whether these had much practical value is debatable: the rudimentary doctors appear to have been mainly laymen who, without the benefit of a monastic education, may well have been unable to read. In addition, village herbalists, many of whose remedies relied on traditions of magic and the occult, would almost certainly have been illiterate. So the ecclesiastical scholars who copiously compiled records of known cures would have done this solely for the academic purpose of preserving what was evidently an extensive medical tradition. Their remedies range from herbal recipes drawn from Greek and Roman works to folk cures, prayers and hopelessly implausible charms. Among salves for such conditions as dandruff (to be washed away with watercress seeds mixed with goose grease) and 'granulations', or pimples, on a woman's face (seen off with 'great wort' root stirred into oil), are treatments for anything from leprosy and snakebite to wounds and warts. In general, the more outlandish remedies existed for conditions over which the physician would have been least able to help. Problems in pregnancy frequently fall into this category and in particular there are several 'cures' for the retention of a dead foetus. 'The woman who may have a dead bairn in her inwards,' reads one 'if she drinketh wolf's milk mingled with wine and honey in like quantities, soon it healeth.'[12] Another remedy for this complication is composed of dried and pounded hare's heart combined with frankincense dust.

With poor diet and lack of protein, especially among the *ceorl* class, child mortality was common. In the case of repeated deaths there appears to have been little hope but to resort to charm:

Let the woman who cannot bring her child to maturity go to the barrow of a deceased man, and step thrice over the barrow, and then thrice say these words
> *May this be my boot*
> *Of the loathsome late birth*
> *May this be my boot*
> *Of the heavy swart birth*
> *May this be my boot*
> *Of the loathsome lame birth*[13]

A MISCELLANY OF ANGLO-SAXON REMEDIES

A salve for 'flying venom' (in other words, epidemics) and for sudden pustules

Take a hand full of hammerwort and a handful of maythe and a handful of waybroad together with the roots of waterdock, avoiding flat roots. Mix with one eggshell full of clean honey. Then add clean butter [the amount unspecified], preferably melted, or clarified, three times. Sing one mass over the worts [or herbs], before they are mixed with the other ingredients and the salve is composed.

Ear problems – including tinnitus

If there are insects in ears, collect the juice of green earthgall, or juice of horehound, or juice of wormwood, whatsoever of these you choose. Pour the juice into the ear, this will draw the worm out. If there is a dinning [or buzzing] in the ears; take oil, apply on to ewes wool, and when going to bed close up the ear with the wool. Remove it on waking.

Bladder troubles

For a sore bladder, and in case any stones are waxing there, collect Dwarf dwosle, or Pennyroula. Pound it well and add two draughts of wine. Mix together vigorously and then drink. The bladder will soon be in a better state and within a few days the plant will heal the infirmity and force out the stones that are inside

Chapped lips

For sore lips: smear the lips with honey, then take the film of an egg, add pepper and apply to the honey coating.

Baldness

If a man's hair fall off, collect the juice of the wort called nasturtium, and by another name cress. Anoint the nose with it, and the hair shall wax.

From *Leechdoms, Wortcunning and Starcraft of Early England*, collected and edited by Revd Oswald Cockayne, London 1864

Only marginally less occult advice is given for conception. 'To make a woman pregnant give to drink in wine a hares runnet [probably rennet] by weight of four pennies to the woman from a female hare, the man from a male hare and then let them do their concubitus and after that let them forbear; then quickly she will be pregnant; and for meat she shall for some while use mushrooms and, instead of a bath, smearing [anointing with oils], wonderfully she will be pregnant.'[14] Hares in particular appear to have been key ingredients for fertility. In one potion for the conception of a male child, a dried hare's belly is to be cut into shreds and added to a drink that must be consumed by both partners.

Emma may have had children who did not survive infancy. She was to produce an adequately respectable number with Aethelred: between 1005 and 1013 a daughter, Godgifu, and another son, Alfred, were born. Her duties of childbirth done, she was not a hands-on mother. Nor were most noble ladies of her time. There is no surviving evidence as to how Godgifu and Alfred were raised in their early lives, and by whom. However, two records of dubious authenticity may, at a pinch, provide some small clues as to Edward's upbringing. The first is a document confirming a donation of land to Westminster church. Here Edward's foster mother is named as Leofrun, the wife of one 'Earl Tostig'. The record is almost undoubtedly a forgery on the part of the monks of Westminster, but this particular detail could be true for the simple reason that it was in no one's interests to fabricate the name. The second possible clue is more of a long shot: a history of Ely Abbey, written in the twelfth century, contains a story that Emma conferred Edward on Ely monastery so that he could be brought up there as a monk. It is at best an eccentric claim: it would have been extremely unusual for the King's son to be dedicated to the Church, and it is highly unlikely that Emma's ambitions for her eldest child were so unworldly. Yet there may be an inkling of a fact here in that it is possible Edward was sent to Ely to receive some education.

Given that Emma was married to Aethelred for fourteen years her brood of three children does not compare favourably to the fecundity of Aethelred's previous wife (or even wives), who produced at least ten offspring. Later chroniclers suggest that Emma's relationship with her first husband was less than rosy. Working in the twelfth century, William of Malmesbury gossips that Aethelred was such a louche and distasteful man he would rarely let his wife sleep with him and instead 'brought the royal majesty into disrepute by tumbling with concubines'.[15] Writing in the early-thirteenth century, Roger of Wendover, a monk at St Albans, also confides that the King 'would scarcely admit [Emma] to his bed'.[16] It is possible that these medieval historians concocted their comments from contemporary stories now lost, but more probably – and more prosaically – such colour comes from their knowledge of Aethelred's disasters shortly after his marriage to Emma. The years from 1006 to 1013 were particularly marked by misfortune, and by bad judgement on the part of the King.

Bloody intrigue at court appears to have been the start of the downward spiral in the King's already troubled reign. By 1005 two of Aethelred's oldest and most trusted advisers seem to have retired to religious establishments: his uncle Ordulf and his kinsman Aethelmaer, ealdorman of western Wessex, disappear from court records. With these senior noblemen no longer in the King's close confidence, the *Anglo-Saxon Chronicles* then report startling developments in 1006. Wulfgeat, another valued councillor, abruptly falls from grace and all his lands are confiscated – because of 'unjust judgements and arrogant deeds' according to the twelfth-century chronicler Florence of Worcester.[17] Meanwhile Aelfhelm, ealdorman of southern Northumbria, is killed and his two sons are blinded. Florence of Worcester fills in the details: he maintains that Aelfhelm was murdered while on a hunting expedition in Shropshire – an act of skulduggery on the part of an ambitious courtier, Eadric 'Streona', or 'the Acquisitor', so named because of his reputation for rapaciously seizing church land and money. Aelfhelm's sons, writes Florence, were blinded shortly afterwards, a severe punishment for unspecified crimes, on the order of the King himself. It would be impossible to prove that all these events were related; however, it seems a remarkable coincidence that in one year four of the King's stalwart advisers were disgraced or killed. The gap was at least partially filled by Eadric Streona, who married Aethelred's daughter Edith, was made ealdorman of Mercia, and proceeded to become probably the most powerful and certainly the most nefarious nobleman in the country.

Emma was a mere bystander to the plots and political manoeuvres. But the brutal treatment meted out to Aelfhelm of Northumbria and his two sons was to have dramatic repercussions for her. Not surprisingly, Aelfhelm's family turned against the King and his court. They were no doubt quick to support Swein Forkbeard and his Danish troops when they invaded England. And at some point over the next eight years Aelfhelm's now-fatherless daughter was married to Swein's son. She was yet another Aelfgifu, and she was to become a thorn in Emma's side – a woman whose determination and cunning were to rival that of the Norman-born queen.

In July 1006 the Vikings returned with a vengeance. Arriving at Sandwich they 'did all just as they were accustomed: raided and burned and killed as they travelled'.[18] Aethelred took defensive action by calling all men in Wessex and Mercia – southern and mid-westerly England – to arms. It may have been the only option open to him but it must have done little to ease the famine conditions that were prevailing: the *Anglo-Saxon Chronicles* point out that the men were away campaigning during harvest time. And they seem to have been pretty ineffective. That winter the Vikings swarmed through Hampshire, Berkshire and Oxfordshire. After burning much of Wallingford they took themselves and their booty away. Winchester was apparently spared; the *Anglo-Saxon Chronicles* describe how the citizens glimpsed the departing Danes from their defensive walls.

Armed resistance on land having failed, Aethelred and his councillors had no alternative but to pay the raiders yet more tribute, in both money and supplies. Food stocks – quantities of wheat and oats, dried meat and even live pigs and sheep – were requisitioned and given to the Vikings. Thirty thousand pounds was raised and paid. Thereafter a truce was agreed. However, there was no lasting peace. The payment merely bought Aethelred time to prepare his defences against the next invasion. He must have been forewarned that there was to be a major onslaught: in 1008 he issued orders that warships were to be built with funds levied from all parts of the country, one ship for every 300 or so hides. These vessels would have been Viking-style warships, crafted with considerable skill for maximum flexibility on the water and capable of holding about fifty men. There is no indication as to how many were actually delivered – perhaps 200 or so: the *Anglo-Saxon Chronicles* maintain that the fleet was larger than 'ever there had been in England in the days of any king'.[19]

In 1009 the armada was ready and duly gathered at Sandwich, near Canterbury, which was a strategic landing point for the Viking raiders. So far so good: a force of about 10,000 men in ships must have been quite some show of power. However, Aethelred's plans then went spectacularly awry. An argument broke out between two noblemen, one alleging that another had been treacherous to the King. The accused abruptly took off with twenty of the ships and started his own personal raiding ventures along the English coast. The accuser, purportedly the brother of Eadric Streona, subsequently set out to stop him, taking eighty more of the fleet. But a sudden storm came down, damaging or destroying many of the ships. Those that managed to reach land did not survive long before being set on fire by the raiding nobleman.

There is no information as to what subsequently happened to either of the brawling aristocrats. A sentence of banishment may have been imposed. However, in the case of the raiding nobleman – accompanied by his family and supporters – this could not have been a long-term punishment: he is believed to have been the father of Godwine who was later to be the most powerful nobleman in the country and whose own son, Harold, subsequently became the last Anglo-Saxon king of England. Nevertheless, the allegation of treason was probably well founded. Such sedition is less likely to have been related to support for the Vikings than to loss of faith over the King's ability to deal with the Danish invaders: Aethelred's eldest sons may increasingly have been seen as a better bet, with many resulting court plots, and counter plots.

Back in Sandwich Aethelred gave further cause to doubt his leadership: in the ensuing confusion over what had happened to half his fleet he simply gave up and retreated back to one of his properties. Abandoned by their king, the rest of the fleet limped off to London, leaving the coast of Kent exposed to the Vikings.

In August that year they arrived. An immense and frightening army landed at Sandwich. The troops were led by the formidable commander Thorkell 'the Tall', a type of super-Viking from the elite squad known as Jomsvikings. He and his men proceeded to loot their way around Kent until the local people themselves paid for peace.

It is at this juncture that the book Emma later commissioned becomes a valuable resource. In the first half of the work the author tells us very little about Emma herself but a great deal about the Danes, and the information he provides is written from a very different perspective to that of the *Anglo-Saxon Chronicles*. According to his version of events (which may well have been suggested to him by Emma), Thorkell was granted licence to ravage England by his king, Swein Forkbeard. It was, the author maintains, an act of vengeance for Thorkell's brother, who had been killed by the English. Perhaps. The size of their army suggests that the Danes also had bigger ambitions.

While Thorkell's troops moved on to plunder and burn their way around Sussex, Hampshire and Berkshire, Aethelred and his people turned to God. The King issued an edict, written by his sonorous archbishop Wulfstan, to the effect that three days of prayer and fasting should be observed across the entire nation just before Michaelmas, the feast day of the archangel St Michael on 29 September. Only bread, herbs and water were to be consumed; everybody in England was to come barefoot to church 'without gold or ornaments'; slaves were to be freed for the three days in order to participate; fairly substantial amounts of money were to be extracted – one penny from each hide as well as one penny from every member of every household; mass was to be held each day at which the people should (in all seriousness) sing the psalm *Domine, quid multiplicati sunt*, or 'O Lord, how they are multiplied'; and anyone failing to obey these commands was to be fined or punished (*thegns* by thirty shillings, *ceorls* by thirty pennies, slaves with a flogging). 'God help us. Amen' ends the decree.[20] The collective act of penance may have been intended to lend the nation moral courage, but it seems more likely to have added to a pervading sense of doom and despair.

Towards the end of 1009, all able men were called up to defend the land. They had some, very limited, success – at one stage the King and his troops managed to cut the Vikings off from their ships and they were apparently prepared to launch an assault 'but it was Ealdorman Eadric who hindered it'[21], according to the *Anglo-Saxon Chronicles*, although quite how or why is not explained. Thorkell's troops proceeded to 'live off' Essex and attack London. But, 'praise be to God', the old Roman town was reputedly the one place that was always able to hold out against the Vikings.

After a brief respite the following spring when the Danes were repairing their boats in Kent, East Anglia at first bore the brunt of Thorkell's ferocity, followed by raids into Oxfordshire and Bedfordshire. On the face of it, defence strategies seem to have been almost laughably misconceived. When the enemy was 'in the east, then [the English] army was kept in the west: and when they were in the south, then our army was in the north' the *Anglo-Saxon Chronicles* comment. Yet the situation was not necessarily quite as mad as it may appear. Despite the heroics described in the epic poetry of the period, the armies of the time existed more for a show of aggression than for the gruesome realities of battle. The Vikings and the English would both have been at pains to avoid a head-on collision. Aethelred's troops would have made menacing moves a healthy distance away from the enemy. Meantime Thorkell's men would have been deliberately skirting well clear of the Anglo-Saxon army so as to be able to spread out and plunder the land at minimum risk of a military confrontation.

Such mutually evasive action was evidently more beneficial to the Vikings. By 1011 they had overrun not only Kent, East Anglia, Oxfordshire and Bedfordshire but also Hertfordshire, Buckinghamshire, Surrey, Berkshire, Hampshire and 'much in Wiltshire'. Aethelred and his *witan* paid yet more tribute money, but any truce agreed was not respected for long. In September Canterbury was besieged. Like Exeter, the town was strongly fortified and its defences were considered impregnable. But Canterbury was swiftly taken by the Vikings, and, as in the defeat of Exeter, this was blamed on connivance from within the walls. Florence of Worcester names the traitor as archdeacon Aelfmaer before describing the carnage that followed the Viking victory. Some townsmen 'were slain by the sword,' he writes 'others were consumed by fire, many were cast headlong from the walls, no small number perished from being hung up by their testicles. Matrons, dragged through the streets of the city by their hair, were thrown at last into the flames to die. Infants, torn from the mothers' breasts, were either cut to pieces with spears or ground to bits under cartwheels.'[22]

A number of people were also taken prisoner, among them the Archbishop of Canterbury, Aelfheah, formerly Bishop of Winchester. The *Anglo-Saxon Chronicles* spell out the humiliation: 'And he who was the head of the English race and of Christendom was a roped thing.'

After seven months in captivity at Greenwich Aelfheah staunchly refused to allow anyone to meet demands of 3,000 pounds for his ransom, despite the fact that Eadric Streona had already organised a large payment of tribute money to the Danes. Aelfheah's captors were infuriated. After a drunken 'feast' on Saturday 19 April 1012 – when 'wine from the south'[23] seems to have been the chief substance consumed – they brought him before their assembly and pelted him with cattle bones. Florence of Worcester describes how one man called Thrum, whom Aelfheah had confirmed into the church only the day before, finished off the archbishop by splitting his head open with a battle-axe. A national martyr, Aelfheah was taken into London and buried with great honour at the minster church of St Paul.

In the midst of the crisis Aethelred continued to conduct court business. Perhaps it was to celebrate the birth of Alfred that he granted Emma a small chunk of Winchester in 1012[24] – she was later to build a house on this property of 'Godbegot', or good bargain because it was exempt from taxation. It lay close to the New Minster and to the royal residence in the town. In the same year the King also instituted a formal system of taxation to pay for the defence of the realm: this *heregeld*, literally 'army tax', was also to be known as *Danegeld*. The enormous amounts of tribute money already paid to the Vikings had, by contrast, been raised on an *ad hoc* basis. *Heregeld* was a land tax, was much resented, and was to remain a compulsory payment for almost forty years.

Aethelred needed such a guaranteed source of income because of a dramatic development in 1012. Appalled by the brutal behaviour of the

Danish troops and mortified at the murder of Archbishop Aelfheah, Thorkell himself suddenly switched sides and agreed to serve the English king. The *Anglo-Saxon Chronicles* suggest that he defected with forty-five of his warships; Emma's author maintains that he brought with him forty ships 'manned from among the best Danish warriors', all of whom would have expected to be fed, clothed and generally well rewarded. Meanwhile, according to the take on events in Emma's book, back in Denmark Swein Forkbeard was once again enraged.

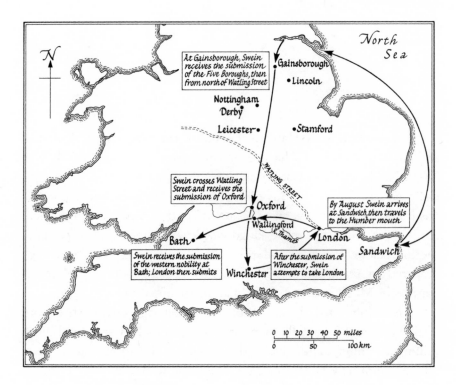

North
Sea

At Gainsborough, Swein
receives the submission
of the Five Boroughs, then
from north of Watling Street

● Gainsborough

● Lincoln

Nottingham ●
Derby ●

Leicester ●

● Stamford

WATLING STREET

Swein crosses Watling
Street and receives the
submission of Oxford

● Oxford

Wallingford
R. Thames

By August Swein arrives
at Sandwich, then travels
to the Humber mouth

Bath ●

London

Swein receives the submission
of the western nobility at
Bath; London then submits

Winchester

After the submission of
Winchester, Swein
attempts to take London

Sandwich

0 10 20 30 40 50 miles

0   50   100 km

CHAPTER FIVE

Defeat

Since the defection of Thorkell the Tall to the King's army Aethelred and his military leaders have been anticipating another attack from Swein Forkbeard. The Danish king's retaliation is expected to be especially vicious. An outright invasion of England is possible and Aethelred has been warned by several of his courtiers that Swein could be planning to take over his entire kingdom. Several months have passed – the lull before the storm – during which troops and ships have been prepared in readiness along the Kentish coast, particularly around Sandwich, which is the preferred landing point of the Vikings.

In mid-July of 1013 an enormous fleet approaches the port. Aethelred's and Thorkell's ships are swiftly launched and amid much yelling and thumping of shields the soldiers on board manage to drive off the dauntingly large armada, chasing the fleet well away from the shore. On land, the local people of Kent shout out great cheers of triumph: the Vikings have gone.

But where, and for how long? A few days later exhausted messengers arrive in Kent bringing unwelcome news for the King: the foreign fleet has been seen rounding the curve of East Anglia and heading north-west, not away from the coast but towards it. Down in the south, there is nothing Aethelred and his men can do. The King simply hopes and prays that his northern subjects are well prepared – and will remain loyal to their monarch.

There is another portentous pause. No further reports are received. Aethelred, his queen and their entourage continue court business, receiving ecclesiastic visitors, entertaining the local nobility and holding council meetings to discuss possible military tactics. Then appalling intelligence is abruptly delivered to them by breathless and agitated scouts: the people of the Danelaw have deserted their king.

Aethelred is informed that the Viking forces, led by Swein Forkbeard and his son Cnut, have made their way inland having sailed up the River Humber and along the River Trent to Gainsborough. The towns-folk there barely put up a fight and seem almost to have welcomed the Scandinavian overlord. Swein has now made Gainsborough his base and, with his men hardly needing to raise a sword in threat or aggression, he has been receiving the submission of nearly all the Danelaw landholders. Almost every single person of power and note has come to him, laid down his arms and offered up hostages as surety of the new allegiance. The scouts report with some awkwardness that among the first to capitulate was the ealdorman of Northumbria himself, Uhtred who is married to the King's daughter Aelfgifu.

News of the Danelaw defection quickly spreads among the southerners. Some are horrified, barely able to believe that the King's own ealdormen and other nobles were not violently intimidated into such renegade action. Some say they are not entirely surprised – after all, many of the northerners are little more than Vikings themselves: their Scandinavian blood runs deep and their affiliations to their Anglo-Saxon lord and sovereign have always been dubious. Meanwhile, other more disaffected folk mutter that the turncoats have been very wise to give up on their weak and ineffective king. And rumour has it that the Queen herself is not without sympathy for the latter view. She is believed to have lost all confidence in her husband's current defensive capabilities and is said to be urging him to move the court – and her young children – to a place of greater security: Kent is too exposed to possible Viking incursions by sea, and besides, the Lady is apparently unconvinced as to the patriotism of the people of this area.

With more reports reaching him that Swein Forkbeard is demanding provisions for his troops and is planning to take his army south, Aethelred does issue orders for the court to decamp. His army is insufficiently strong for an all-out offensive against the Viking forces, which would by now be swelled by English recruits from the north, so his best option is to protect himself and his sovereignty by relocating to a place with strong defences. Accompanied by the King's soldiers and by Thorkell and his men, the court migrates to London. The people of this garrison city are known to be staunch supporters of the monarch.

Once installed there, the sequestered king and queen receive increasingly alarming messages about the activities of Swein, who is now clearly intent on conquering the entire country. Having left his many northern hostages under the guard of his son Cnut in Gainsborough, he is marching down England with his men, looting and burning farms and villages as he progresses. Some scouts report that it is as if the whole of England is smouldering. With dismay the royal household hears that Swein has reached Oxford and that the towns-folk there have had little option but to surrender. Winchester swiftly follows suit. Swein then turns east: London itself appears to be the next target.

The Danish-led troops approach and – a moment of glee on the part of the Londoners – a number of their army are drowned when they misjudge the Thames and attempt to ford it rather than take on the soldiers defending the bridge at Southwark.[1] Undaunted, Swein presses on. He reaches London's old Roman fortifications. But any hopes he has that the townspeople will surrender swiftly flounder. The stalwart Londoners, backed by Aethelred's army and Thorkell's men (who, praise be, are very willing to fight their fellow Danes – at a price), put up a menacing show of aggression. Swein's forces are forced to retreat.

The Danish invader proceeds to Wallingford and from there to Bath, demanding submission from the terrified townsfolk and taking hostages as he goes. In the face of this widespread surrender London is unlikely to hold out for much longer. The townsfolk hear rumours that the Queen herself is expecting the worst, and anticipates that the city will soon be overrun by Swein Forkbeard. She is apparently insisting that she leaves immediately and places herself under the protection of her brother in Normandy. Sometime before the Viking forces turn back towards London the Lady does indeed depart. Her flight from England is a very risky undertaking: if captured by the Vikings she and her entourage will become prize hostages.

And how appallingly different her return to Normandy is from her departure for England eleven years beforehand. No fanfare, no majesty: her homecoming is the flight of a fugitive. Accompanied by Aelfsige, the abbot of Peterborough, she and her retainers set off in boats crewed by well-armed, highly paid men. The journey is particularly tense as they sail away from the English coast, and even when they reach open water every man and woman on board remains vigilant, constantly scanning the horizon for signs of aggressive warships. But Swein Forkbeard is more intent on conquering the whole of England than patrolling its shores, and the refugees slip away successfully, giving great thanks to God when they reach the coast of Normandy. Having crossed the Channel, the Queen despatches agents back to England entrusted with the message that it is safe for her children to follow her. In the care of the Bishop of London they duly arrive.

The people of London, meanwhile, are forced to submit to Swein Forkbeard and Aethelred has no option but to flee, a king without a kingdom. For a few months he lingers on the fringes of England and sets up a base with Thorkell the Tall on the Isle of Wight. He also enlists the help of one of Swein Forkbeard's most aggressive Viking enemies, the Norwegian chieftain Olaf Haroldson. Aethelred thereby becomes almost totally dependent on two different Viking commanders for his protection – Thorkell the Dane and Olaf the Norwegian.

It is an ignominious situation, quite as much for the Lady as for her husband. Back in her homeland, Aethelred's wife may be out of danger, but she is deeply humiliated. Loss of status is not the only blow to her pride. Having returned as a powerless exile, it is galling for her to see that her mother is still a figure of some authority in the Norman court. And in neighbouring Brittany, her sister Hawise has become the *de facto* ruler: since the death of her husband, Duke Geoffrey I, in 1008 she has been acting as regent on behalf of her sons Alan and Odo.[2]

To make matters worse, the Lady learns that her brother has been establishing new alliances with the very man who has overrun England. With flagrant opportunism, Richard has ignored his previous *entente* with Aethelred and has been quick to make overtures to Swein Forkbeard, offering the Danish leader a treaty of peace, a secure base for any of his wounded men, and the (profitable) opportunity to sell his booty in Normandy.[3] Meanwhile Aethelred himself is imminently to join his family in exile, and Richard seems unperturbed at the prospect of welcoming his brother-in-law while doing brisk business with the King's Viking enemies.

*   *   *

In his undignified situation as exiled monarch, it is possible Aethelred was simply hoping that the barbarity of England's new Viking ruler would prove too much for the people and that they would rise up against him, allowing their king to make a swift return. An impressive warrior, Swein Forkbeard hardly had a reputation for prosperously peaceful government. First and foremost his immediate ancestors were war leaders, while he himself had come to power through the sword.

Swein was from the third generation of Denmark's ruling dynasty. The current monarchy of the country can trace its roots back to his grandfather, Gorm the Old, who is largely credited with the creation of Denmark as an entity. During the early-tenth century much of this region of small states had fallen under the control of Swedish kings, but around the 930s the pagan warrior Gorm imposed himself on the area he was to call Denmark, and sometime during that decade he established a 'royal' base at Jelling in Jutland. What little is known about the first Danish king comes mainly from the thoroughly biased quills of later, Christian, chroniclers. Writing in the 1070s, Adam of Bremen compiled a history of the see of Hamburg and its northern outposts in which he describes Gorm as a 'savage worm' who tortured the Christian missionaries in his territory to death.[4] In contrast to this allegation of brutality, Gorm was evidently a loving husband. At Jelling a stone carved in runes, the mystical Germanic alphabet used for inscriptions and divination, still stands in memory of his queen. It reads 'King Gorm made this memorial to his wife Thyri, the adornment of Denmark.' After Gorm's death, his son, Harold Blue Tooth, consolidated his father's powerbase, added extensive military camps, and converted to Christianity – no doubt in part to gain wider political credibility and to establish himself as something of an imperial ruler. As a mark of his new faith he reinterred both his parents at Jelling, in Denmark's first church. He also raised a great runestone there in their memory. It was as an emblem of his own grandeur as well: 'King Harold' it is inscribed, 'ordered this memorial to be made for Gorm his father and Thyri his mother. That Harold who won for himself all of Denmark and Norway and made the Danes Christian.' Although whether he ever occupied much of Norway is very questionable.

Harold Blue Tooth's own son, Swein Forkbeard, was a great deal less filially inclined and, it would seem, less Christian. According to Adam of Bremen he persecuted Christians, at least for a while. The author maintains that this was part of a plot: Swein teamed up with those who 'had against their will been compelled to Christianity' and incited them to rebel against his father, with the aim of declaring himself king. Civil war ensued and Harold, having sustained injuries in battle, fled to the 'land of the Slavs' where he died. His body was brought back to Denmark and buried with due honour at the church he had founded in Roskilde, which was to become a significant religious and naval centre. Meanwhile Swein, so Adam writes, was driven out of Denmark by the King of the Swedes and sought exile in Scotland. There he apparently remained for a number of years until the death of the Swedish king (in 995) when he returned to claim the Danish crown – and thereafter became a vigorous Christian.

The book Emma commissioned also takes up the story of Swein's accession to the throne of Denmark. It offers a rather different outlook on events, with no allusion to pagan and Christian rivalry – and no Caledonian interlude. Swein, her author reports, was loved by all except his father, whose hatred was due only to envy. Overcome with jealousy at Swein's popularity, Harold Blue Tooth attempted to disown his son, whereupon his own army rose up against him. Harold was subsequently wounded and later died, and Swein 'held his throne undisturbed'.

Swein strengthened Denmark's fortresses, Emma's document continues while remaining silent about his military incursions. He disciplined his army, earned the unswerving loyalty of his troops – and baulked at the treachery of his commander, Thorkell, when he deserted and not only joined the King of England but also, apparently, took possession of the south of the country, which he then churlishly refused to share with his own King. Writing in the early 1040s, some twenty-seven years after the Danish monarch had forced Aethelred into exile, Emma's author infers that Swein had no option but to wreak revenge in England, and he builds up a majestic image of the Danish king's departure to bring the land of the Anglo-Saxons under his rule 'by force or stratagem'. His fleet of longships was particularly magnificent: 'On one side lions moulded in gold were to be seen on the ships, on the other birds on the tops of the masts indicated by their movements the winds as they blew, or dragons of various kinds poured fire from their nostrils. Here there were glittering men of solid gold or silver nearly comparable to live ones, there bulls with necks raised high and legs outstretched were fashioned leaping and roaring like live ones.'

Emma's author records that Swein had two sons 'of excellent qualities', Harold and Cnut – a more phonetically apposite, if risqué, spelling of Canute. The author, probably erroneously, names Cnut as the elder brother and may have conferred this seniority on him to build up his importance. But there is little doubt that the writer was correct in reporting that Swein entrusted his kingdom to Harold while he and the warrior Cnut set off to subdue Thorkell and the Anglo-Saxon people.

Emma's author describes how the brave Danish king and his son led their men to an unidentified harbour in England; how they battled against 'severe resistance'; how they scattered the enemy; and how they proceeded to conquer other ports in a similar fashion until the whole of England was in their power. This was not exactly the easy subjugation that the *Anglo-Saxon Chronicles* record. But in her later years Emma was evidently at pains to vindicate the Danish takeover of England on the grounds of their superior might and courage. Back in 1013 when she was driven into exile in Normandy it is extremely unlikely that she had any such admiration and enthusiasm for the men who had robbed her of her power and prestige. As the wife of a fugitive, failed king, her future at that stage must have looked very bleak. But the tumultuous course of the next four years was to revolutionise her life – even if her prospects were to plummet a long way before they improved.

The *Anglo-Saxon Chronicles* maintain that towards the end of 1013 Swein was accepted as 'full king' of England, although it is doubtful that he was ever formally crowned. The court annals give no indication as to conditions in the country at this juncture; however, William of Malmesbury, writing in the early-twelfth century, claims that Swein oppressed England 'with rapine and slaughter'. He describes how chaos apparently ensued, with much looting and kidnapping for the slave trade while 'private and public wealth was carried down to the ships, and hostages with it, because Swein was no lawful lord but a most atrocious tyrant'. Yet the people of England did not have to suffer for long. The *Anglo-Saxon Chronicles* abruptly record 'the happy event' of Swein's death at Candlemas, 2 February 1014.

Whether this was an act of murder or a life cut short by illness or accident is not consistently clear. Emma's book implies that Swein died from poor heath, having felt that 'the dissolution of his body was threatening him'. Later chroniclers,[5] somewhat tongue in cheek, offer the folklore story that his death was an act of semi-divine retribution: Swein Forkbeard was killed by St Edmund.

It is a neat tale of comeuppance for the Vikings. In the 860s and 70s St Edmund had been king of East Anglia, where he was captured by Scandinavian invaders who attempted to make him renounce his Christianity. On his refusal, he was gruesomely put to death: according to some stories, St Sebastian-like, he was shot in a hail of arrows, and then beheaded; other versions have him spread-eagled as an offering to the northern gods. A prominent martyr, Edmund was subsequently sanctified, and for obvious reasons his cult became especially strong during the second wave of Scandinavian raids in the tenth and early-eleventh centuries. In 1014 the holy hero is said to have become incensed by Swein from beyond the grave. The new king of England had either ravaged the lands around Bury St Edmunds where the saint's incorrupt body lay or, according to different tales, had demanded huge tax payments from the people there. Edmund purportedly took his revenge by manifesting himself to a terrified Swein and then variously striking him hard on the head or running him through with a spear. In any event, the Danish conqueror reputedly died in a satisfactory spasm of terrible pain.

The author of Emma's book reports that before his death Swein had named Cnut the heir of his new kingdom. Certainly, the people of the north-east appear to have supported the claims of the Danish youth, who would at this stage have been aged eighteen or nineteen. Yet according to the *Anglo-Saxon Chronicles*, most of the nobles in the rest of the country had other thoughts. They elected to invite Aethelred back from Normandy 'and declared that no lord was dearer to them than their natural lord – if he would govern them more justly than he did before'.[6] It is a loaded statement. The strong implication is that the (former) supreme lord of England was obliged to agree terms with his own subjects before he was allowed to return. He is apparently accused of injustices. These may have been the sudden and harsh taxes he had demanded as tribute money for the Vikings and the brutal punishment he inflicted on those unable to meet the payments. However, there is no evidence to suggest that in the confused months after he regained the throne Aethelred made any strenuous efforts to amend such unpalatable practice and institute any reform – *Danegeld*, for instance, continued to be an official tax long after his reign. However, a pact of some description between the King and his nobles was undoubtedly made. The *Anglo-Saxon Chronicles* report that, somewhat precociously, Edward, no more than eleven years old at the time, was despatched across the Channel ahead of his father to broker the deal – or at the least to act as a hostage to his good intentions.

In the spring of 1014, Aethelred returned to England. But resuming control of the country was not, apparently, an entirely straightforward exercise. According to Scandinavian stories,[7] he and his Norwegian ally Olaf Haroldsson encountered major problems around London, where the Danish forces held out against the reinstated king. The biggest obstacle there was London's bridge, which linked the city with the market town of Southwark. In occupying this large wooden structure the Danes had a great strategic advantage and were able to check any naval attacks from the River Thames below. Olaf, however, had an ingenious solution. He sneaked up to the bridge, fastened cables around the piles that supported it and took these lines to ships waiting downstream. When the tide was right, his oarsmen rowed with all their might, the bridge fell and London was liberated. The nursery rhyme 'London

Bridge is falling down' is thought to have originated from this Norwegian act of deliverance.

In the *Anglo-Saxon Chronicles*, however, Aethelred's first act was to rally an army and, personally, to lead it swiftly to the north-east where Cnut held sway. There he launched a savage offensive. In the ensuing blood-bath when 'all human kind that could be got at were raided and burned and killed'[8] by Aethelred's troops, Cnut abandoned his English supporters, marshalled the Danish fleet that had remained in the north, and sailed away taking with him at least some of the hostages with whom he had been entrusted by his late father. He made for Sandwich, where he released these prisoners, having first chopped off their hands and noses – some sources record that their ears were also removed, and Florence of Worcester maintains that their nostrils were slit rather than entire noses being sliced away. The detail of this mutilation stands out against Aethelred's vaguely reported butchery in the north no doubt because the chroniclers were wanting to emphasise the barbarity of the retreating Danes.

Cnut then sailed on to Denmark while Aethelred attempted to re-establish peace, and his authority, throughout the kingdom. Emma may well have returned from Normandy at this point with Alfred and Godgifu. She would have found a country in turmoil. According to Archbishop Wulfstan, society itself was almost falling to pieces. One of his most famous homilies, Sermon of 'Wolf' to the English, was written in this year, blasting out at the sins of the people that had brought about the sorry state of the nation: 'Here are slayers of men and slayers of kinsmen and killers of priests and enemies of the monasteries; and here are perjurers and murderers; and here are whores and those who kill children and many foul fornicating adulterers; and here are wizards and witches; and here are plunderers and robbers and those who despoil; and, to be brief, countless numbers of all crimes and deeds'.[9] If Wulfstan is to be taken at face value, witchcraft and the occult were never far from the surface of life and a reversion to paganism was almost inevitable when civilised order broke down.

* * *

Meanwhile an increasing division was emerging between Aethelred and his surviving elder children. Of his six sons by his former marriage(s), three had apparently died by the time of his exile: Egbert, Eadred and Edgar may have been killed in battle or sustained fatal wounds – they variously disappear from court records between 1005 and 1012. During the months of Swein's occupation, Emma's remaining three stepsons had stayed in England, presumably in hiding – at least there is no evidence to suggest that they sought exile abroad. On the Danish king's death some of them were no doubt angling for the crown rather than encouraging the overtures to bring their father back. In the summer of 1014, Aethelstan, thought to have been the eldest, died. The fact that he made a will, which still survives, suggests that he was either sick or badly wounded and knew that his days were numbered. Among bequests to Aelfmaer, his dish-thegn (who was to receive eight hides at Catherington along with one pied stallion and a notched sword), and Aelfnoth, his sword polisher (who was left another notched sword), are legacies to the Church, to his father (who was bequeathed land as well as a silver-hilted sword and a coat of mail), to his brother Eadwig (a silver-hilted sword) and to his brother Edmund (the sword that 'King Offa owned', a silver-coated blast horn and property in East Anglia as well as other estates). There is no mention of Emma's children.

Edmund, later to earn the title 'Ironside' because of his unflinching valour, had evidently been close to Aethelstan, and after his elder brother's death clearly considered himself well in line to the throne. So much so that he began acting against his father. In 1015, during a meeting of the *witan* at Oxford, the infamous Eadric Streona orchestrated the murder of two disaffected noblemen, Siferth and Morcar, probably on the orders of the King. Aethelred, presumably having wind of a further plot, removed Siferth's widow to the security of the convent at Malmesbury. But, in defiance of the King, Edmund Ironside promptly abducted her and the couple swiftly got married. For the warrior-prince this was not so much a love match as a useful means of gaining support in the north midlands where the families of Siferth and Morcar had large estates – and where he headed with all speed to rally his own army.

But while Edmund Ironside was whipping up a northern rebellion against the King, Cnut was on his way back to England with a mighty fleet. According to Emma's author, on his return to Denmark Cnut had lovingly embraced his brother Harold, had shed tears for the death of their father, and had then suggested that they divide the kingdom of the Danes between them and together conquer the land of the Anglo-Saxons, with Harold subsequently taking the pick of whichever nation he liked. Harold, the writer records, quite reasonably refused but offered his brother every assistance possible for his invasion of England (undoubtedly a shrewd move to divert Cnut's attention from the Danish throne). Preparations were made and as summer approached Thorkell deserted the English king, returned to Denmark and swore allegiance to Cnut.[10]

Bolstered by the Danish commander's inside knowledge of England's defensive capabilities, Cnut set sail. Once more, Emma's author enthuses over the spectacle of the departing Danish armada: so great 'was the ornamentation of the ships, that the eyes of the beholders were dazzled, and to those looking from afar they seemed of flame rather than of wood. For if at any time the sun cast the splendour of its rays among them, the flashing of arms shone in one place, in another the flames of suspended shields.'

It is entirely apposite, of course, that the writer emphasises these ships – with or without the warriors on board holding their shields over each side in traditional battlemongering mode. The enormous success of Viking warfare – and trade – had resulted mainly from the expertise of Scandinavian shipwrights. Almost unbelievably these astute technicians made no records – no drawings or sketches – of their designs. Apart from runic inscriptions, the Scandinavians of this period were a non-literate, non-documentary society relying instead on memory, observation and oral traditions. Finely tuned boat-building skills were passed down through word of mouth among a people who appear to have had an innate understanding of water dynamics and the composition of wood. Different timbers were used for specific types of vessel – from fishing boats of pine to top-quality war vessels of oak. The boat-builders had no saws: axes were used to create planks of unbroken grain

that had great elasticity in water: the nimblest of the ships would effectively snake their way through the sea. Long and lean, the warships in
particular could proceed through very shallow water and enable their
crews to make surprise attacks by their capacity to be sailed right on
to flattish beaches. By the early-eleventh century these vessels were as
much as thirty metres long and carried about 100 men – sixty rowers
and perhaps forty others who manned the large wool sail (treated with
tar, ochre and fat) and acted as shield bearers. The most splendid of
the ships were known as *drekkars*, or dragons, suitably and elaborately
adorned and seemingly alive as they moved with immense speed and
flexibility through the waves.

The *Anglo-Saxon Chronicles* report that the Danish fleet, composed
of 160 ships (no doubt most of them dragons), arrived once again at
Sandwich, and raided Kent and Wessex while 'the king lay sick at
Cosham', near Portsmouth. Meantime the slippery Eadric Streona made
a complete volte-face and, taking forty ships (with armed crew) from
the English fleet, offered his services to Cnut. Other nobles, too, were
soon forced to join the Danish leader. Famously, in the spring of 1016
Uhtred of Northumbria, Aethelred's son-in-law, was outmanoeuvred
and during his formal surrender was treacherously murdered by Cnut's
men – prompting a bloodfeud that was to continue for more than half
a century.

Meanwhile, Edmund Ironside apparently abandoned his attempted
rebellion and tried to precipitate his father into taking the lead over
the defence of the realm. But Aethelred by then appears to have been
too poorly supported, and was probably too ill, to be of much help.
After an abortive effort to join Edmund and his troops he retreated to
London, where he died on St George's Day, 23 April 1016, 'after great
toil and difficulties in his life' the *Anglo-Saxon Chronicles* concede –
finally – with some sympathy. He was buried at the church of St Paul's
in the city that had latterly become his base and that had shown him
such staunch support.

Aethelred's death left Emma in an extremely precarious position.
However much she may have held her first husband in low esteem, she
would not have welcomed his demise. Emma was now a widow with a

very uncertain future – particularly if Cnut were to conquer the country. Aethelred's laws of 1008 imply that even in peacetime widowhood was a vulnerable situation: 'And every widow who conducts herself correctly is to be under the protection of God and the king' one ruling stipulates, with the underlying inference that these lone (and well-behaved) women had a distinct need for such support. But other than her immediate family, a dowager queen had no one to turn to for help, a dicey position that in Emma's case would have been compounded by the fact that the country was being very brutally invaded. Her movements at this juncture are not recorded. She may have attempted to return to the safety of her brother's court in Normandy but it is more likely that she willingly remained in England, and probably in London, where she could at least monitor developments and keep a wavering grip on her scattered properties.

In the midst of her dilemma, her intentions that one of her own sons should succeed Aethelred must quickly have evaporated. Edmund Ironside had clearly placed himself in prime position. According to Scandinavian stories, she sent her eldest child, Edward, to fight alongside his half-brother – which if true was a sensible, and opportunistic, move to smooth over any factionalism. Aged about twelve Edward was too young to have been considered a serious claimant to the throne, particularly in view of ugly memories of the fate of his uncle Edward the Martyr and of the experiences of his own father, both of whom had been crowned while still minors. So, however antagonistic Emma's previous relations with Edmund had been, at this stage her best hope for maintaining some vestige of her status and some claim on her estates would have rested with her ambitious, and without doubt courageous, stepson. Latterly at least, she appears to have had much respect for him: the book that she was to commission depicts Edmund Ironside as a gallant hero, almost – but not quite – as brave as Cnut.

In Emma's version of events, Edmund is presented as an eager, and valiant, whippersnapper while the Danish leader is portrayed as a sagacious commander, although in reality Cnut would have been as much as ten years younger than his English rival. The *Anglo-Saxon Chronicles* record that on Aethelred's death the nobility in London elected Edmund

king. Not that this cut much ice with many other leading aristocrats
and churchmen who had gathered in Southampton: they voted in
support of Cnut – and his apparently superior force. How binding these
decisions were is not clear.

During 1016 law and order seems largely to have broken down while
the armies of the two contenders sailed or clattered around the country,
clashing several times. After the fourth confrontation Eadric Streona
expediently changed sides in favour of Edmund, who appeared to be
gaining the upper hand. However, Cnut's army was ultimately to prove
the stronger. In October that year the two forces fought for the last
time. At the Battle of Ashingdon, in Essex, Edmund was defeated and
fled – while Eadric rapidly threw in his lot with Cnut once again. There
matters might have rested for a while, with the Danish leader in control
of England and Edmund Ironside on the prowl, but the two men were
persuaded to meet and come to a binding agreement.[11] The chief archi-
tect of the pact was apparently none other than Eadric Streona who
seems, somewhat masterfully, to have been attempting to keep a foot
in both camps simultaneously. He insisted that in the best interests of
the country Edmund and Cnut should come to a formal compromise –
there would be no lasting peace otherwise. However valid this view
might have been, a bizarre arrangement followed.

On an island in the River Severn near Deerhurst, Gloucestershire,
the two leaders came face to face. They swapped hostages, settled the
amount that the defeated English king should pay Cnut's army, then
swore an oath of friendship and agreed to split the country. Edmund
Ironside was to take the region of Wessex in the south-east; Cnut was
to have the rest of the kingdom.

For the people of England this cannot have been a very happy
prospect, particularly for those of the governing nobility who owned
land on both sides of the divide. But they did not have much opportunity to find out whether the partition was at all workable. On 30
November 1016 a far simpler solution was provided: the death of
Edmund Ironside.

The *Anglo-Saxon Chronicles* elliptically record that Edmund died and
was buried alongside his revered grandfather, King Edgar, at Glastonbury

Abbey. Emma's book speciously states that God himself intervened and graciously 'took away Edmund from the body, lest it should chance that if both [Edmund and Cnut] survived neither should rule securely, and that the kingdom should be continually wasted by renewed conflict'. Later chroniclers, however, revel in allegations of murder that purportedly took place amid much treachery and gore. Eadric Streona is widely held to be behind the perpetration of regicide. He is variously said to have ordered his son or bribed a couple of Edmund's retainers to hide in the royal privy house (according to Henry of Huntingdon, the murderer was, unhygienically, 'concealed in the pit'[12]). When Edmund subsequently retired there 'for the purpose of easing nature'[13] he was stabbed in the backside or bowels and died shortly afterwards. The twelfth-century Norman historian Geoffrey Gaimar adds an enterprising twist by asserting that Eadric masterminded the creation of a type of crossbow machine from which an arrow, at remote control, struck Edmund 'in the fundament'. Excruciatingly, it 'went up as far as the lungs', leaving no trace of feathers at the point of entrance.

By whatever means it was arranged, the assassination of the unfortunate Edmund brought an era of immense fear and uncertainty to a close. England had endured at least thirty-five years of Scandinavian raids and extortion and with more than half the country already under the authority of Cnut, it seems that at this stage there was no further opposition to him. The governing nobility of Wessex, former heartland of the monarchy, simply gave up and along with the rest of the country submitted to Cnut. The claims of Aethelred's other sons and indeed of Edmund Ironside's two tiny male heirs were ignored in the face of a very large and very evident Danish army. And so a teenage Viking – warrior of the waves and prince without significant claim to property in his homeland – became the overlord of all the Anglo-Saxon people.

PART II

VIKING QUEEN

CHAPTER SIX

Captive Bride

London in the spring of 1017 is a town very much under occupation. Cnut's troops are posted along the walls and at all points of entry. His men search every trading vessel arriving at both the old and new harbours – Queenhithe beyond the big bridge over to Southwark, and Billingsgate downriver, where large ships from the Holy Roman Empire, Flanders, Normandy, and other Continental states have started to return, trading at the wide jetties that flank the river banks. The army is also a menacing presence within the town, quick to pick up on the slightest signs of intrigue or belligerence.

While not exactly sympathetic to such edginess, the Londoners have some proud appreciation as to why there is a strong show of vigilance. They are well aware that theirs is probably the most important town in the entire country: it is in a key position not only as a trading centre but also as the gateway to thoroughfare along the Thames. The new King of England needs to ensure that there is no trouble here. However, the townsfolk do not have much stomach for fight or rebellion. For a great many months they held out against Cnut's troops, but now that they have been forced to recognise the Scandinavian warrior as their monarch they simply want to pick up the pieces of their lives. At the moment they have a far greater desire to re-establish their markets and workshops than to organise a revolt against the Danish conqueror.

With a population of some 8,000,[1] London in the early-eleventh century is a very large city by the standards of the day. Nevertheless, it is only partly occupied and there are sizeable stretches of open land within the walls. The town occupies the site of England's ancient

Roman capital, although most of the current city was built at a much later date. The remains of its immediate predecessor, a smaller Anglo-Saxon settlement called Lundenwic,[2] lie beyond the western walls. This exposed trading centre was badly attacked during the first wave of Viking invasions, and in 886 King Alfred the Great re-established the town inside the stone fortifications of the neighbouring Roman city which had otherwise been lying largely derelict for centuries. It has not yet filled up.

The residents of Lundenburg, as this newer town is known, mainly inhabit an area in the south of the enclosed space. Stretching back from the river, a grid of dirt-track streets is lined with small, chimneyless houses of wood and thatch and is sporadically punctuated with wells, cesspits and rubbish tips. In the west, the old stone-built minster of St Paul's rubs shoulders with the churches of St Gregory and St Faith. It is in this vicinity that folkmoots, or open-air assemblies, take place for important proclamations – the death of King Aethelred, the formal acknowledgement of King Cnut among them. Towards the centre of the town's most heavily populated area are the churches of St Mildred Poultry and St Benet Sherehog, which lie close to the big cheap, or market, where cattle, pigs and other farm produce are sold. Not that there was a great deal of activity here during the recent war with the Danes. Cripplingly, business at the neighbouring workshops of black-smiths, stonecarvers and boneworkers (producing cups, combs and other domestic items) came to a halt then, and Cheapside has only just begun to bustle once more. It is of course a relief, too, that trade has now also resumed at London's eastern market, or Eastcheap, and that down on the wharves fish and imported goods are again being sold amid much banter – although the noise is still just an echo of the clamour that was once such a feature of this international depot.

After King Aethelred's death less than a year ago, the people of London endured two grim sieges and countless attacks from Cnut's army. They had remained fiercely loyal to the Anglo-Saxon monarch and had protected him and his family who gathered around him during his last days as he lay sick at the royal palace within the north-west walls. When Aethelred died they staunchly supported the claims of his son Edmund Ironside – and almost immediately became the focus of Danish aggression.

That May, barely two weeks after Aethelred had passed away, Cnut's ships arrived in Greenwich – several miles south on the opposite side of the Thames. His warriors proceeded to launch a bold campaign to take the well-guarded city and capture or kill Edmund Ironside, who was at that point still within the city walls. Their biggest impediment was London's large bridge: even with the masts of their warships taken down it would have been difficult for a large number of vessels to negotiate a passage through the shallow waters under the low span. Besides, any troops passing beneath the timbers were at an enormous disadvantage and were likely to be picked off by local defence forces above them. So Cnut's men created an alternative route[3] – grudgingly the Londoners concede that it was a plan of great ingenuity which was executed with much skill and hard labour. The Danish-led troops dug a huge trench that arched around the southern end of this obstacle. It was a muddy operation, and a masterfully conceived plan: they created a bypass and then pulled many of their ships through this new channel.

Having established a naval blockade at both western and eastern ends of London's river front, Cnut's troops set about besieging the landside of the city. Edmund Ironside and a group of his supporters, however, managed to escape while their enemies were creating a second trench. It was to extend all the way around the fortifications of the city while the earth extracted was piled up behind it as a counterscarp. The overall effect was that London then had two walls and ditches mirroring each other, the defensive stonework and its moat facing a barricading dyke and earthwork embankment. So even if any of the city's inhabitants managed to escape from their own fortifications they still had to contend with the enemy's obstruction.

The Londoners were completely trapped, King Aethelred's widow among them.[4] They could only hope that Edmund Ironside would, as promised, return with troops to liberate the city. They knew they could survive fairly comfortably for several weeks – after that it would be a struggle to feed the many people who remained within the walls: traders, craftsmen and noblemen who were all expected to take up arms in defence of their property and of their vulnerable women and children.

Yet although cut off from the outside world the Londoners still had fairly wide expanses within the northern and eastern areas of their walls where their cattle, pigs, sheep and goats could be grazed and fattened. They had their market gardens, too, growing leeks, onions, cabbages, parsnips and carrots. And they had sufficient water from streams, in addition to their wells. But they faced a major problem over lack of grain supplies – they had been reliant on deliveries by oxcart or ship, which were unable to get through the blockades. Dwindling stocks of oats, for broth and porridge, were of only marginally less concern than the stores of wheat and barley that were quickly depleted to make bread.

Grain was not the only worry. Cnut's troops intermittently launched attacks on the city, attempting to burn the gates, scale the walls and terrorise the inhabitants into surrendering. But the men of London resolutely fought back and held them out. After nearly three months ensnared within their own fortress, the Londoners were freed by Edmund Ironside and his forces.

They arrived almost straight from battle in Wiltshire, where they had contended with other deployments of Cnut's troops[5] – a messy encounter in which neither side emerged victorious. Edmund had greater success over London: he and his men managed to drive the Danish-led army back to their ships and then chased many of the vessels away.

However, the relief was short-lived. The army was needed elsewhere in the country. With few troops left to defend London, just a couple of weeks later a section of Cnut's army regrouped, returned and besieged the city once more. For almost another three months the townsfolk, with their dowager queen among them, were subjected to frightening assaults by the surrounding Danish-led troops. But still the enemy could not penetrate their walls. Meanwhile the Londoners' food stocks were rapidly diminishing.

When news got through to them of Edmund Ironside's defeat at the Battle of Ashingdon they held on to hopes – and fervently prayed – that their own chosen king would, and could, still rally a force to repel the Danish invaders. And, amid deteriorating conditions, they continued to withstand their besieging enemy. So it was with some sense

of bitter betrayal that they subsequently learnt of Edmund's pact with
Cnut. Late in the month of October, messengers arrived with official
notification that England was to be divided – the Anglo-Saxon king
was to be monarch of Wessex only; Cnut was to rule the rest of the
country, including London. The people of Lundenburg had no option
but to negotiate with the Danish-led forces, who were quick to release
the city only to establish a strong military presence within the walls.

The financial terms are punitive. The Londoners are still struggling
to raise the remainder of the 11,000 pounds they were forced to agree
in order to free themselves from the Danish stranglehold. It is a hefty
charge, well in excess of one pound for every person in the city, a sum
quite beyond the means of most of the population and the extensive
shortfall must be provided from other sources, notably trading dues.
Last December, when the death of Edmund Ironside was announced at
the folkmoot – amid muttered suspicions of foul murder – much genuine
sorrow was expressed, as well as several rearguard and snide remarks
about the way this Anglo-Saxon king, a man of their own blood, had
let the Londoners down, as if he were to blame for the burden of debt.

The people of Lundenburg are, however, unanimous in their sympathy
for Aethelred's widowed queen. The Lady Aelfgifu, or Emma, has not
only suffered months of siege along with the citizens; since the blockades were lifted she has been even more circumscribed and is held as
a prisoner by Cnut's men. In late October troops surrounded the enclosures of the royal palace and the Lady has not been seen since. What
will happen to this heavily guarded captive? There is much speculation
that Cnut will demand that she become his wife – a noble symbol of
the submission of the Anglo-Saxon people.

* * *

Emma was indeed to marry Cnut. In her book, the prelude to this
arrangement is couched in fairy-tale terms. The new King of England
lacks for nothing but a suitable wife, so he sends out search parties to
find an appropriately noble woman and 'obtain her hand lawfully'. It is
a tall order. The quest, through many lands and cities, is long and
arduous, but eventually the King's men turn up trumps in Normandy,
where they locate 'the most distinguished of the women of her time for

delightful beauty and wisdom'. Messengers are sent to woo her, royal gifts are lavishly bestowed and after much negotiation the incomparable lady finally agrees to become 'the partner of his rule'. This romance, if not a blatant falsehood, is at the least exceedingly liberal with the truth. It is very unlikely, for a start, that Emma was back in Normandy at this stage; and, rather than being wooed, she would have had little choice but to marry Cnut.

By contrast, under the year 1017 the *Anglo-Saxon Chronicles* tersely report that 'before 1 August the King ordered the widow of the former king Aethelred, Richard's daughter, to be fetched to him as queen'.[6] The chroniclers may have been deliberately exaggerating such commanding abruptness in order to play up the coarse Danish background of the new king: these court annals imply that there was a brazen show of conquering machismo – which carries overtones of the Scandinavian tradition of marriage by seizure. Some forty years later, the Norman chronicler William of Jumièges[7] expanded on this idea and wrote that Cnut not only seized Emma as his wife but in return handed over her weight in gold and silver to 'the army', the well-rewarded troops presumably being those Danish soldiers who delivered the captive to him unraped and otherwise unharmed. Yet however embellished the suggestion that the Danish warlord captured and forcibly married the queen of the defeated kingdom, this version of events is likely to have been far closer to reality than Emma's once-upon-a-time story.

Emma would not have been aghast at the prospect of marrying her dead husband's enemy. Indeed, the orders for the mandatory match are unlikely to have come as a shock. Among the ruling classes in Europe during this period it was not unusual for a widow to be married on to her husband's successor.[8] Emma was to be more than a trophy of triumph along with swords, coats of mail and other spoils of conquest. As a second-hand queen she would provide valuable links between the old and new regimes. If on her first marriage Emma had been a peaceweaver between hostile states, this time round she was a figure of both subjugation and *détente*. From her perspective it would not have been an entirely humiliating situation: her importance would be recognised; her conciliatory role could place her in a position of great power; and, of far more immediate concern, she would retain her own estates across the country.

As Cnut's captive, she had no option but to do pretty much as he wished, a position in which she must have known she risked putting herself when she chose to remain in England on Aethelred's death. Her own children had variously fled. Before Cnut's troops arrived to besiege London, and possibly even before Aethelred died, she must hastily have entrusted Godgifu and Alfred – accompanied by assorted foster mothers and attendants – back into the care of her brother's court. They were certainly safely in Normandy when Cnut took over the whole of England and set about stamping his authority on the country with swift brutality. Edward, the young warrior, appears to have travelled to France separately. By Christmas Day, 1016, he had left England and was evidently well on his way to his uncle's court: on that date the teenage prince had circuitously reached Flanders, where he issued a charter[9] to the monastery of St Peter, Ghent, to the effect that once (rather then if) he became King of England all the property that the establishment had owned in his native land would be restored.·

The reason for Emma's resolve to remain in her adopted country must have involved claims over property. Without her estates and wealth in England, she would have been entirely dependent on her Norman family and would, once again, have become little more than a pawn for her brother Richard to sequester or trade more or less as he wished. It is unlikely that she could simply have returned to his court with the aim of remaining there *ad infinitum*, a superfluous lady without status. Richard might have packed her off to a convent, a safe and convenient parking place for widows, or, more probably, given that she was still of childbearing age, married her off in another alliance with a nearby state.

And so the prospects in Normandy were extremely uninviting to Emma. Therefore why not stay in England and face whatever fate unfolded there? She may even have gambled that if Cnut succeeded in conquering the country he would be unlikely to risk antagonising the Normans by ordering her execution – although plenty of others were to meet this end. He might, though, have insisted that she leave the country, in which case she would have sailed back to her brother, having simply delayed her return to his authority by several months. Indeed, under the circumstances marriage to this new king may have been her preferred lot. In England, at least, she had become an estab-lished figure; for the last fifteen years she had observed the ins and outs of court life; she knew those of the churchmen and nobility who had survived the Danish onslaught; and she had an understanding of the country and the Anglo-Saxon people that might enable her to make a significant, and powerful, contribution to the future of the kingdom.

Personal details would not have been a primary consideration, but for Emma there may have been some attraction in the prospect of acquiring a young, and evidently dynamic, husband. She was at this stage about thirty, give or take a couple of years. The man she was to marry was roughly ten years her junior. How very different from the outlook on her wedding to Aethelred when, as little more than a child, she had become bound to an inept, middle-aged monarch some twenty years older than her.

Whether her marriage to Cnut met with the full approval of all Emma's family is very doubtful. A surviving volume of contemporary poems dedicated to her second brother, Robert the Archbishop of Rouen, contains the satire *Semiramis*. In all likelihood its quasi-classical verse reveals the Norman view of Emma's conduct at this stage. The poem tells the story of a queen, Semiramis, who has died and is separated from the land of the living by a great sea. In her parallel universe she has started an unnatural and distasteful affair with a bull, who is Jupiter in unseemly disguise. 'What prostitute in the whole world could have been more debased? His dewlaps make her purple robes seem worth-less, in the green grass Semiramis learns to low, under a young moon [she] delights [in] the bull's mounting',[10] the unnamed author comments with contempt. From across the water, her horrified brother attempts to call Semiramis back. But the Queen, a 'most renowned likeness of an illustrious mother', scornfully mocks him and wilfully continues the rampant bestiality.

According to some interpretations,[11] this royal lady is Emma, separated from her family by a watery divide and potentially dead to them because of her behaviour. The bull is Cnut, a king (of the gods) but a monarch of a base nature. The brother, possibly Robert or even Richard, fails to stop his sister's outrageous exploits despite his remonstrations and his invocations of their mother, the dowager countess Gunnor. The poem seems, by implication, to be as much a criticism of the Norman ruling family and their inability to curb Emma's actions – and her independence – as it is a condemnation of their sister's shameful match.

There was further reason for the Normans to regard the marriage as disreputable. In their poem the bull is introduced as an adulterous beast; in reality Cnut already had a wife.

Bigamy had not, of course, been seen as a problem by Emma's Norman forebears. Although her father had simply kept a string of concubines along with just the one wife at any given time, her grandfather and great-grandfather had both been married to two different women simultaneously. But while their arrangements had reflected an expedient blend of Christian and pagan Scandinavian practices, Emma and her brothers were of a generation altogether more dominated by the Church – and wary of its strictures. Cnut, too, was a Christian: yet, much like Emma's Scandinavian ancestors, evidently one with a cavalier attitude to canon law.

Cnut's first wife was an Englishwoman called Aelfgifu – confusingly also the name that Emma had been made to adopt when she married Aethelred and by which she continued to be known in England. This other Aelfgifu was of very noble stock, and as a young girl may even have been introduced to Emma at court. She was the daughter of Aelfhelm, that ealdorman of southern Northumbria who was once a much trusted adviser to Aethelred and who had been murdered back in 1006. She had been further afflicted by tragedy that year when two of her brothers, also prominent courtiers, were blinded – in all likelihood at the behest of Aethelred himself. So the surviving members of Aelgifu's family would have had good reason to support action against the Anglo-Saxon king and his court. Their powerbase was in Northamptonshire, where they held extensive lands and from where they were no doubt among the first to submit to the leadership of Swein

Forkbeard and his warrior son when they arrived in Gainsborough in the summer of 1013.

An aristocratic Midlander, Aelfgifu of Northampton was related to Siferth, the nobleman murdered in 1015 and whose widow subsequently married Edmund Ironside. As Cnut's wife, Aelfgifu therefore connected the Danish and Anglo-Saxon rivals for the English throne. This extended kinship goes some way to explaining why, on defeating the English claimant, Cnut then seemed not unwilling to reach a compromise with him. And why, according to some stories, he was later horrified on hearing of Edmund's murder.

There are no records to indicate exactly when Aelfgifu of Northampton married the Danish invader nor what type of wedding ceremony took place: it may have been a purely secular formality without the blessing of a priest. This marriage evidently did not end when Emma became Cnut's second wife. Although unwanted wives were frequently, and formally, divorced for whatever trumped-up reasons and then roundly shrugged off by being placed in a convent, this was not the fate of Aelfgifu of Northampton. She remained at large in England, with Cnut later to appoint her to a powerful position alongside one of her sons. She is known to have had at least two children with the Danish conqueror: Swein and Harold, named after their Scandinavian grandfather and great-grandfather respectively. If Emma's book is to be believed, they were both born before their father's marriage to her in 1017 – which at least adds an element of respectability to the situation.

Crucially, the author of the book asserts that Emma herself negotiated the terms of her marriage with new King of England and struck a deal to the effect that only *her* sons by Cnut would be considered the rightful inheritors of the throne. The writer alleges that Emma adamantly refused to become the wife of the Danish conqueror 'unless he would affirm to her by oath that he would never set up the son of any wife other than herself to rule after him . . . For she had information that the King had had sons by some other woman'.[12] In the early-eleventh century the swearing of an oath was the equivalent of signing a binding legal document. However, it seems somewhat unlikely that the captive Emma was in a position to demand this of the man who now controlled England by force.

Her apparent preoccupation with sons as yet unborn rather begs the question as to what her intentions were with regard to her existing children by Aethelred. It is conceivable that there was a trade-off between Emma and Cnut whereby she agreed to become his wife and relinquish these three children if he in turn would effectively disinherit his sons by his first wife. Yet whether or not this was the case, Emma does appear phlegmatically to have abandoned Edward, Godgifu and Alfred. They were living with their uncles and the Norman court and there they would remain. On the face of it their circumstances were not dissimilar to the system of fostering that was prevalent among the nobility, particularly for boys. But whereas most aristocratic sons could expect ultimately to return to their original homes – and their inheritance – Emma's boys had no such prospect. Meanwhile her daughter was left to be married to whomever the Norman ruler chose – with a dowry presumably to be supplied by him.

The corollary, though, is that there was no alternative for Emma's children, whether or not their mother married Cnut. Had she returned to Normandy – placing herself once again under the power of her brother Richard – the situation would not have been different: if Richard had subsequently sent Emma to a convent her children would have remained landless wards of the Norman court, as they would if he had married her off to another stately warlord. Whatever their mother's course of action, at this point the future would have looked decidedly unpromising for Edward, Godgifu and Alfred.

It is in stories over the fate of Aethelred's family that Emma starts to emerge as a heartless and steely figure. Thietmar of Merseberg in the German, or Holy Roman, empire provides an account of her conduct over her sons.[13] It is a decidedly garbled version of events, but it does have some historic merit: Thietmar was writing very shortly after the Danish conquest of England and his tale must, to a large degree, reflect contemporary views about Emma, indicating that on the Continent at least she was earning a dastardly reputation. The widowed queen, says Thietmar, grieves for her husband inside the besieged city of London, where she is staying in a garrison with her two sons, curiously named Athelstan and Edmund. After six exhausting months she sends messengers to the Danish troops to broker peace. Their terms are that she pay a tribute of 15,000 pounds, hand over all the city's coats of mail (of which, amazingly, Thietmar claims 'there was an incredible number of 24,000'), provide 300 hostages – and give up her sons to be put to death by the Danish troops. The Queen, writes Thietmar, agrees to these conditions, admittedly after some deliberation. In other words, she is prepared to sacrifice her sons for her own liberation. Thietmar maintains, however, that they manage to escape – with one later wounded in a skirmish and the other valiantly pressing on to rally troops in an effort to rescue his mother.

Misconstrued though it may be, Thietmar's story does highlight the certainty that Emma's sons would have been killed had they fallen into Danish hands. Edward and Alfred had a clear, legitimate claim to the English throne and were now two of just three surviving sons of Aethelred. By 1017, the princes Aethelstan, Egbert, Edmund (Ironside), Eadred and Edgar had all died, leaving Eadwig the only remaining son of Aethelred's first (or second) marriage.

The new ruler of England was brusque and bloody in sweeping out any potential opposition to his regime. The *Anglo-Saxon Chronicles* record that on becoming king of all the nation Cnut divided the country in four, which must have been a move to reward his chief supporters and to enforce a temporary military government through the individual armies they commanded. East Anglia went to Thorkell the Tall, Merica (largely the Midlands) to Eadric Streona, Northumbria to the Norwegian earl Eric of Hlathir, who had originally been allied with Cnut's father. Wessex, traditionally the homeland of the monarchy, the new King kept under his own control. He then ordered the execution of many prominent, and dangerous, Anglo-Saxon nobles.

Emma's author implies that the carnage was extensive. He claims, somewhat piously, that Cnut 'loved' those who had fought nobly and faithfully for his rival, Edmund Ironside, but had such strong feelings against any man known to have oscillated opportunistically between the two leaders that he ordered 'the execution of many chiefs for deceit of this kind'. And on this issue his allocation of the country to four strong military leaders was at least in part short-lived: Eadric Streona, Cnut's newly appointed commander of Mercia, was suddenly dealt the *coup de grâce*. This son-in-law of Aethelred had, after all, shamelessly betrayed Edmund, while the fact that he had been responsible for the murder of Aelfhelm, father of Cnut's first wife, may also have contributed to his death sentence.

Stories of Eadric's execution are recounted with delight by many chroniclers, and it is in tones of distinct satisfaction that Emma's author dwells on this episode. He maintains that when Eadric demanded rewards for his war deeds Cnut majestically summoned Eric the Norwegian and said 'Pay this man what we owe him: that is to say, kill him, lest he play us false'. Eric, as a good Scandinavian warlord, imme-diately raised his axe and neatly chopped off Eadric's head with a mighty blow. Henry of Huntingdon,[14] writing some hundred years later, drew from different sources with his version of events. Eadric's execution was, Henry claims, the direct upshot of his involvement in the murder of Edmund Ironside: when Eadric proudly reported this act to Cnut, the new king apparently rejoined, 'For this deed I will exalt you, as it merits, higher than all the nobles of England.' And he promptly ordered that Eadric be decapitated and his head 'placed upon a pole on the highest battlement of the tower of London' – although the allusion to such a building in London at this date is probably anachronistic.[15] What subse-quently happened to Eadric's wretched widow Edith, Aethelred's daughter, is not known.

Meanwhile, Aethelred's son Eadwig was not long for this world. According to a version of *Anglo-Saxon Chronicles* compiled in Abingdon, 'King Cnut put to flight the aethling [or prince] Eadwig and had him killed'.[16] One down, but four remaining: quite apart from Edward and Alfred safely ensconced in Normandy there were two further claimants to the English throne. In the short interval between his marriage in 1015 and his death in November the following year, Edmund Ironside had fathered two sons (unless they were twins, one of them would have been born after Edmund was murdered). These tiny children were hastily squirreled out of the country, while the fate of their twice-widowed mother, again, remains a mystery. They are known to have fetched up at the royal court of Hungary, where the younger boy, Edmund, died, and where his elder brother, Edward, later married and produced three children – Christina, who became a nun; Margaret, who married King Malcolm of Scotland in about 1070; and Edgar, who was to be a claimant to the English throne in 1066 and who subsequently sought sanctuary in Scotland.

In a tale recounted by the Norman chronicler Geoffrey Gaimar,[17] Emma herself plays a pitiless and highly manipulative part in the fate of Edmund Ironside's sons. Writing in the late 1130s, Gaimar claims that on becoming king Cnut had sent these small boys to the monastery of Westminster, which was several miles west of London. But his queen, Emma, persuades him that they are too dangerous to be allowed to remain in England and as a consequence they are entrusted to a nobleman who removes them to Denmark. Wishing them 'much ill' the Queen then convinces her husband that the boys pose an imminent threat to his reign and so he despatches instructions over to Denmark, ordering that they be maimed so badly they will never recover. However, the nobleman intervenes and manages to save his charges by sending them on to Hungary, safely beyond the reach of both Cnut and Emma.

It is, though, extremely unlikely that any of Aethelred's sons or grandsons were still in England by the time that Emma was married to Cnut. The ceremony was held in the summer of 1017, a good seven months after the Danish Viking had been proclaimed King of England and within that time he would have made sure that all threats to his regime were removed. The wedding probably took place in London and may well have been incorporated into Cnut's formal coronation, with Emma almost literally the crowning glory and with the bishops nervously turning a blind eye to the existence of Cnut's concurrent wife. Changes to the coronation rites known to have been made before 1044[18] plausibly took effect specifically for the ceremonial ascension of Cnut: the new – and foreign – king needed to gain credibility from the Church while it, in turn, would have used the opportunity to redirect the duties of the monarch, particularly in the light of Aethelred's faltering regime. The rites stress the King's undertakings as a just and peaceful ruler, rather than a leader of power and might, while his queen is to act as a partner to his rule, words echoed in Emma's book when describing her own position. And there is little doubt that on her second marriage Emma would once again have been consecrated Queen of England, an emblem of continuity and of balm. Hers was an old role redefined – which also offered a new beginning.

CHAPTER SEVEN

Partner

A good 2,000 people have descended on Oxford: it is such a throng the townsfolk say that there must barely be anyone left elsewhere in the country. Well, nobody of importance at any rate. Literally all the great and the good have gathered here. And what a spectacle they are. The top-ranking noblemen make a big show of their riches and their status, with gold finger rings, ornate buckles fastening the belts of their tunics, and large, elaborate brooches ostentatiously securing their cloaks across the shoulders. There are now many more governing aristocrats than the three commanders the King appointed nearly two years ago. Among them are other Scandinavian warriors he has seen fit to promote as *jarls* – earl is the term some Anglo-Saxon people have started to use in their own rendition of this foreign word, even though the role seems little different from the former office of ealdorman. What really matters is that these are men of land and power, however newly acquired. And the Scandinavian earls are groomed for the part, jangling with jewellery and with beards trimmed and hair well combed. In contrast, the assembled Anglo-Saxon bishops and abbots are, of course, altogether more modest in their daily apparel, although during church officiation they look resplendent in liturgical vestments of embroidered silks and godweb, thick silken fabric which for church apparel is dyed purple.

It is almost a year since King Cnut was crowned, and he has convened this great gathering at Oxford to bring the Anglo-Saxon and Scandinavian elite together and to smooth over the antagonism to his rule. As befits the most powerful people in England, all these great men are accompanied by hosts of attendants: the churchmen with their priests and clerics; the earls and other noblemen with their sons, foster sons and retainers. And they have each brought a large retinue of servants, in part for practical purposes, in part as a further show of importance. Many of these staff are accommodated in tents that have been erected outside Oxford's earthwork fortifications. The temporary housing now forms something of an ancillary village to the town, which normally contains about 3,000 people but whose population has been swelled to more than bursting point. Pack animals are tethered near the flimsy shelters beyond the walls, and wattle enclosures have hastily been put up to contain the cattle, pigs, goats, sheep and fowl that were driven to the town as a moving larder. Meanwhile a watchful eye is kept on supplies of vegetables, grain, ale and beor that are stored in temporary sheds – although plenty goes missing. Wine, most of it imported, is more closely and jealously guarded.

Living conditions for those staying outside the town's walls are infinitely preferable to the circumstances of many people lodged within. The stench, squalor and noise inside the boundaries of Oxford are in some parts appalling: the crowded situation has led to overflowing cesspits; large heaps of food waste rot in untidy piles and are fought over by dogs whose scraps continue long into the night; the noise of drunken human revelry and arguments vies with the canine quarrels until well after daybreak.

Of course the King and Queen do not have to contend with such disturbances, or insanitation. They and the privileged members of their entourage are accommodated in comparatively spacious comfort, complete with royal privy house, near the great hall. It is here that the conferences the King has ordered are taking place. The new, and foreign, monarch of England may have started his reign by the sword, and has certainly shown himself capable of dispensing very savage justice, but he is now apparently eager to dispel this brutish reputation.

Although there has been little armed resistance to his regime since he was acknowledged King of all England, feelings are still bitter about the 72,000 pounds he demanded from the people as tribute money to pay off his army. This sum is in addition to the 11,000 pounds extracted from the Londoners when their city was under siege: 83,000 pounds in total is an appalling amount to have demanded from the beleaguered Anglo-Saxons. However, King Cnut recently earned some approval from his new subjects: he has dismissed most of his well-rewarded army, sending the majority of his ships back to Denmark but retaining a fleet of forty vessels. The crews of these warships number around 4,000, a much diminished force and far less intimidating than the large deployments of Scandinavian troops that were posted around the country up until a few months ago.

Many people are amazed that the brutal conqueror is now showing himself to be a man of peace and wisdom, despite his youth. Others, more familiar with Scandinavian customs, say that the new King of England is following a practice well established in his homeland: after bitter warfare and slaughter the men of the North will frequently hold a great assembly, known as a 'thing' in their own tongue, in order to put the bloodshed behind them and agree on a compatible path for the future.

King Cnut arrived in Oxford accompanied by an enormous band of followers and flunkeys. A long, straggling train of oxcarts loaded with food supplies, and a huge herd of farm animals driven by several stockmen brought up the rear. The King himself rode ahead with his bodyguards. The townsfolk have been told that these escorts are known as housecarls and are, apparently, rather more important than the guards of previous – Anglo-Saxon – monarchs. The King's coterie of Scandinavian warriors certainly behaves with a great deal of arrogance, barely acknowledging common folk and making deliberate display of the large, jewelled sword hilts hanging from their belts. Many people say that King Cnut's cabal is modelled on the fabled and ferocious Jomsvikings, a brotherhood of the finest and fittest fighting men who once occupied the fortress of Jom in Pomerania, although this Scandinavian pirate force has recently been dissolved as a result of warfare in the northern countries. King Cnut's housecarls are understood to have sworn an oath of fellowship to each other, to live under very strict rules of conduct, and to enjoy a special, indeed exclusive, relationship with the new lord of all England.

Meanwhile the Queen and her Anglo-Saxon retainers are reassuringly familiar figures. The Lady Aelfgifu, or Emma, is regarded as something of a talisman, representing the past as well as a hope for the future. Among the more voyeuristic townspeople, there was some salacious expectation that the Danish king would arrive with a great train of wives and concubines, for it is rumoured that he is semi-pagan and keeps several women. Others maintain that King Cnut is a devout Christian and that the Lady is his one true, Christian wife – and they say there were many witnesses at her recent wedding and second cor-o-nation who can verify that she is the only rightful Queen of England. The Lady was in the midst of the royal entourage when it reached Oxford and was borne there with great dignity in a splendidly adorned horse litter. This in itself is a striking show of wealth: a curtained couch suspended on poles between two fine beasts. Some people gossip that it is in fact an extremely uncomfortable mode of transport – and an extravagant, if impressive, waste of horsepower: why use two animals to carry just one person? The Lady's accompanying womenfolk travel far more economically astride individual horses, wrapped tightly in their cloaks and with the ends of their voluminous wimples occasionally billowing behind them in the wind.

The Lady is often present during the King's meetings with his earls and churchmen. Given that both her parents were of Scandinavian origin, she understands the native language of this foreign monarch and can clarify to him the detail of more complex discussions that are being held. But more than that, the King appears to rely greatly on her judgement and guidance.

The Archbishop of York is another frequent adviser. It is to the new king's credit that he has been quick to seek the counsel of this great man of God. Archbishop Wulfstan is an old, outspoken and venerable churchman. He has frequently railed against the people and accused them of all manner of heinous sins, and he is feared and revered by the Anglo-Saxons in almost equal measure. The aged ecclesiastic and the young warrior king make a striking contrast. There are many people who hold that quite apart from the Queen, who is after all a foreigner in origin, the Archbishop of York is the saving grace of the Anglo-Saxon people. He already has sufficient power and influence to prevent the king from turning England into a northern-style state of only semi-godliness.

*   *   *

How Scandinavian the country may have become under Cnut's govern-ance is difficult to gauge. This is partly because of a lack of surviving records from this period – partly, indeed, because there may have been little documentation in the first place.

The *Anglo-Saxon Chronicles*, for example, are sparse in their entries during Cnut's rule of England: possibly an indication of antipathy; possibly a reflection of the non-literate, non-documentary Scandinavian background of Cnut, which could have resulted in a distancing between the Viking ruler and the chief record-makers of the day.

But the overwhelming reason as to why relatively little is known about Cnut's reign – and the extent of its Scandinavian influence – is because, less than fifty years after the coronation of the young Viking, the Anglo-Saxon kingdom was invaded once again, this time by Emma's relatives. The Norman Conquest had momentous, and far-reaching, repercussions on the country, which subsumed the effects of the Danish rule of England and rendered it simply a historical blip.

However, there were clearly two highly significant differences in the leadership of the conquering rulers. After 1066 Duke William of Normandy imposed a militaristic regime on the former Anglo-Saxon kingdom. In 1018 Cnut the Viking sent most of his army home – and Anglo-Saxon England was left relatively free of an occupying force. Of equal, if not greater, importance is the fact that after 1066 William the Conqueror filled many prominent church positions with Norman eccle-siastics. Cnut, by contrast, came from a part of Europe that had only newly, and partly, converted to Christianity: after his coronation in 1017 he not only left the existing Anglo-Saxon bishops and archbishops in place but also relied heavily on their guidance.

If, in the realms of giddy speculation, the Norman Conquest had never happened, or Emma's great-nephew William had been defeated in 1066, would England have evolved along more Scandinavian lines? Probably not. Emma's son Edward (later known as 'the Confessor'), was to play his part in the making of the country. When he became King after many years of exile in Normandy, he ushered in a period of Norman influence. Aristocrats and churchmen from Normandy had a significant place in the English court long before the rule of his cousin William. How much they vied with the Anglo-Danish nobility is not entirely clear, but in any event Scandinavian domination would have been offset by the developing role of the Church, increasingly turning all eyes to Rome – and the Continent.

The extent of the Pope's jurisdiction when Cnut came to the English throne is debatable, and how far Wulfstan, Archbishop of York, and his counterpart Lyfing, Archbishop of Canterbury, were directly answerable to Rome is a muddy matter. It is clear, however, that Wulfstan, who had been a weighty, critical and apocalyptic figure during Aethelred's reign, continued to exert enormous moral, and by extension legalistic, control over the kingdom.

Cnut's troops had mainly been mercenaries recruited in his brother Harold's kingdom of Denmark. In paying them off and sending most of the men away the new king indicated that he had little intention of turning England into a warrior state suppressed by an aggressive over-lord – with hired help. His subsequent objective of stamping his peace-able, if punitive, authority over the Anglo-Saxon people can only have been carried out with the support of England's major clergymen. The great meeting he orchestrated at Oxford in 1018 publicly marked his desire for conciliation and consensus, neither of which could be achieved without a hefty input from the prominent church leaders.

The *Anglo-Saxon Chronicles* are extremely slight in their reference to what must have been a seminal occasion, simply stating, without any preamble about a national assembly, that 'And at Oxford Danes and English were agreed on Edgar's law'.[1] This one sentence not only implies that the new and old aristocracies of the country came to terms with each other, however grudgingly. It also infers that the Danish king showed himself willing to follow English traditions: King Edgar the Peaceable had ruled England between 959 and 975 and his laws had heavily influenced those of his son Aethelred – whose own legal codes had been drawn up by Archbishop Wulfstan. But invoking the laws of Edgar did not entirely indicate a return to business as usual. King Edgar had been a peacemaker and had also instigated a period of church reform. The archbishops Lyfing and Wulfstan were probably keen to continue such measures while also harking back to an ostensibly golden era in order to redefine the role of the king – and so to avoid repeating the mess that had been Aethelred's rule. However much they may initially have abhorred the accession of the foreign king, these archbishops made the most of a convenient opportunity to direct the ruler of the land.

It was at about this time that Wulfstan wrote one of his most influential works, *Institutes of Polity*, a copy of which still survives today. It is an exposition of the duties of representatives of both the Church and the state: king; earls; reeves (an increasingly important position as local collector of taxes and general factotum for the monarchy); bishops; priests; nuns and so on. Although Cnut was probably unable to read the document, he was no doubt forced to listen to it being declaimed. It behoves the king, Wulfstan pontificates, to advance and protect the Church and 'with just laws to bring peace and reconciliation to all people'.[2] So far so good: this appears to be exactly what Cnut was aiming for. And, Wulfstan continues, he must be a thoroughly Christian monarch, which was perhaps partly a nudge at Cnut's barbarous background. For, Wulfstan adds, 'through an unwise king, the people will be made wretched not once but very often, because of his misdirection' – a slightly baffling *non sequitur* which must be an allusion to Aethelred's unfortunate reign.

Wulfstan's document makes no reference to the duties of a queen. Yet there were coronation rites specifically written for the king's wife, and ones that in all probability had recently been redevised, possibly by the Archbishop of York himself. Despite Wulfstan's silence on this role it was clearly considered a station of some responsibility.

A description of the traditional duties of a queen exists in the *Exeter Book*, a volume of poetry written down in the mid- to late-tenth century. It contains a series of maxims, or poems of folk wisdom, that would have been passed down through generations. According to one of these, 'A king shall buy a queen with goods, with beakers and bracelets . . . the woman shall thrive, beloved by her people, be cheerful of mind,

keep counsel, be liberal with horses and treasure, everywhere at all times
before the band of comrades greet first the protector of the nobles with
mead, present straightway the first goblets to the prince's hand, and
shall know wise counsel for them both together'.[3]

So the ideal Anglo-Saxon queen of folklore was an admirable hostess
as well as a prudent and deferential companion to her husband. Emma
was hardly 'bought' with goblets and jewellery but in her marriages to
both Aethelred and Cnut she would have been expected generally to
conform to such a prototype. Yet while her liaison with her first husband
may well have been formal, and possibly slightly frosty, her relationship
with Cnut became radically different from the norm of most royal
marriages. Given the circumstances just before her second wedding, let
alone the existence of another wife, the prospects for this match would,
at the outset, have been regarded as fairly dismal. But no doubt to the
surprise of many, including herself, Emma was apparently to enjoy being
married to her Danish husband – if her own version of events can be
taken at face value. Her book, which otherwise gives little information
about the early years of Cnut's rule, makes much of what seems quickly
to have become a bond of mutual admiration. The author writes that
'it is hard to credit how vast a magnitude of delight in one another
arose in them both. For the King rejoiced that he had unexpectedly
entered upon a most noble marriage; the lady, on the other hand, was
inspired . . . by the excellence of her husband.'

It is, of course, impossible to verify the personal nature of the marriage
between this older woman and the young, vigorous king. But surviving
charters and other documents do show that Cnut and Emma developed, at the very least, an extremely close working relationship, one
that may initially have arisen from the Scandinavian background that
to some extent they shared. And Emma does indeed appear to have
become a real partner in Cnut's rule, as her book claims.

One of the earliest extant documents from the reign of Cnut is a
record in Latin of a grant of land to Lyfing, Archbishop of Canterbury.[4]
It is dated 1018, deemed authentic, and states that 'King Cnut, at the
request of Queen Aelfgifu' gave a copse at Ticehurst in Sussex to this
churchman. This stretch of land adjoined one of the archbishop's estates

on the boundaries of Kent, and Emma would have lobbied her new husband to bestow the small piece of woodland on the senior ecclesiastic in an attempt to dissolve a considerable amount of ill will emanating from Canterbury. The town had suffered badly during the Viking attacks and their archbishop, Aelfheah, had been killed by Scandinavian troops. The grant shows that fairly soon after his marriage to Emma Cnut was acting on her advice – and shrewdly trying to pour oil on very troubled waters.

Of course the grant also tells us who were considered important people of the day. There are twenty-one witnesses listed at the end of this document: Wulfstan's name appears immediately below that of Cnut himself; Emma, still known in the English court as Aelfgifu, ranks just beneath this Archbishop of York. Thorkell, military commander turned statesman, is listed thirteenth, after assorted bishops and abbots. Significantly, fourteenth is one Godwine 'dux' – in other words duke, or ealdorman or earl, all of which were roughly equivalent titles. It is the first surviving indication of this nobleman's rise to power. He was to become enormously rich, enormously influential and enormously underhand in his dealings with Emma and her family.

Godwine is believed to have been the son of Wulfnoth, the courtier responsible for the destruction of a large number of Aethelred's fleet in 1009. Whatever disgrace his family suffered as a result of the fiasco, it had apparently been put behind them in 1014. In that year Aethelred's son Aethelstan had drawn up his will, and in it he restored to Godwine land at Compton in Sussex which had once belonged to his father (and which until then had presumably been confiscated). Whether Godwine subsequently allied himself with Cnut during the upheavals of 1016 is not known. He may simply have made himself very amenable to the new king once Cnut had conquered the country. In, or just after, 1018 Godwine reinforced his position at court by marrying Cnut's sister-in-law, Gytha. She was to produce at least nine children with Godwine, and she was to attract much gossip. The twelfth-century chronicler William of Malmesbury maintains that Gytha became a rapacious trader and operated a lucrative racket in sending slaves from England to Denmark – particularly, pretty girls for whom, so it seems, there was an ever-ready market in Scandinavia. Whatever the truth of this racy allegation, it is fairly well established that Gytha came from a respected Danish family: her father was the gloriously named warrior Thurgils Sprakaleg, said to have been descended from a bear; one brother, Ulf, was married to Cnut's sister Estrith; another brother, Eilaf, was a worthy war veteran whom Cnut had rewarded with an English earldom.

With several Scandinavian earls in place and selected members of the English aristocracy also elevated to such governing positions, towards the end of 1019 Cnut evidently felt sufficiently confident in his most senior courtiers to leave them running the country for a few months while he went back to Scandinavia. He had an urgent reason to do so: his brother Harold had suddenly died, childless, and Cnut needed to return to Denmark to claim that kingdom for himself. And so his empire began to evolve.

Not that Cnut explained the motive for his trip in acquisitive terms to his Anglo-Saxon subjects. From Denmark he sent a remarkable letter addressed to the English people. A copy of the original document survived from this period, tucked into a book of gospels in York Cathedral, along with some land surveys and short sermons by Wulfstan. In his astute missive, Cnut maintains that he had been informed of great danger approaching England – in other words more Viking attacks. Hence, so he says, his return to Denmark where he has 'taken measures so that never henceforth shall hostility reach you from there'.[5] He claims he has paid his own money to settle the issue, although this could have been composed of publically raised Danegeld. He may have been buying off Danish aggressors; he may have been paying for Danish help in stymieing other potential Viking attacks. But whatever the nature of the negotiations, the guarantee of no more northern aggression would have been a very persuasive reason for the battle-weary English to knuckle down under Cnut's leadership: after years of being brutalised and bullied by Scandinavian-led pirates it was a big plus finally to have a really effective protector. Although safeguarding England was not the primary cause of his Danish venture, the new king turned out to be as good as his word: the country was not to suffer any major Viking onslaught during his reign.

Cnut's letter was no doubt read out to his English subjects at public assemblies across the kingdom. It salutes his archbishops, bishops, Earl Thorkell and the other earls, and then all the people of the country 'whether of twelve-hundred wergild or two-hundred, ecclesiastic or lay'. Significantly, it states that 'I have borne in mind the letters and messages which Archbishop Lyfing brought me from Rome from the Pope, that I should everywhere exalt God's praise and suppress wrong and establish full security'. So evidently since Cnut had become King of England his senior archbishop had made a long and arduous visit to Rome and established contact with the Pope on his king's behalf – and this Danish king was at least prepared to consider the resulting advice from Rome. The letter also reaffirms the basic tenet 'all men have agreed and sworn to at Oxford' that Edgar's law should be 'steadfastly' obeyed. And it singles out Thorkell as having jurisdiction over the country while the King is away.

It is very unlikely that Emma accompanied Cnut to Denmark. It was not a return trip to be undertaken lightly: Adam of Bremen, writing towards the end of the eleventh century states that it is 'a three-day sail from Denmark to England with a southeast wind blowing',[6] which were the most advantageous weather conditions. This estimate would not have taken into account added complications of trundling across each country on horseback or in a horselitter – with a requisite band of retainers – to reach the chosen ports. But in any case Emma was no doubt of far greater help to Cnut as his eyes and ears in the English court. In her husband's absence she may well have had some responsibilities as a quasi co-regent with Thorkell, although there is no evidence that this was formally arranged.

While Cnut had made sure that he could entrust England to a group of loyal nobles, similarly in Denmark he required a body of staunch and reliable courtiers to help govern his new kingdom. And this may have been of great benefit to the English aristocracy: a number of Cnut's Danish warriors who might otherwise have settled into powerful positions in England returned with the King to their homeland. Having claimed Denmark, Cnut spent the winter of 1018 there, just long enough to put his own men in place. Leaving his brother-in-law Ulf in charge, early in 1019 he turned tail for England. Judging from the amount of time Cnut was to spend in each country, it appears that he regarded the Anglo-Saxon kingdom as the more significant nation. With good reason, too: in spite of more than thirty-five years of Viking raids, it remained infinitely richer than any Scandinavian state.

On his return to this much prized possession, Cnut embarked on a programme of further reconciliation with his Anglo-Saxon subjects. In 1020, Cnut revisited Ashingdon in Essex, where he had defeated Edmund Ironside in 1016 with much bloodshed on either side. The trip probably took place in October on the anniversary of the battle. One version of the *Anglo-Saxon Chronicles* reports that Cnut had a minster, or church 'built there of stone and mortar for the souls of those men who had been slain there, and gave it to his own priest, whose name was Stigand'.[7] This is the first significant reference to a singular ecclesiastic who was to be one of Emma's most trusted advisers – as well as a notorious political operator: although his career initially shadowed the sharp changes of the Queen's own fortunes, after Emma's death he was to become the last Anglo-Saxon Archbishop of Canterbury and later to ingratiate himself with her great-nephew William the Conqueror. Stigand even features in the Bayeux Tapestry – tonsured but with otherwise slightly wild hair, waving his pallium in his left hand and with his name embroidered into the fabric above him.

It is through church business that Emma's participation in Cnut's rule is most apparent. On 12 June 1020, Archbishop Lyfing died and Aethelnoth, Dean of Christ Church Cathedral, was appointed to replace him as Archbishop of Canterbury. That Emma had a hand in the matter is evident in a surviving letter from Archbishop Wulfstan, written to update the King and Queen as to how the formalities are progressing. He 'greets humbly King Cnut his lord and the Lady Aelfgifu. And I inform you both, beloved, that we have acted concerning Bishop Aethelnoth according as notice came to us from you: that we have now consecrated him.'[8] And he goes on to express his hopes that the King and Queen will grant Aethelnoth the rights and dignities that previous Archbishops of Canterbury have enjoyed.

It was also in 1020 that over in northern France the Cathedral of Chartres burnt down. Cnut despatched messengers with a donation for its refoundation. This act of generosity was almost undoubtedly prompted by Emma, who had emotional ties with the town: her brother, Robert Danus, was buried at Chartres; her sister Matilde had died there; and her mother was a great benefactor of its churches. Emma would also have been well aware of the political mileage to be gained from overseas patronage. A letter of thanks was duly despatched from Fulbert, Bishop of Chartres, to Cnut. This surviving document demonstrates how badly at this stage the Danish King of England was perceived on the Continent, and how the gift had been a wise move. Fulbert confesses that he has been amazed to receive the donation. He is surprised that Cnut has shown himself to be a man of such wisdom and piety and implies that he had previously thought the King too barbarous to be bothered with finer spiritual matters: not only is Cnut a distant foreigner, but the bishop had also heard him 'to be a ruler of pagans, not only of Christians'.[9] Fulbert addresses Cnut as 'the most noble King of Denmark' making no mention of his rule over England, but he must have known that Cnut was also the monarch of the Anglo-Saxon people. He probably chose not to acknowledge this position because it was still a contentious issue on the Continent. After all, nearby in Normandy Emma's two sons, legitimate heirs to the English throne, were living in exile.

The sorry prospects for Edward, Alfred and their sister Godgifu would hardly have improved when the Norman court received news of the birth of Emma's two children by Cnut. Before 1022[10] she produced a son and a daughter who were both given Scandinavian names: Harthacnut appears to have been a name by which Cnut's great-grandfather Gorm the Old was also known;[11] Gunnhild was probably so called after Cnut's grandmother, the wife of Harold Blue Tooth. There may additionally have been other children who did not survive sufficiently long for their existence to be documented.

Emma's author makes no mention of Gunnhild, but devotes quite some space to the fact that 'the most noble queen bore a son' to whom Cnut pledged 'the whole realm which was subject to his command'. The child's name, Emma's author explains, was a composite of his father's name and a Scandinavian word, *harde*, meaning swift or strong

and indeed the boy was to excel over 'all men of his time by superi-
ority in all high qualities'.

This excellent child may well have been raised with the expectation
of becoming King of England, but he did, of course, have two sets of
half-brothers who could also claim to be rightful heirs to the throne.
On his mother's side, Edward and Alfred, ensconced in Normandy, were
of ancient royal Anglo-Saxon descent. On his father's side, Swein and
Harold, the sons of Aelfgifu of Northampton, were more immediate
contenders and, at least during the first few years of Harthacnut's life,
were being brought up in England.

It is probable that after Cnut married Emma, his first wife retreated
to her family estates in the Midlands with her children. There is no
evidence from surviving charters to suggest that Aelfgifu of
Northampton played a part in court life during the early years of Cnut's
rule. This was Emma's domain and she would not have tolerated the
presence of a rival. But Cnut's first wife may subtly have made her mark
in other ways. An Aelfgifu appears in the surviving list of benefactors
to a church in Cambridgeshire: in the *Liber Vitae* of Thorney Abbey
the name is among a group of prominent royals and ecclesiastics and
is listed immediately after 'Imma Reginae' or Queen Emma, somewhat
unusually referred to here by her Norman name.[12]

Understandably, the great moralist Wulfstan was distinctly unimpressed
by his king's marital arrangements and the worthy Archbishop of York
attempted to stop the spread of any similar moral degradation. During
1020 he drew up a new series of laws for Cnut, based on the famous
laws of Edgar in which he made it plain to the rest of the country that
having more than one wife was totally unacceptable.

The laws are divided into ecclesiastic and secular ordinances, in other
words church-related law and more general laws of society, albeit that
the latter are coloured by the promotion of a very Christian way of life.
In each section there are clear instructions as to marital monogamy.
Within the 'ecclesiastic' statutes it is forbidden for a man 'to have more
wives than one, and this is to be his wedded wife, but he is to remain
with one as long as she lives – he who wishes to heed God's law aright

and to protect his soul from hell-fire'.[13] Monogamy is also stressed in the 'secular' grouping: 'And if anyone has a lawful wife and also a concubine, no priest is to do for him any of the offices which must be done for a Christian man, until he desists and atones for it as deeply as the bishop directs him; and desists from such for ever.' The possibility of being excommunicated from the Church was no mean threat. And just in case any Scandinavians living in England might feel such rulings are not applicable to them, the laws continue: 'Foreigners, if they will not regularise their marriages are to depart from the land with their goods and their sins.'

Sinful though he was, Cnut himself approved the laws. The long, thoroughly Christian code shows a commitment to maintain justice, uphold public order and protect the weak and vulnerable. The legislation ranges from an enumeration of what financial dues the public must pay to the Church, and when, to the itemising of fines and other punishments for specified misconducts. Trading is forbidden on Sundays, as is hunting and any type of work unrelated to church duties. If a slave is forced to labour on a feast day then his master is to be fined and is to forfeit the serf, who then becomes a freeman. Meanwhile the (fairly limited) rights of free women are to be respected: widows are not to be immured in convents 'too hastily'; 'and neither a widow nor a maiden is ever to be forced to marry a man whom she herself dislikes'.

Not that there was very much equality between the sexes when it came to retribution for marital sin. It is, for example, 'a wicked adultery' for a married man to 'commit fornication' with a single woman – worse if the women is married or is a nun. But there the matter rests, with no punishment directly suggested. However, a married woman who commits adultery becomes 'a public disgrace, and her lawful husband is to have all that she owned; and she is to forfeit her nose and ears'.

The threat of mutilation seems more in keeping with Scandinavian methods of punishment than English traditions and may possibly have been suggested by the King himself – or his Danish courtiers. In contrast, another law infers that pagan Scandinavian customs were a worrying influence for church leaders. 'It is heathen practice,' it reads, for a person to worship 'heathen gods, and the sun or the moon, fire or flood, wells or stone or any kind of forest trees.' In the legislation Wulfstan drew up for Aethelred in 1008 there is no mention of such subcultures, and it may be that with a Danish king in place there was an open surge of these beliefs in the Danelaw area of the country.

Whether in the Danish-dominated town of York or the quintessentially Anglo-Saxon stronghold of Winchester, the new laws would have been read out loud to the people during public gatherings throughout the country, hence the dramatic language. 'And we enjoin eagerly also every man that he always have in his mind the fear of God, and day and night be in terror of sins, dread Doomsday and tremble at the thought of hell, and ever expect his last day at hand' admonishes one such ruling, the spectre of Wulfstan almost visibly looming behind it.

Indeed the first law of the land was that the people should love and honour God and be unanimously Christian. They should also 'love King Cnut with true fidelity'. Failure to comply with this clause may have been the undoing of Cnut's right-hand man, Thorkell the Tall. Under the year 1021 there is just one entry in the Peterborough manuscript of the *Anglo-Saxon Chronicles*: at Martinmas, the feast of St Martin of Tours celebrated on 11 November, King Cnut's erstwhile commander was outlawed. No further explanation is given. Quite possibly Thorkell had simply become too powerful for Cnut to control comfortably. The Scandinavian warrior departed, leaving a vacuum at court to be filled by whom: Godwine? Emma? Possibly both.

CHAPTER EIGHT

Saints and Sinners

On a June morning in 1023, a long procession snakes slowly towards Canterbury. The group is composed of several hundred people, singing psalms and hymns – all known by heart. They are led by monks from Christ Church Cathedral and it is these ecclesiastics who set the chanting that is picked up in a gentle ripple effect along the walking train of pilgrims. The front and back of this large body are so far apart that at times different canticles resound from either end.

It is a solemn yet joyful occasion. Although the main focus of the event is evidently a coffin, this is no funeral march. The great crowd of monks and members of the laity have gathered to rebury a martyr – and in the process confirm his status as a saint.

Immediately following the psalm-setting monks is a coterie of senior churchmen. Among them are the Bishops of Wells and Winchester as well as the Archbishop of Canterbury himself, Aethelnoth, who since the death of Wulfstan earlier in the year has become the most influential ecclesiastic in the country. He utters prayers and blessings as he sprinkles holy water on the ground at his feet. Behind him is the saint's coffin, draped in silks and other finely woven cloth. It is carried in relays by strong and sturdy monks who have been specially selected for this great honour. The King, flanked by a number of his housecarls, walks directly after the coffin. In his wake is the Queen, veiled and wearing outer robes of the best godweb – she needs no cloak on this warm June morning. The Lady is accompanied by several almost equally well-dressed female attendants, one of whom carries the small aethling, or prince. It is the first public excursion of Harthacnut, and many people take this appearance to indicate that without a doubt the young child is the heir to the throne.

The royal entourage is followed by a cluster of senior aristocrats, including Earl Godwine and his wife Gytha as well as Leofric, another increasingly important adviser to the King, who has joined the procession with his wife Godgifu. There is much gossip about the growing rivalry between these two powerful families and others in the throng are eyeing them up to see how much they appear deliberately to be avoiding each other. Stretching back behind the group of nobles are more monks, a few parties of nuns, a big turnout of parish priests and a great many members of the laity. This large number of men, women and children has come to join the procession not just from Canterbury and its neighbouring localities, but also from Sandwich, Dover, Rochester, Winchester, Oxford and other further-flung parts of southern England.

The coffin contains the body of the holy martyr Aelfheah, the Archbishop of Canterbury who was cruelly killed by Viking invaders back in 1012. Eleven years after his death and his funeral in London, Aelfheah is being taken back to Canterbury to be splendidly interred as a saint in Christ Church Cathedral.[1]

The monks and the people of Canterbury are quietly jubilant that Aelfheah will once again be among them, resting on the north side of Christ's altar in the great church. And there will without doubt be many pilgrims coming to seek help beside the new tomb of this holy man. But the Canterbury folk know full well that their gain is London's loss. And there is a certain smug satisfaction about this, particularly among the senior ecclesiastics. Until a few days ago Aelfheah lay buried in St Paul's minster in the heart of London.

It is said that on Aelfheah's death at Southwark, across the Thames from London, the Viking army had intended to sink the Archbishop's body in the river but that some of his captors, whom Aelfheah himself had converted to Christianity, refused to allow such ignominy. So it was that he was handed over to the Londoners, who laid him to rest in a fitting tomb in St Paul's from where a great number of miracle cures have subsequently been reported. But three days ago, on 8 June, St

Aelfheah was exhumed at the behest of King Cnut. No wonder that, in the build-up to the occasion over the last two years, Earl Thorkell was outlawed: it was his men, after all, who were responsible for killing the sainted Archbishop and no matter how much the Viking commander might have tried to make amends he has never been forgiven by the people of London and of Canterbury. Although some people say that Thorkell's banishment was for other political reasons, many monks maintain that he was forced out of England by the King because Cnut himself was fearful of the vengeance that would otherwise be wrought by the saint.

The removal of Aelfheah's body has been bitterly resented in London. Not just by the ecclesiastics at St Paul's but also by the citizens, who were enormously angry to see the saint being forcibly taken away from them. It is rumoured that on the day the saint was taken out of his grave the King sent several of his housecarls to different parts of the city to cause violent disturbances and so distract the people's attention from the events at St Paul's. He also ordered a number of troops to stand guard by Archbishop Aethelnoth and the Canterbury monks as they broke open St Aelfheah's tomb.

Many of the monks say that there they found the holy body marvellously intact, looking exactly as it would have done when it was placed there eleven years before. They claim that it had not stiffened in the manner of ordinary mortals: the joints were still supple, so it was perfectly possible to bend the saintly corpse and move it into a new coffin without damage. St Aelfheah was then carried over the bridge to Southwark, although in view of the standoff between groups of threatening soldiers and surly citizens, the monks confess that this was achieved with only a small degree of dignity.[2]

Once the party reached Southwark the menacing mood lifted and with mounting excitement the coffin was conveyed on board a ship specially decked out for the occasion. Here King Cnut was waiting to greet the Archbishop and the monks attending the coffin. Accompanied by other vessels, the resplendent ship was then rowed over to Rochester. The Canterbury monks say that King Cnut himself steered on this most stately of occasions.

From Rochester they have proceeded on foot towards Canterbury, joined by the Queen and other nobles and by ever-growing numbers of well-wishers who have come to marvel at the glory and the sanctity of the occasion. It will take eight days for St Aelfheah to complete his journey from St Paul's minster to Christ Church in Canterbury, allowing plenty of time for the increasing throng to witness the majesty of the procession. And although many of them will not be able to crush into the Cathedral to see the final rites of the saint's re-interment they will have contributed to the veneration of the event – and will be able to testify as to the great piety of the King and Queen.

*   *   *

In 1023, when Cnut orchestrated the removal of Aelfheah's body from London to Canterbury, he was playing a deft political hand. And without doubt he was working in consultation with Emma – possibly even at her instigation. There were a number of factors behind the masterful move. Not least of which was the situation in London. The city appears to have been a big problem for Cnut: whereas Aethelred had adopted London as something of a base, the Scandinavian king was unwelcome there and instead increasingly developed Winchester as his quasi head-quarters. Meanwhile, five years after Cnut's coronation, Aelfheah's body in London's largest church had become the focus of anti-Danish senti-ments. The King felt that removing this troublesome emblem would defuse the increasingly volatile situation. At the same time he had to address difficulties in Canterbury. Memories of the Viking barbarities inflicted on this town were still vivid and the King was not popular there either. But in bestowing an Anglo-Saxon saint on Canterbury he provided the people there with the enormous spiritual and financial benefit of a pilgrimage site, for which they could not but be grateful. So in a flourish of near alchemy he turned relics imbued with antago-nism into a benevolent and gracious gift and also placed himself in the position of devout and generous provider.

For about the next two centuries St Aelfheah's remains were to draw huge numbers of pilgrims to the town. The saint was even, apparently, invoked in the dying breath of Thomas Becket in 1170 after he was famously stabbed in Canterbury Cathedral by the henchmen of Henry

II. Ultimately, though, the cult of this other martyr and Archbishop of Canterbury was to overshadow that of St Aelfheah and by the end of the thirteenth century the town had become associated principally with St Thomas.

At the time Thomas Becket was canonised in 1173, the pope had taken some, limited, control over the creation of saints. However, back in the early-eleventh century there was no formal mechanism for elevating an individual in such a way – either from Rome or even more narrowly within England. The actual definition of a saint was vague. The Latin *sanctus* simply means holy. Saints at this period were usually martyrs although sometimes they were just thoroughly good (and dead) men and women. Often fairly recently deceased, they were considered worthy of their exalted and godly title mainly through popular appeal, although their resulting cults were much encouraged by the Church.

In essence saints were venerated because they had a direct line to God: since they enjoyed a particularly close relationship with the Almighty they were able to address him on behalf of supplicants who might as a consequence be absolved of their sins – and thereby receive miracle cures. A type of lateral tradition also evolved whereby a saint's corpse, in turn, was believed to have miracle properties and purportedly did not putrefy for a great many years after the death of the sublime person. Underlying such apparent revelations was the practice of exhuming the saintly bodies in order to rebury them with much fanfare. This started as a means of safeguarding the holy relics, moving them from dilapidated and poorly maintained churches or from small shrines that had become inadequate for the number of visiting pilgrims. But by the eleventh century the Church was deliberately using the exhumations to draw attention to the saint, build up the cult and profit from a new, improved pilgrimage trail. The monarchs, too, had realised the benefits of re-interring, or 'translating', saints' corpses. It would be anachronistically cynical to suggest that the kings' involvement was devoid of any genuine belief; however, by associating themselves with saints they were well aware that they would duly gain prestige and increased credibility. And in promoting the cults the kings were often able to address sticky political predicaments as well. In 997 Aethelred had been involved in the translation of the relics of his half-sister Edith to a new shrine at Wilton Abbey, and a few years later had declared his murdered half-brother, Edward, a saint when he, too, was ceremoniously reburied. The moves were at least partly an attempt to persuade the English people of the royal family's spiritual supremacy at a time of particular vulnerability and intense Viking attacks.

Emma herself was later to try to turn one of her own sons by Aethelred into a saint. Her efforts came to no avail although, somewhat ironically, long after her death another of her children – Edward the Confessor – was to be elevated to sainthood. Back in 1023 she would have known full well that an association with Anglo-Saxon saints would be an expedient measure for her Scandinavian husband: he would be following a practice of previous, indigenous kings; he would be showing penance; and he would be seen as a great Christian leader. Aelfheah's was not the only corpse to be shifted around the country at the injunctions of Cnut. He was also to sanction the translation of St Mildreth's body from the Isle of Thanet to St Augustine's Abbey in Canterbury and that of St Wystan, a Mercian prince murdered in the ninth century, from Repton to Evesham. But the re-interment of Aelfheah was the first and probably most glorious of such occasions.

During the year of the martyred Archbishop's translation to Canterbury, Christ Church Cathedral also received other riches from Cnut.[3] The King granted the community there the port of Sandwich. Given the amount of customs dues and other trading taxes this extensive harbour levied, it was no small gift. The surviving records of the grant are in fact forgeries made after the Norman Conquest, probably because the first charter was lost. But their wording suggests they were closely modelled on a much earlier, and probably original, document. As well as detailing tolls and landing procedures, they state that in addition King Cnut gave Christ Church his crown of gold and that he himself placed it on the altar of the Cathedral. And here, quite possibly, is the genesis of the famous myth about Cnut and the waves.

The earliest known source of this legend is Henry of Huntingdon's *History of England*, written in the first half of the twelfth century. Rather

than being a tale about Cnut's vanity and witlessness that culminated
in the King being soaked as he tried to turn back the incoming tide,
as became the popular interpretation, the story illustrates the
Scandinavian monarch's respect for God and his wry wisdom, his seemingly arrogant behaviour an exercise to teach his courtiers a lesson in
humility. According to Henry, Cnut ordered his attendants to set out
a chair for him on a seashore – the locality of which is not specified.
As the tide came in the seated king shouted at the waves to stop,
commanding them not to wet the feet or robes of his royal personage.
When the sea blithely failed to obey him, the King leapt back and
admonished his fawning retinue, telling them that this showed how
empty the power of kings was in the face of God, 'He whom heaven,
earth and sea obey by eternal laws'. Thereafter, writes Henry, Cnut
never wore his crown of gold but instead dedicated it to Christ. And
this latter act may be a direct echo of the gift of royal regalia described
in the grant to Christ Church in Canterbury.[4]

Disappointingly, Emma's book provides no specific details of Cnut's
peacetime activities in England – and certainly no flamboyant inter-
ludes of damp feet and abject humility. But it does stress the King's
close association with the Church. He was, her author enthuses, so in-
timate with the country's ecclesiastics that he 'seemed to bishops to be
a brother bishop for his maintenance of perfect religion'. The writer
goes on to extol the King for devoting himself solely 'to things pleasing
God'. This was not, of course, entirely the case. Cnut may have made
every effort to be seen as a peaceable and model Christian king, but he
also had other preoccupations. He was the supreme ruler of Denmark
as well as England, and he needed not just to promote spiritual harmony
but to maintain order in both countries and also to protect them.

It may be for this reason that he made a *rapprochement* with Thorkell,
his erstwhile commander and statesman, sometime in 1023. Since his
banishment from England nearly two years before, Thorkell had
remained a threat to both of Cnut's kingdoms. Having been roundly
rejected from the Anglo-Saxon realm, he would have returned to
Scandinavia, where he no doubt resumed his activities as a Viking

warlord and recruited his own private army. An elliptical entry in the
Anglo-Saxon Chronicles states that in 1022 King Cnut took a fleet over
to the Isle of Wight.[5] The reason for this is not given, although it may
have been a move to head off an imminent attack by Thorkell and his
men.[6] Denmark would also have been in danger. Whether Cnut briefly
returned there in 1023 to negotiate with the Viking aggressor is not
recorded but according to one manuscript of the *Anglo-Saxon Chronicles*[7]
that year the two men came to an agreement: they swapped sons, who
became honourable hostages, and Thorkell was appointed to 'guard'
Denmark along with Cnut's boy while the King of England and Denmark
was to bring up the Viking leader's child at his court. There, frustrat-
ingly, any established information about Thorkell abruptly ends: he may
have died shortly afterwards, which would explain the lack of further
details. Meanwhile his son appears to have thrived under Cnut's
patronage: he married the King's niece Gunnhild[8] and is known to have
been still at the English court in 1042.

Which of Cnut's own boys was entrusted to Thorkell, and for how
long, is not entirely clear. However, the child must have been one of
Aelfgifu of Northampton's offspring – Swein or Harold. Emma's young
son, Harthacnut, was very much in evidence at St Aelfheah's re-
interment, which probably took place just after Cnut's negotiations
with the Scandinavian chieftain. But Harthacnut was also shortly to
be shipped northwards. According to Scandinavian stories he became
a foster son to Ulf, the most powerful of the Danish nobles. Ulf was
married to Cnut's sister, Estrith, and was also the King's regent in
Denmark – presumably at one stage sharing control of the country
with Thorkell.

It is possible that Harthacnut first arrived in Scandinavia with his
father on a trip Cnut made there in 1025. Under that year, the *Anglo-
Saxon Chronicles* very briefly report that the King returned to his homeland to do battle, unsuccessfully as it turned out, against the Swedes.

More details about this and other of Cnut's activities in the area are
provided by Scandinavian sources. However, there is a big credibility
problem here: the material was written down for the very first time only
after an extremely long interval from many of the recorded events. It

was mainly because of a strong oral tradition, and a corresponding lack of reliance on the written word, that Scandinavian histories were not documented until the mid-twelfth century (as opposed, for example, to the earliest known history of Anglo-Saxon England, written by the Venerable Bede before the 730s). The resulting works often contain a greater element of folk tale than reliable fact. At times the Scandinavian accounts also seem very garbled. One of the most respected authors of these histories was, in fact, a resident of Iceland rather than Scandinavia *per se* – although the relatively remote island was populated with Norse people and had been ruled by Norway for a good three centuries. This Icelandic writer, Snorri Sturluson, was a wealthy politician, scholar and prolific compiler of historical prose narratives known as sagas. In particular, his *Heimskringla* of the early-thirteenth century charts the development of Norway through sixteen sagas and among these *St Olaf's Saga* is especially pertinent to Cnut.

This Olaf (and, confusingly, there were a number of prominent Olafs at the time) was the Norwegian Viking who, with his wandering mercenary army, had supported Aethelred when he was forced into exile. Variously known as Olaf Haroldsson and Olaf the Stout, the pirate leader had converted to Christianity when with Aethelred and Emma in Normandy and had later helped the English king expel the Danish army from his country by pulling down London Bridge. After being handsomely paid for his efforts Olaf had returned to Scandinavia, where he had taken control of what was effectively Norway.

According to Snorri, after Cnut came to power in Denmark, he attempted to make Olaf the Stout accept him as overlord. The demand would not have come out of the blue: Cnut's father, Swein Forkbeard, had previously exercised control over Norway. But the Norwegian chief refused to submit to the Danish monarch and teamed up with Onund, the King of the Swedes, in defiance of Cnut. It was partly in retaliation and partly because these two leaders had begun to pose a threat to his Scandinavian realm that Cnut returned there in 1025. He raised a large army, probably composed of English as well as Danish fighters, and in a great dragon warship led his men to 'Holy River', thought to be Helga A in Skane, southern Sweden. There, through the cunning of Olaf and Onund, he was defeated. The *Anglo-Saxon Chronicles* suggest that this was also partly due to the defection of his brother-in-law Ulf, although Snorri makes no such allegation.

In Snorri's version of events Emma accompanied her husband to Denmark on this occasion – improbable though not impossible. Snorri subsequently maintains that Emma was responsible for much subterfuge, culminating in the murder of Ulf. In Snorri's story, Harthacnut had been sent over to Denmark some months beforehand. Here he was to act as regent with his uncle Ulf. Unhappy with the arrangement of having an absentee king, Ulf then readily accepted instructions in a letter bearing Cnut's seal that Harthacnut was to be accepted as the full monarch of Denmark. But this was, in fact, a ploy on the part of Emma, who had stolen her husband's seal in order to issue fake orders and thereby gain power for her son. Ulf and Harthacnut, innocent of such machinations, realised they had unwittingly overstepped the mark and tried to make amends on Cnut's arrival in Denmark. On the intercession of Emma, whose hand in the matter remained unknown, Harthacnut was readily forgiven. But after the defeat at Holy River Ulf did not fare so well.

Recovering from the battle, Cnut and Ulf spent an evening at the royal base in Roskilde, absorbed in a game of chess – apparently the King of Denmark and England was a keen player. Cnut made a bad move, Ulf took a knight from him and the session ended in an argument. The following morning Cnut ordered one of his attendants to kill his brother-in-law. The man returned saying that he had been unable to carry out his task because Ulf was in Roskilde's church – which was dedicated to the third-century pope St Lucius and which Cnut himself had patronised and promoted. Unmoved, the King commanded another retainer, Norwegian by birth, to carry out his murderous objective. This accomplice had no qualms and came back bearing a sword dripping with blood, having plunged it through Ulf while he was praying in the choir.

Evidently Cnut's attempts to establish a reputation as an ideal Christian king did not see much success in Scandinavia. However far-fetched Snorri's tales may be, they were not invented entirely out of thin air. That Ulf died at this point is pretty much unquestionable. Whether Cnut was actually responsible for this bloodshed – and inside a church, too – is another matter. But the allegation does at the least show that later Scandinavians saw him as a cold-blooded murderer with a dismissive attitude to the Church. Emma, too, clearly acquired a dubious reputation in the North. Was she really a scheming and overly ambitious mother? Almost without doubt, yes. But perhaps not quite at this juncture. In 1025 Harthacnut would have been seven years old at the most and even Emma would have blenched at trying to bamboozle a nation into accepting a leader so young.

With Harthacnut being brought up in Denmark, Emma was now separated from four of her five children. This was not a remarkable state of affairs for a noble woman, but she may around this time have had some latent concern about her sons in Normandy. By this stage they were young adults: Edward would have been about twenty years old; Alfred in his mid-teens (twelve being the age when a boy was considered grown up[9]). Meanwhile her daughter by Aethelred, Godgifu, had been married off to the Count of Amiens and the Vexin, probably at the instigation of Emma's brother Richard.[10] It is unlikely that Emma herself had any involvement at all in her daughter's wedding. Shortly after this event, however, there was a distinct wobble in the political situation in Normandy. In the mid-1020s Duke Richard II died, leaving the principality to his eldest son, also called Richard. This Richard was not popular and survived little more than a year in office before being terminally poisoned at a feast. On his death his younger brother Robert became duke. Whether he had a hand in his sibling's early demise is not proven. Emma, at any rate, must have been anxious to make formal contact with this suddenly powerful nephew. She seized a neat opportunity to forge an alliance between her Norman and Scandinavian family groups: Robert was unmarried; Cnut's sister Estrith, newly widowed after the murder of Ulf, was available for a political match.

The marriage was a disaster. Perhaps Estrith lacked the acumen – that Emma evidently possessed – to make an unlikely match work. At any rate, Robert fairly swiftly managed to divorce Cnut's sister. What

Cnut and Emma present a cross to the New
Minster, Winchester. In the picture Emma is
given her Anglo-Saxon name 'Aelfgifu'

Queen Emma receives her book

REGEM
DANORŪ
SUEINUM

INQVAM
ueridica
comperi relati
one omnium sui teporis
regum ferme fortunatissimu
extitisse, adeo·ut(quod raro
contingi solet) principiis
felicibus secundum dm &
sctm, multo felicior respon
dere extitit. Hic deniq;

The opening lines of Book I of the manuscript
Emma commissioned

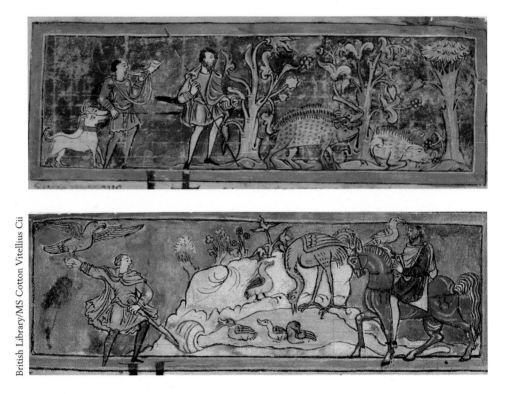

Scenes from an early eleventh-century calendar: pig feeding in
September and hawking in October

Coins issued during the reign of King Cnut: 'Quatrefoil',
'pointed helmet' and 'short cross' pennies

Page from a herbal produced in the early eleventh century
at Christ Church, Canterbury

A copy of an illustration in the 'Utrecht Psalter', made at
Christ Church, Canterbury in the early eleventh century

· C V I ·

eruint ;   eiuſ filiiſ hominum ;

enteſ. ani   Quia ſatiauit animam in

pſiſ defecit ;   anem . & animã eſurien

addnm   tem ſatiauit boniſ ;

Wading to longships

Transporting horses by longship

The Bayeux Tapestry: Emma's priest Stigand, who
became Archbishop of Canterbury after her death

happened to her thereafter is not clear, although the rejection of Estrith must have done little to promote Norman relations with the Danish King of England. Estrith's legacy, however, is important. With Ulf, she had at least one child, Swein, who was ultimately to become King of Denmark and so to continue the bloodline of Gorm the Old, which can be traced through to the current Danish monarch. She had no children with Robert. Had she done so she might possibly have seen two of her offspring ruling different parts of Europe. As it was, Robert's illegitimate son, William, was to succeed him – and change the course of English history.

But long beforehand, Emma's second husband continued to make an impact on England, and indeed Europe, however briefly this reverberated. Leaving Harthacnut with regents in Denmark, Cnut returned to his Anglo-Saxon kingdom in 1026, where he made yet more acts of penance for past woes. Roger of Wendover,[11] writing around the same period as Snorri Sturluson, claims that he ceremoniously visited Edmund Ironside's tomb at Glastonbury, on which he is said to have bestowed an elaborate pall intricately decorated with peacock designs. Cnut's attentiveness to Edmund's grave may have been a move to show due honour to this former rival while subtly defusing efforts to turn the one-time Anglo-Saxon king into yet another saint. But Cnut's most significant activities around this time lay well beyond England.

Over the next couple of years the country was largely left in the care of Cnut's council while their king was otherwise occupied. Godwine, the Earl of Wessex, was ever powerful. Meanwhile Leofric, a Midlands aristocrat, was becoming increasingly prominent – and was to be appointed Earl of Merica. Emma, too, may have been entrusted with responsibilities. It is unlikely that she accompanied her husband on his journeys that would, by sea and on horseback, have been physically very challenging. She was certainly not with Cnut when he undertook a great pilgrimage to Rome in 1027. The author of her book makes no mention of her on this occasion: he himself was a witness to Cnut's piety and generosity en route to the holy city and in his subsequent descriptions of the King's trip would certainly have included reference to Emma had she been there.

The writer was a monk resident at the monastery of Saint Bertin in St Omer in 1027, and he rubbed shoulders with Cnut then as the King of England passed through this city – which is now in France but was part of Flanders at the time. The author claims he saw with his own eyes how the King entered monasteries 'in a manner wonderfully reverent . . . freely pouring forth . . . rivers of tears'; how he prostrated himself at the high altars of the churches in these establishments, pressing kisses on the ground and beating his chest in humility; and how he would then give a sign to his attendants to produce an offering – which would perhaps have been a golden crucifix or an elaborate casket for relics. These were evidently extremely ostentatious: the St Omer monk writes that inevitably the gift would not be 'a mean one, nor such as might be shut in any bag, but a man brought it, huge as it was, in the ample fold of his cloak'. This Cnut would then place on the altar with his own hands – an act of due drama. And, the author continues, the King would not limit his attention to the prominent altars but would liberally bestow other presents, as well as grovelling kisses, elsewhere in the churches.

Such appears to have been Cnut's somewhat flashy progress along a route that took in Flanders as well as France and northern Italy on the way to Rome. The trip very publicly established the monarch of England and Denmark not only as a devout king but also as an international political player of stature. The visit to Rome was timed to coincide with the coronation there of the German king, Conrad II, as Roman Emperor in March of 1027. Cnut made good use of his new contacts and during this occasion started negotiations to betroth his (and Emma's) daughter, Gunnhild, to Conrad's son and heir apparent, Henry. Gunnhild was not yet of marriageable age – she would have been no more than eight years old – so the wedding was a slightly distant event, but the prospective alliance was a big coup for Cnut: a once barbaric Viking leader had become an accepted member of Europe's noblest elite.

On reaching Rome, the King issued a letter to his English subjects, which, like the previous missive he had sent to the Anglo-Saxon people back in 1019, would have been read out across the country. The document has not survived but it is paraphrased by the early-twelfth-century chronicler, William of Malmesbury,[12] who was probably writing with direct reference to an original source. According to William, the letter made it plain that the royal journey had not been made entirely for the sake of the King's soul. There were also thorny commercial issues that Cnut had proudly been able to resolve. From what William reports, it is clear that pilgrims and traders from both of Cnut's kingdoms had been subject to heavy taxes on their travels through the Continent to the holy city. The King said he had been able to negotiate on this matter with the new Roman Emperor, with the Pope, and with other European leaders and he apparently claimed that binding oaths were then sworn to guarantee that Anglo-Saxons and Danes would no longer have to shell out immense sums of money when moving around mainland Europe. The surprising implication was that at the time there was a large volume of human traffic from Denmark and England across the Continent. Whether his itinerant subjects actually did enjoy entirely toll-free passage thereafter is not known. But what would really have mattered to Cnut was being able to tell his people that he had sufficient credibility among world leaders to make such demands.

Flushed with success, he returned to England and then promptly took on the Scots. The *Anglo-Saxon Chronicles* record that in the year of his pilgrimage to Rome[13] he also travelled to the bellicose kingdom of Scotland, where he succeeded in obtaining the submission of chieftains Malcolm, Iehmarc and Maelbeth – probably the real Macbeth of Shakespeare's play.

With one set of enemies vanquished, the following year Cnut headed out to Scandinavia to settle old scores there. The *Anglo-Saxon Chronicles* succinctly record that in 1028 he went to Norway, drove King Olaf out and 'appropriated that land for himself'.[14] Snorri Sturluson, writing about two centuries later, provides rather more details.

Snorri maintains that since being defeated by Kings Olaf and Onund, Cnut had been running a campaign to buy his way into Norway and that the country had been infiltrated by his spies who offered rich rewards to anyone willing to swear loyalty to him. For Cnut, it seems, was well practised in the arts of bribery: Snorri writes that it 'is to be said of King Knut [Cnut] that everyone he got to know and who seemed to him to be a man of some mettle and inclined to attach himself to him, got his handfuls of money'.[15]

So, with the ground well prepared by ready blandishments of gold and silver, Cnut sailed north along the Norwegian coast to the Trondheim district, stopping to accept the submission of people along the way. On reaching his destination he called an assembly in which the local aristocracy unanimously proclaimed him King. He repeated this exercise in other districts of the country until, says Snorri, he won the whole of Norway 'without shedding a drop of blood'.

The eleventh-century German monk and chronicler, Adam of Bremen[16] also offers details of Cnut's acquisition of Norway – inevitably from an evangelical angle. Rather than attributing the takeover to an open-purse policy on the part of the King of Denmark and England, Adam suggests that this happened principally because his enemy, Olaf, was a thoroughly decent Christian. Norway, Adam maintains, was a miserably backward and barbarous land full of magicians, soothsayers and other 'satellites of Anti-Christ'. And he claims that Olaf was over-thrown in a rebellion by Norwegian nobles who objected to the fact that the King had arrested their wives for practising witchcraft. Cnut opportunely filled the vacuum.

Whatever the truth of Adam's and Snorri's stories, it seems that Olaf fled and that Cnut was indeed subsequently accepted as the country's overlord by the Norwegian nobility. Having appointed one of his chief warriors, Hakon, as regent he then sailed back to his Anglo-Saxon kingdom. Hakon, however, was drowned when his ship capsized on a trip back to England. Olaf then re-emerged, attempted to reclaim the kingdom but was killed by his own people during the Battle of Stiklestad, near Trondheim.[17] Cnut's rule resumed unopposed.

And at this stage he must have decided that Norway could provide him with a solution to his long-standing domestic problems. Needing a new regent who could be wholeheartedly trusted, Cnut sent his first wife, Aelfigu of Northampton, and their son Swein to govern the country on his behalf, thus honourably and very publicly relocating Emma's rival.

If Snorri is to be believed – and he was, after all, writing from a Norwegian perspective – Aelfgifu and Swein made themselves very unpopular in their new territory. They promptly imposed extremely harsh and self-serving laws: anyone leaving the country without permission was to forfeit their land to these new rulers; farmers were in duty bound to build all the houses needed on their royal estates; if a man was outlawed any inheritance that he had was to become their property – and so on. Some Norwegians, says Snorri, grumbled greatly about Swein, but most blamed Aelfgifu for the stringent measures.

These were enough to induce them to view Olaf's rule in a golden hue of nostalgia, and the monarch's grave near Trondheim became the focus of nationalist feeling. Despite having been slaughtered by his own people, Olaf rapidly came to be regarded as a Norwegian saint. Swein, at least, was diplomatically sensitive to the situation and gave permission for the former king's remains to be exhumed by church leaders. Aelfgifu, meanwhile, was on her mettle.

When the coffin was duly opened, says Snorri, there lay Olaf's body wonderfully whole, showing not the slightest sign of decomposition. At which point, the Icelandic writer asserts, Aelfgifu commented that of course this would be the case since Olaf had been buried in sand, which she claimed had preserving properties. The only visible difference, indeed, between Olaf the man and Olaf the corpse was a remarkable increase in the length of hair. The presiding bishop then whipped out a knife and neatly trimmed Olaf's whiskers, collecting material for sacred relics. Aelfgifu, however, said that the cut hair could only be regarded as holy if it was able to withstand fire. The bishop, writes Snorri, obligingly placed it in a censer, where miraculously it did not burn. Unsatisfied, Aelfgifu demanded that the experiment be repeated, whereupon 'hard language' was used against her and Olaf was pronounced a true saint.

Despite their poor reputation, Aelfgifu and Swein appear to have governed Norway unopposed until about 1035, when they were driven out by Olaf's son, Magnus the Good. According to Snorri, Swein fled to Denmark, then governed by his half-brother Harthacnut, who somewhat implausibly is said to have offered to share control of the kingdom with him. Swein, however, died soon after arrival there, from what cause is not known. Meanwhile, unfortunately for Emma, Aelfgifu returned to England. There she was to display the sharp and demanding characteristics Snorri later attributed to her in his saga – with an added twist of distinctly foul play. But while Aelfgifu had been exercising rapacious power in Scandinavia, Emma had been placing herself very much centre-stage in Cnut's rule of England.

CHAPTER NINE

Image and Empire

There was, the old monk recalls, much hushed respect, even a sense of awe. Everyone who had gathered at the Church of Christ was very aware of the commanding presence of the Lady. And everyone, ecclesiastic and lay, wondered at her wealth and wisdom. She did, in fact, confer a great many riches on this church but the arm bone of St Bartholomew was her finest and most exotic gift.

The elderly ecclesiastic walks slowly along the cloisters on the north side of Christ Church Cathedral in Canterbury. He is recounting to one of his younger brethren a story from a long time ago. The aged monk, Edwin, joined the holy order here as a child, several decades before England was invaded by Duke William of Normandy, and his experiences are of great interest to his companion Eadmer, who has literary ambitions and intends to become a chronicler.

Like many ecclesiastics of his generation, born just prior to the conquest, Eadmer is anxious to learn about the old times and to preserve this history – since the Normans took control of the country some fifteen violent years ago the Anglo-Saxon ecclesiastics have been fearful that their culture and collective memory will be wiped out. Eadmer has been listening intently to the old man's recollections. Among his tales, memories of that other conqueror, King Cnut, and his powerful wife, intrigue the younger brother most. In particular, the aged monk witnessed one of the Norman-born queen's most colourful acts of patronage and it is this event that he is describing, with evident enjoyment in the drama and detail.[1]

The story of St Bartholomew's arm, says the old monk Edwin settling into narrative flow, actually starts far from England. Some time ago, a terrible famine was expected in Apulia, a fair distance south of the holy city of Rome. Fearing the worst for the people of this province, the bishop of the church of Benevento set out to raise money for them in advance of the calamity. He took with him the most precious and sacred treasure belonging to this church, an arm bone of that apostle and unflinching Christian martyr who was flayed alive beside the Caspian Sea in the first century after Christ – namely St Bartholomew. The bishop knew that this relic would fetch a princely sum if only he could find a sufficiently wealthy buyer.

He travelled north, Edwin continues, and was received with courtesy wherever he stayed. And everywhere he went he told his hosts of the impending troubles in his homeland. He gladly accepted from them very many gifts of money and treasures – most of which were at intervals entrusted to his servants to take back to Benevento, it being unwise to journey while burdened with much richness. As he progressed through the land of the Frankish king, the bishop increasingly heard of the piety, wealth and bounty of the Queen of the Anglo-Saxon kingdom, for there was widespread renown about the generosity she showed to Christ's churches. In the light of the patronage others had received from this lady, he felt sure that he would obtain the greatest amount for his holy relic from her – and more besides. And he made plans to visit her.

So it was, Edwin recounts, that the bishop set sail for England, where he was graciously welcomed at the royal court. He was duly granted an interview with the Queen, during which he spoke at length about the difficulties his people faced. He was not disappointed in the response. Moved by his story, the Lady liberally donated some of her own money and urged him to return to his country in order to help the good Christians there. The bishop, however, knew that he had not yet raised quite enough for his purposes. Besides, he still had in his possession the sacred bone of St Bartholomew. So he made it known that this was for sale and ensured that word spread among the Queen's close advisers – of whom there were several ecclesiastics, including Stigand, who had not yet become a bishop, and had not then displeased the authorities in Rome as he was later to do.

These councillors made enquiries as to whether the Queen would be prepared to buy the relic, which thereafter would become her own property, continues Edwin. Through her intermediaries, the Lady issued a message to the effect that indeed she would be happy to pay a good price for the bone, but she would do so only if the bishop could satisfy her and others that it really had been part of an arm of St Bartholomew. This could be achieved if he swore – without equivocation or duplicity of any kind – at Christ's altar and over the holy relics of other saints that the bone had truly come from the apostle's sacred body.

The bishop readily agreed.

He received instructions to travel on to Canterbury, where the King and Queen commanded that a great ceremony be held at this very Church of Christ. A host of people was swiftly summoned to attend the occasion: laymen and women, both young and old; bishops; abbots; abbesses; priests; nuns; monks – Edwin adds that he himself, then but a boy, was included in the number. On the appointed day, he says, the Bishop of Benevento, dressed with due splendour, proceeded up the nave of the church and put the bone with deference but dignity in the centre of the high altar, between assembled reliquaries of the church – among them the head of St Swithun and the relics of St Wilfrid of York. Then, in the sight of the King and Queen as well as members of the clergy, and in the hearing of the laity – who were, of course, situated in the nave of the church and therefore separated by the rood screen from the spectacle taking place in the choir – the bishop did indeed swear on the altar and on the holy relics of the saints, positively affirming that the very bone he had placed there was from the body of St Bartholomew the Apostle. And all who were gathered in the church, Edwin says with quiet emphasis, were witness to the occasion and henceforward knew and believed with certainty that the bone was a veritable holy relic. And we all, he adds, told many others of this truth.

After that, Edwin continues, the Lady paid the bishop many pounds of silver. But she did not keep the sacred treasure for herself, graciously bestowing the arm bone of St Bartholomew on the Church of Christ on behalf of King Cnut and herself. Moved by her gesture, and as a mark of this very great occasion, the Archbishop of Canterbury,

Aethelnoth by name, then gave the Bishop of Benevento a magnificent cope of the very finest cloth and adorned with a golden fringe. It was a symbol to show how much value was attached to the acquisition of the holy relic from distant lands – for which God, indeed, be praised.

* * *

Years later Eadmer incorporated this tale into his *History of Recent Events in England*, written in the last decade of the eleventh century. That the anticipation, rather than the existence, of a natural disaster was credible cause for an itinerant bishop to set out to seek a fortune is in itself striking, although Eadmer appeared to find this relatively unremarkable. He seemed far more interested in Emma's conduct: her generosity; her ability to strike a deal; her deft handling of what might at first have seemed a dubious proposition. Once the bishop gave his word, would Emma herself have been fully convinced that the bone was a true relic? Probably. This was, after all, an age of faith and of complete respect for sworn, verbal statements – supercilious doubt would have been an alien concept. It was not unusual for relics to be authenticated through altarside affidavits but what was important in this instance was the great crowd of people who bore witness to the event.

Eadmer's story is, of course, part fable, part fact. Ostensible reports from eyewitnesses were fairly frequently employed by the writers of saints' lives as a means of lending credence to claims of miraculous happenings. In his historical chronicle, Eadmer took the device several stages further. He not only cited the testimony of the elderly monk Edwin, but backed this up by noting that the tale of St Bartholomew's bone was additionally told to him, with very similar details, by two other witnesses, aged ecclesiastics named Blackman and Farman. And he later rounded off the story by offering first-hand evidence of his own. Eadmer wrote that some years after hearing the tale of St Bartholomew's arm, church business took him all the way to Bari in Apulia. There he had occasion to meet the very same Bishop of Benevento – who coincidentally was wearing a striking, golden-fringed cope, or liturgical cloak, at the time. Eadmer asked the bishop if this was the actual garment given to him by Aethelnoth of Canterbury. He replied that indeed it was and then also confirmed that the circumstances under which it was given to him were exactly the same as had been previously recounted to Eadmer. All of which indicates how eager Eadmer was to prove the truth of the story – and how much he regarded Emma's acquisition as a sensational purchase.

The traffic of relics from the Continent to England had started very shortly after the first wave of missionaries arrived in the early-seventh century. The majority of these were secondary relics – grave cloths and the like. Initially, the Church in Rome did not condone the dismembering of human remains. The very practice of exhuming saintly skeletons and removing them from one resting place to an ostensibly more glorious site was deemed controversial, and any fragmentation of the body officially very much frowned upon. By the eleventh century, however, the translation of saints and the profiteering from the sale of alleged holy bodily parts was widespread across Europe. Yet few of England's own saints were dismembered in this fashion. St Oswald appears to have been an exception, although this was due to the fact that the seventh-century King of Northumbria (and martyr) was mutilated by his pagan enemies. His head was buried at Lindisfarne; his arms at Bamburgh (and taken thence to Ely, with both Durham and Gloucester subsequently maintaining that they held an appendage); and his body at Oswestry, from where it was removed to Gloucester, with later claims that it was dug up once again and given to Bergues in Flanders. Meanwhile secondary relics of English saints were avidly collected. On St Cuthbert's exhumation, the hair of the seventh-century bishop of Lindisfarne was removed for distribution, along with his shoes; when Cnut orchestrated St Mildreth's reburial at St Augustine's in Canterbury, dust from the saint's original grave at Minster in Thanet was assiduously retained so that miracles could continue to take place there.

Emma's gift of St Bartholomew's arm bone, however, was in a different league. Bartholomew was, of course, no home-grown saint but an apostle whose remains were highly valued on an international level. Installed at Christ Church, doubtless in a suitably ornate casket, the bone was an object of great honour and veneration for hundreds of years. However, what ultimately happened to this item is not clear. Most probably it, along with a great many relics from the Anglo-Saxon era, was burnt or otherwise lost in the upheavals of the Reformation during the sixteenth century.

Emma's other recorded (and presumably, special) offerings to Christ Church, Canterbury – given in her own right – were two great cloaks with gold tassels, two elaborate altar cloths, a large chalice of gold, and an illustrated gospel book adorned, again, in gold.[2] She may also have presented this church with the body of St Ouen, a seventh-century evangelist and Bishop of Rouen. One theory, as expounded by Eadmer, holds that the bones of St Ouen actually arrived in England during the tenth century, well before Emma's era. Eadmer claims they were brought over from Normandy by mysterious clerics during the reign of King Edgar and entrusted to the then Archbishop of Canterbury, Oda – who in the course of time also became a saint. However, in another story, as told by Eadmer's contemporary William of Malmesbury,[3] it was Emma who conveyed the skeleton of this saint from Normandy to England. According to William, she bought it when in exile back in 1013, later conferring most of the body on Canterbury Cathedral but keeping the head for herself. One wonders what she might have done with this item as her personal property: it may have been an object to gloat over, an early medieval precursor to a private art collection; Emma may have performed private acts of godly devotion over the grinning skull; or she may simply have kept it as a valuable resource to be richly handed on, as and when expedient. If William is to be believed, St Ouen's head was indeed later found among Emma's many treasures.

Whether Emma presented any largesse to the English Church during Aethelred's reign is not recorded. Possibly the country was at that stage too war-torn for indulgent acts of benevolence. Possibly her later gift-giving was a reflection of her increased power – and her wish to demonstrate this. It was during Cnut's rule that she became a very energetic, very public patron, often in conjunction with her Danish husband.

Christ Church, Canterbury was by no means the only beneficiary of Emma's devout if calculating generosity. The large and hugely rich church at Abingdon received a very valuable reliquary from Emma and Cnut, in which the remains of the fourth-century Spanish martyr,

St Vincent, were subsequently housed.[4] An inscription on this casket
ostentatiously announced that it was cast from a staggering 230 smoul-
dered gold coins mixed with twenty-two pounds of silver. Evesham
Abbey, where the remains of St Wystan had been reburied at the
instigation of Cnut, also benefited from royal patronage. Emma and
her Danish husband furnished it with costly vestments and other elaborate offerings.

However, Emma and Cnut's most famous gift was a great gold cross.
It numbers among many riches grandly donated by them to the New
Minster in Winchester, the composite magnificence of these offerings
inspiring William of Malmesbury later to claim with characteristic ebul-
lience that 'the quantity of metals terrifies the minds of strangers and
the splendour of the gems lashes the eyes of onlookers'.[5] The gift-giving
was, he says, prompted by Emma, who handed out treasure with 'holy
prodigality' while her husband was campaigning in foreign lands. Fairly
shortly after William made these comments the cross itself fell victim
to the havoc of the wars between Stephen and Matilda, who clattered
around the country battling for the crown throughout most of the 1140s.
During the siege of Winchester in 1141 the glittering icon was apparently melted down and the resulting 500 pounds of silver and thirty
marks of gold was carried off by Henry of Blois, brother of Stephen and
Bishop of Winchester.[6]

Yet the cross remains enormously significant because of a remarkable record made of this gift. Donors to churches were often listed in
books known as *Liber Vitae*, as in the *Liber Vitae* of Thorney Abbey in
Cambridgeshire in which Emma's name appears. Such volumes were so
called after the heavenly 'Book of Life' described in the Bible: according
to Revelation,[7] this book is to be opened on Judgement Day and the
dead assessed from what is written against their names; those who are
not found listed are to be cast into a lake of fire. By being entered in
an earthly 'Book of Life' a mortal might avoid such a fate, since it was
expected that the name would also appear in the divine volume. Perhaps
being pictured in one of these books, as Emma and Cnut are, was an
even greater guarantee of heavenly inclusion.

The frontispiece to the *Liber Vitae* of the New Minster, Winchester,

is a line drawing with green, ochre and red tints. It shows Emma and
Cnut placing their vast golden cross on the high altar of the church –
or at least Cnut's hand is on the cross, Emma's wavers nearby. The
implication is that theirs is almost, but not quite, an equal partnership.
Below the royal couple, seven witnesses peer up between rounded arches
whilst above are hovering angels topped by floating images of the Virgin
Mary, Christ and St Peter. All the divine and mortal figures feature
enormous and expressive hands – pointing, praying, outstretched – that
are so engagingly characteristic of Anglo-Saxon art. Between this picture
and the list of donors' names are another drawing, the Day of Judgement,
and a history of the church. The text was written in 1031 by a monk
and priest named Aelfsige, who may also have penned the rendition of
the royal donors. And this visual documentation is one of the very few
remaining records of Cnut's activities after his northern conquests.

The illustration is extremely stylised, there being little attempt at
distinctive portraiture – at least for English royals – until the second
half of the fourteenth century when Richard II was painted complete
with wispy moustache and slightly bulbous nose, and later rendered in
a reasonably lifelike effigy on his tomb at Westminster Abbey. In the
early-eleventh-century *Liber Vitae* of Winchester's New Minster, the
King and Queen are very largely representational figures. The picture,
though, has the great merit of showing how they would have dressed
– and what sort of image they wished to project. Emma is presented
with a slightly square jaw, which is very similar to that of the image of
the Virgin Mary above her. She wears a series of garments that are
pretty much all-encompassing: long-sleeved robes that almost reach the
ground but are held up by one of her hands; a baggy hood that covers
her head and tapers into trailing, decorated ties. This headgear appears
to be kept off her face by an elaborate band worn across the forehead.
Her feet, apparently clad in shoes, are tiny but less minuscule than
those of St Mary at the top of the illustration. An angel fluttering over-
head bestows a veil on her.

In contrast, another angel places a huge crown on Cnut, who faces
Emma. He is dressed in a knee-length, wrist-length garment topped
with a cloak that appears to be slipping off the right shoulder despite

being flamboyantly fastened with ties similarly elaborate to those of Emma's hood. On his lower legs he sports long sock-like items that are topped with embroidered braids, while on his feet he wears shoes that seem to be decorated just below openings at the ankle. As a mark of his Viking ancestry he has a good crop of hair and a well-grown beard, while, somewhat worryingly for a religiously inspired image, he is shown clutching his sword in his left hand. This gesture is undoubtedly symbolic of his power and might, the sword itself piercing the red and green lines framing the picture.

As the property of the New Minster, the illustration would, of course, have been seen by just a limited number of Cnut's subjects – for the most part ecclesiastics connected with this church as well, possibly, as other of its wealthy donors. So would the average English person have had any access at all to a visual reference of their monarch and his wife? The Queen, who would publically have appeared fairly well obscured in a hood and probably a veil, may have been of marginal interest in this respect. But a king would readily have shown his face and, certainly, representations of him were ubiquitous, if decidedly rough: the coinage of the country was stamped with an image of his head.

Two sizeable sectors of society, the very poor and the very religious, would not have possessed or handled money but everyone else was familiar with an outline of the regal face through their coins. However crude his likeness on these, the monarch of England controlled a monetary system that was very sophisticated by comparison to the prevailing standards elsewhere in Europe. Its regulation and its uniformity across the country were particularly advanced. Indeed Cnut is thought to have adapted aspects of English coin production (principally weight and metal mix) for his Scandinavian kingdoms so as to bring the currency units of his entire empire into line.[8]

England's coinage system had been increasingly regulated by the monarchs since King Offa of Mercia introduced a form of silver penny in the latter part of the eighth century. This subsequently became the sole issue of currency. The value of a penny was high: laws[9] from the early-tenth century stipulate that a sheep is worth two coins; a pig, ten.

Small change was evidently needed, and to produce this the penny was quite literally halved and quartered – sometimes a cross was engraved on the obverse side to provide basic cutout lines. Later in the tenth century Aethelred's father, King Edgar, effectively confirmed his control over a unified England by reforming and standardising the issue of currency, with strict rules governing its production.

By the eleventh century all legal coins were stamped with hieroglyphics indicating where the penny had been issued and by whom. Around the circumference of two surviving pennies from Cnut's reign, minted sometime after 1029, are inscriptions indicating that they were variously produced by Leofric of Hertford and Edred of London. Both Leofric and Edred would have been licensed moneyers who had paid for this privilege, and for the potential of a very profitable business. Coins were bartered or exchanged at mints up and down the country. There were as many as seventy of these production points, principally in market towns. However, there were only a limited number of centres issuing the actual engraved stamps, or dies, from which the pennies were individually struck. Small squares of well-prepared metal were hammered into one mould engraved with the moneyer's details, and then bashed from on top with the die bearing the regal face. During the reigns of both Aethelred and Cnut, these dies were reissued at intervals of about six years – which seems to have been a cunning ploy not just to retain tight control over the currency but also to levy a form of wealth tax. On production of a new issue, the former coin designs ceased to be legal tender and people were obliged to redeem their now-defunct pennies at a mint, either directly paying a fee or receiving fewer new coins in return.

During Cnut's rule there were three issues of the silver penny – and therefore three different images of the Danish king sequentially in circulation. Between 1017 and 1023, while Cnut was establishing himself as monarch, the 'Quatrefoil' penny was produced, so called because of the decorative emblem, shaped a little like a four-leafed clover, which frames Cnut's head. He is shown in profile with a long, straight nose and a somewhat bulging eye that seems in danger of being crushed by the weight of the enormous crown above it. Evidently what is being emphasised here is the crown, and the notion of kingship. During the period of Cnut's northern conquests a coin portraying the King in war-mongering mode was in circulation. Again he appears in profile with the long nose and the big eye, but this time instead of a crown he wears a conical or pointed helmet, similar to those later portrayed in the Bayeux Tapestry. Finally, from about 1029, he takes on a distinctly classical mien – and unlike the illustration in the book at Winchester's New Minster, which was drawn around this date, he has no Viking-style beard. Still in profile, his head is uncovered and is garlanded with a laurel-like arrangement of bands loosely fastened at the back, above the neck. It is the image of an emperor[10] – and, latterly, this is how he wished to be seen by his English subjects.

The author of Emma's book offers sparse detail about Cnut's rule of England but does claim that he was 'the Emperor of five kingdoms . . . Denmark, England, Wales, Scotland and Norway'. The assertion that the Danish conqueror ruled all of Scotland is undoubtedly an exaggeration, while the inclusion of Wales among the kingdoms he governed may be wishful thinking since there is little evidence to support any notion that Cnut brought this area of Britain under his direct control. But quite clearly Emma wanted to emphasise her second husband's grandeur – and his imperial status.

However, in the 1030s, while Cnut was positioning himself as a northern emperor, over in Normandy Emma's eldest son by Aethelred was apparently styling himself as the monarch of England. Edward, a young man still in exile and still without prospects, property or, presumably, any money to speak of, was by now an adjunct at the court of his cousin Robert. In two surviving charters ostensibly from this period he bears the title 'king'. One document records a grant of land by the Duke of Normandy to the abbey at Fécamp. It is witnessed by a number of ecclesiastics and courtiers, including Robert's very small (and illegitimate) son William, and Edward, who is described as 'King'. The other charter seems almost absurdly fantastical: Edward himself, heralded as 'King of the English people' grants St Michael's Mount in Cornwall to the monastery of St Michel in Normandy.

Of course Edward had no real power, so he was hardly in a position

to donate chunks of the Anglo-Saxon kingdom to religious institutions
in Normandy. But to dismiss the document as a blatant forgery on the
part of the monks of St Michel might be an oversight.[11] In making this
supposed grant Edward could have been anticipating a great change in
his fortunes. According to an uncorroborated story by William of
Jumièges,[12] during the 1030s the Normans had plans to restore the
Anglo-Saxon exile to the throne of England.

Writing towards the end of the eleventh century, the Norman monk
from the abbey of Jumièges describes how Duke Robert treated his
cousins Edward and Alfred with great honour and regarded them both
as brothers. He was, apparently, deeply concerned about their frustrating
predicament as exiles and in a spirit of compassion (and, by implication, corresponding aggression to the monarch of England) he sent
envoys to King Cnut to request that he should 'mercifully' give back
to Edward and Alfred 'however late, what was theirs'. In other words,
Robert diplomatically demanded that the two exiles be reinstated and
that Cnut honourably return the crown to the legitimate King of
England. Understandably, the Danish king roundly rejected such overtures and sent the envoys home. At which point Robert became enraged.
So, William of Jumièges writes, he summoned his nobles and ordered
them to assemble a large fleet.

Fully equipped with weapons and crewed by strong warriors, ships
from all the harbours of Normandy quickly gathered at Fécamp.
However, shortly after the fleet set sail a violent storm came down. The
vessels had no option but to make for the island of Jersey where the
attempted invasion was aborted. The Norman monk comments that he
believes this was the will of God, who intended Edward to rule England
in the future but without bloodshed.

Yet William's story does not end there. Another Norman attack on
England appears to have been planned but it was pre-empted by Cnut.
William maintains that he sent messengers to Normandy to broker peace
and inform Duke Robert that he was prepared to return half the kingdom
of England to Aethelred's sons. Writing with the benefit of hindsight,
William alleges that Cnut wanted to make amends because he knew
that he was terminally ill. However, there we are left somewhat in mid-

air. William's tale tapers off inconclusively and no further information is given about the negotiations.

Some aspects of the story might be true. Robert was not on good terms with Cnut, whose sister he had, after all, divorced and it would have suited him very well to have his cousin as King of England instead. He may, indeed, actively have tried to place Edward on the English throne in the expectation of benefiting from the ensuing gratitude. Whether he had any chance of succeeding is very questionable: it seems unlikely that he could have mustered a sufficiently strong army against Cnut. Meanwhile how would Emma have reacted? If the story were even partly credible, she would have been in a very awkward situation: her husband challenged by her two estranged sons, who were backed by her own Norman family.

Subsequently, would the self-styled northern emperor actually have offered half of his richest kingdom to the sons of a notoriously impotent ruler who were effectively living on charity? Such a proposal seems extremely improbable. And did Cnut really know he was about to die?

As it was, Robert himself probably met his death first. Sometime before 1035 he set out on a pilgrimage to Jerusalem, having named his small son William as his heir and having entrusted Normandy to a group of regents on this child's behalf. He did not return alive. William 'the Bastard' duly succeeded. He is said to have been the product of the Duke's liaison with a dancing girl called Herleva. Robert was apparently so smitten with this woman that he slept with her on the night they met[13] and for ever afterwards regarded her as his wife (although failed to marry). Their son was eight years old at the most when he became the Duke of Normandy. It was not a comfortable situation either for him or his subjects. The state was plunged into near anarchy as squabbles broke out between the governing nobles and with neighbouring provinces. In the midst of this turmoil Edward and Alfred could expect no further Norman support for their claims to the English throne.

Meanwhile the government of England also descended into chaos. As in Normandy, the problems started with the death of the country's strong ruler.

Towards the end of 1035 the English royal court had been in Dorset. Here Emma and Cnut visited Sherborne, then a significant religious centre and the seat of a bishop. Its cathedral church contained the shrine of St Wulfsige, Bishop of Sherborne in the 990s, who had been hallowed for his austere principles. Emma is said to have been embarrassed by the contrast between the regal couple, weighed down with jewels and gold ornaments, and the simplicity of the saint's way of life.[14] The church was apparently in a bad state of repair and she gave twenty pounds of silver so that the roof could be refurbished. Cnut was also a dutiful patron to Sherborne. He issued a charter[15] to the church, granting it sixteen hides of land at Corscombe (also in Dorset). In addition, the document records the King's request that the monks of Sherborne offer prayers to God for him and daily expiate his sins through the singing of psalms and the celebration of mass. It was not unusual for a charter to express general wishes of absolution and redemption, but this appears abnormally specific.[16] As such, the request may possibly provide justification for the claims that Cnut had intimations of impending mortality.

The royal entourage had then moved on to Shaftesbury, another pilgrimage site, and a large one, too. It was here that St Edward the Martyr, Aethelred's murdered brother, lay buried. And it was here that Cnut died on 12 November 1035. He was about thirty-eight years old.

After some years of silence about the activities of the monarch, the *Anglo-Saxon Chronicles* record that 'he was king over all England for very nearly twenty years' and that his body was conveyed back to Winchester and buried in the Old Minster there.[17] But according to local legend, his heart was left in Shaftesbury, having been apparently cut out of his body, placed in a glass container and buried near the tomb of St Edward. During the Dissolution of the Monasteries, Shaftesbury Abbey was destroyed but a glass casket thought once to have contained Cnut's heart was saved and given to Winchester Cathedral – where it remains in the church's museum.

'Before him there never was so great a king of England' extolled Henry of Huntingdon[18] in the early-twelfth century. Yet the mighty achievements of this one-time Viking were not sustained and his empire, already recently reduced by the loss of Norway, almost immediately splintered. The major problem was that Cnut had not named a successor, either for his empire as a whole or for the throne of England specifically – an oversight that makes it difficult to believe that he truly knew he was dying. In the resulting uncertainty all hell broke loose for Emma.

PART III
SCHEMERS

CHAPTER TEN

Letters

Within a few weeks of King Cnut's funeral at the Old Minster, Winchester is alive with rumours. Most of them centre on the Lady.

Many townsfolk maintain that almost immediately after her husband died, the widowed queen herself laid claim to the great stash of treasure housed in the city's royal palace. The King's sceptre, his crown of gold, his hoards of coins, cups of precious metals, expensive fabrics and assorted relics of saints are among the many sequestered items. They say that the Lady quickly enlisted the support and well-armed security of King Cnut's housecarls, and that, staunchly protected, she has only rarely emerged from the palace grounds. Certainly, heavily veiled, she was a grieving presence at her husband's funeral but since then she is said to have remained within the royal enclosures, guarding her riches and waiting for her son, the aethling Harthacnut, to arrive and claim the throne of England. He is believed to be detained in Denmark, where he is the ruler of that realm.

Some imagine, with varying sympathy, how echoingly empty the royal complex must seem, despite the presence of the housecarls. In particular, the great hall would be dauntingly quiet. It had been the scene of lavish feasts where King Cnut's northern *scops*, or minstrels, would carouse late into the night, singing verse about his many achievements. Now the might of the Scandinavian king is reflected only in the band of stories sculpted on the walls: a bold and vividly rendered length of stonework depicting heroic tales from the sagas of his homeland.[1]

It would be a lonely vigil for the Lady, and some people wonder why she has taken this isolating and determined stance. She is the dowager queen, her absent son will inherit his father's position – there is little cause for the contentious defence. In contrast, others comment that she has been wise to pursue such a course of action: she has an urgent need to assert Prince Harthacnut's rights to the crown of Anglo-Saxon kingdom, and her armed appropriation of King Cnut's treasure is a very necessary precaution – for there is a strong contender for the throne.

Local gossip has it that this man is known as Harold Harefoot on account of his reputation for agility, or more appropriately political agility. Apparently he is the son of King Cnut by another wife. And it is his mother, most of all, who claims that he is the rightful king of England.

More stories are in circulation, contradicting the suggestions that the Lady Aelfgifu, or Emma as she is otherwise known, is in command of all the royal treasure. Some townspeople say that just after the late king was laid to rest, a group of sword-clad horsemen was seen clattering through the town. These aggressive strangers are believed to have been the henchmen of that other lady – also named Aelfgifu – and her son Harold Harefoot. Several ostensible witnesses allege that the horsemen speedily rode past both the Old and New Minsters straight up to the palace surrounds. What happened thereafter is not known for sure, but it is said that they took those inside the royal enclosure by surprise and savagely demanded that King Cnut's riches be handed over so that they could convey them safely to his son Harold, who they assert is the true heir to the throne. They apparently made off with a great deal of treasure, although some folk believe that the dowager queen managed to hide a good quantity of valuable items.

Many gossip that the mother of this man Harold Harefoot was never married to King Cnut and that he therefore has no legitimate claim to the throne. But a different group says that the other Lady Aelfgifu was indeed the monarch's first wife and that she had two sons with the King, one of whom, named Swein, was until recently the ruler of Norway. He, however, is believed to have passed away in the northern lands a few months ago.

In another twist, an allegation is gaining credence that Harold Harefoot is not, in fact, the son of King Cnut at all. A story is being spread that his mother, unable to have children herself, placed the newborn infant of a serving girl in her bed and ever afterwards pretended that this child was the offspring of herself and the King. But several noble people claim this is a shocking falsehood and that such lies have been made up by the dowager queen herself, who is in an increasingly desperate position. Because the Lady's son Harthacnut is in Denmark, they say that the former council of King Cnut will have little option but to elect Harold Harefoot as the next King of England.

Amidst the mutterings, the gossip and the head-shaking tales, one observation is clear: the Lady is firmly inside the palace and is likely to stay there for as long as possible.

* * *

The confused year following the funeral of Cnut was dominated not so much by the rivalry between the contenders for the throne as the battle on their behalf by their mothers – the late king's two extremely strong-willed widows. Their war of words and lobbying was by no means solely prompted by maternal concern: both these women were seeking their own prestige, wealth and control through their sons.

When he died, Cnut left Emma politically and financially extremely exposed. If she failed to remain in power by virtue of the next king, she would be stripped of much of her property and all of her status. She had one serious option to the contest for continued court control: by now aged about forty-eight, she could simply have chosen to retire gracefully, possibly to lead a worthy life in a convent. Had she done so she would have been remembered as an influential queen, notable for her piety and her authority during her second husband's lifetime. But she had too much fight in her for such a passive climb-down. The next few years were to set her apart: she was to emerge as a remarkable figure with pre-eminent and self-serving powers of determination, manipulation and cunning.

While Emma had a great deal to lose, Aelfgifu of Northampton, on the other hand, had much to gain. She had recently been routed from Norway by Magnus the Good – losing her powerful position as regent as well as her son Swein, who died shortly afterwards – and she must have returned to England in humiliation. Whether Aelfgifu arrived before or after Cnut's death is not clear, but at any rate once he was buried she was quick to grasp a chance to reverse her misfortunes. Almost immediately she projected her surviving son Harold as the heir very apparent to the crown. Although she had never been the Queen of England, and although her position as Cnut's first wife remained a blurred issue, she had the distinct advantage over Emma in that Harold was conveniently and visibly in the country while Harthacnut was very notably absent.

Emma refused to move from the palace at Winchester. By commandeering those of Cnut's housecarls who had remained there she effectively had a private army at her disposal. But a vital ingredient was missing – the troops needed the credibility of a royal, and male, leader and Emma's son remained preoccupied in Denmark, apparently in no hurry to claim his ostensible birthright.

In the vacuum Aelfgifu of Northampton and Harold Harefoot tried to seize control of the country. However, to achieve any lasting results for this coup they needed the acceptance of the regional governors of England. How they attempted to gain this is very much subject to interpretation.

Ultimately Emma created a trump card over her rival in that her version of the events of 1036 were recorded for posterity. The book she later commissioned details the powerplay of this year, and it became a basic record of the very vexed episode following Cnut's death, with later chroniclers variously amplifying, abbreviating and editing it.

Her author, the monk from St Omer, claims that after Cnut's burial Emma remained 'alone in the kingdom', grieving over her husband's death and 'alarmed' that none of her sons were with her (smoothing over the fact the two of them were not in fact Cnut's heirs and in any case had been in exile for a great many years). For, the scribe continues, 'certain Englishmen' deserted the noble sons of the excellent queen and chose one Harold as their king. This man, the author scoffs, was supposedly the progeny of a mere concubine of King Cnut, but in fact 'a great many people' understood him to be of no royal blood at all. 'The more truthful account', the monk confides, was that Harold was actually the illegitimate child of a serving wench. This baby, he asserts, had been appropriated by the concubine, who then claimed that he was her son by the King.

It seems very unlikely that the Viking conqueror who shrewdly won the approval of most of the leading churchmen of England and also masterminded the bloodless takeover of Norway could have been hood-winked into accepting a misbegotten child as his own. Was this a popular myth, or even a slanderous tale concocted by Emma herself? From wher-ever the story emanated, the compilers of the *Anglo-Saxon Chronicles* appear to have swallowed it. Writing fairly shortly after Emma's author composed his book, they tersely record that Harold 'said he was the son of Cnut and the other Aelfgifu – although it was not true'.[2] And they maintain that the ignoble usurper sent his men to the palace in Winchester, where they took from Emma 'all the best treasures which King Cnut possessed'. Meanwhile the Queen 'stayed on inside there as long as she could'.

Florence of Worcester, who wrote his history of this period[3] about eighty years later, provides more colour, and more explanation. He repeats the allegation that Harold Harefoot was not the son of Cnut, and adds as a plausible ramification that neither was Aelfgifu's other purported child. Swein, he says, was believed to be the illegitimate son of a priest while Harold's father was understood to be a mere cobbler. Florence then goes on to describe how Harold Harefoot 'tyrannically deprived' Emma of the greater part of Cnut's riches and how he began to reign England as if he were the true heir to the country. But, Florence comments, stymied by the knowledge that Harthacnut was yet to arrive in England and that this prince had a stronger claim to the throne, Harold was not as powerful as Cnut had been.

Emma's book includes a story of how Harold Harefoot almost imme-diately tried to force Archbishop Aethelnoth into crowning him – it being a legal requirement that the Archbishop of Canterbury should preside over coronation rites. But Aethelnoth, a man of 'high courage and wisdom', demurred. Placing the sceptre and the crown on the holy altar (presumably of Canterbury Cathedral), he cunningly said that he would not refuse to consecrate Harold but nor would he confer on him the royal regalia. And on that altar, Aethelnoth commanded, the glittering emblems of monarchy were to remain – no bishop was to remove them, and certainly no bishop was to offer assistance to Harold. Threats were uttered, bribes attempted but the man who would be king was unable to sway the Archbishop. Harold then loped off in despair and petulantly 'turned from the whole Christian religion'. Emma's author carps that thereafter instead of attending church services Harold went hunting with his dogs or occupied himself with 'utterly paltry matters'.

With or without the scandalously unChristian activities of Harold Harefoot, the situation must have been intolerable to the foremost nobility, who were struggling to find a peaceable solution to the dangerously anarchical problem of succession. For the average Englishman (and woman), the issue would have been of little pressing concern. After all, in essence, the people of England were governed by their immediate superiors, the king being a fairly remote figure who impinged on their lives principally through taxes, laws and warfare. Yet the leading churchmen and aristocrats would have been well aware that the messy predicament could break into violence and ultimately into civil war. They hastily called a gathering of Cnut's former *witan* at Oxford. The *Anglo-Saxon Chronicles*[4] report that the two most powerful noblemen headed opposing factions. Earl Godwine, for the time being a faithful friend to Emma, supported the cause of Harthacnut and the dowager queen. Earl Leofric backed Harold Harefoot and Aelfgifu of Northampton. Leofric being a Midlander would have had much to gain from the association with a future king (and queen mother) from his own part of the country. In addition, it may have been at this juncture that the men of London started to become staunch champions of Harold Harefoot – they were certainly to be among his strongest followers. How much dissension there was at the Oxford convention is not recorded but it is known that an unwieldy compromise was thrashed out there. After much deliberation it was agreed that England would be split: Harold Harefoot was ceded territory north of the Thames while Harthacnut was to control the area roughly south of the river, with Godwine and Emma acting as his proxies until such time as he arrived.

Emma's book skips any mention of this meeting, probably because it weakened her and Harthacnut's cause. But two other contemporary sources testify, respectively, that the gathering of the nobility took place amid much intrigue and that an agreement of sorts was reached to divide England. The first source is a surviving letter written just after the negotiations of the leading nobles in Oxford.[5] It is an extraordinarily colourful document from a German priest to a bishop, and it requires a little tangential explanation. While England was beset by power struggles, arrangements for the wedding of Emma's daughter Gunnhild to the son of the German, or Holy Roman, Emperor, Conrad II, went ahead. The match, as brokered by Cnut eleven years beforehand, was intended to be a glorious reflection of the King of England's greatness and prestige. But who was the monarch now? Under the circumstances the betrothal may have become an embarrassment to the German imperial family, who were honour-bound to proceed with the marriage and host the wedding. This duly took place in June of 1036. Emma would not have attended. She had far too much at stake to be able to leave England, probably even to leave the palace at Winchester. Yet William of Malmesbury, writing in the 1120s, maintains that the ceremony was a lavish event[6] – so much so that he says it remained the subject of a popular song in his own day, some eighty years later. Shortly after this apparently splendid celebration, a priest who was in attendance at the court of the Holy Roman Emperor sent a wonderfully gossiping missive to a senior ecclesiastic, the Bishop of Worms. The priest, one Immo, was clearly well aware of the uncomfortable situation in England, and was full of news he had gleaned through Gunnhild about the latest developments there. Immo writes that the new bride – who has been unwell but, thank the Lord, is now much recovered – recently received messengers from England. He reports that they told her how her 'stepmother', in other words Aelfgifu of Northampton, had herself been the orchestrator of a large meeting of the English nobility, her wicked ploy being to deprive Gunnhild's brother Harthacnut of his rightful inheritance. According to the messengers, Aelfgifu tried all known means of corrupting the leading aristocrats and enlisting their support: pleas, flagrant bribery, demands that they should swear oaths of loyalty to herself and her son Harold. But, the messengers said, her many and varied overtures were roundly rejected. Instead the nobles hastily despatched messengers to Gunnhild's brother, Harthacnut, urging him to return to England post-haste.

The second source reflecting the outcome of the Oxford meeting is the English coinage struck in the latter part of 1036. Surviving pennies produced at this time offer evidence of the division of the Anglo-Saxon kingdom.[7] They also reflect the general confusion. Coins bearing Harold's name were struck at mints in the northerly parts of the country while in the south pennies were issued showing Harthacnut to be king. But in many cases the moneyers also expediently left their options open: in London, Oxford, York and Lincoln various mints simultaneously produced coins for both Harold and Harthacnut. Meanwhile at Wallingford, Cambridge, Exeter, London (again) and a number of other towns some moneyers played it safe and simply continued to produce pennies stamped with the profile and name of the dead and buried Cnut.

The image of Cnut may well have been a reassuring factor in this time of deep uncertainty. The powerful emperor of the north had been a man of good judgement, with a great knack of turning most situations to his advantage. Unfortunately little, if any, of these abilities were inherited by his children. Swein had hardly made himself popular as the ruler of Norway, had been driven out and had subsequently died while still a young man. Harold Harefoot, on his father's death, rapaciously tried to claim the throne of England having made almost no diplomatic effort to secure loyalty and support beforehand. At the same time, Harthacnut failed to seize a good opportunity when it came his way and dallied in Denmark: he may have had reasonable cause for this in that Magnus the Good of Norway was creating problems for the Danish kingdom[8] during this period, but it seems remarkable that he was unable to entrust the country to his commanders in order to seek greater strength, and riches, by staking a claim on England. Meanwhile Cnut's daughter Gunnhild lacked the wiles to survive for long at the court of the Holy Roman Emperor.

According to William of Malmesbury, after a fairy-tale beginning Gunnhild's marriage went horribly wrong. Although she was reputedly a dutiful wife, Gunnhild was accused of adultery. In William's story she was offered a chance to prove her innocence through man-to-man combat. Gunnhild herself was not expected to participate: the informant of her alleged infidelity would take on a representative to fight on her behalf. The accuser, William claims, was a man of gigantic proportions and against this daunting individual the unfortunate Gunnhild could find no one willing to defend her except a small pageboy, who was the keeper of a pet starling she had brought with her from England. However, in a David-and-Goliath-like contest, the pageboy won and, triumphant, Gunnhild refused ever to sleep with her husband, Henry, again. William writes that she subsequently divorced him, became a nun and lived 'to a leisurely old age in the service of God'.

Quite when this fight is supposed to have happened is not recorded. Gunnhild had at least one child with her husband – Beatrice, who later became the abbess of Quedlinburg, then a significant cultural and political centre in the Germanic empire – so she may have endured her marriage for more than a year or two. How Emma reacted to her daughter's predicament and potential disgrace is similarly unknown. It is tempting to judge this steely queen as a remote, uncaring mother but few eleventh-century noblewomen would have been directly involved in raising their offspring and most would have had, at best, a formal relationship with their children in later life. Yet Emma does appear to have had a particular track record for becoming involved with her children only when it was to her material advantage.

In 1036 Harthacnut was, at most, nineteen years old (roughly the same age, coincidentally, that Cnut had been when he was accepted as king of all the Anglo-Saxon kingdom). For at least the last ten years he had been living in Denmark, and since the age of about five he would not have seen his mother except, possibly, during short trips to England. Harthacnut may well have had little inclination to rush to her support, even if this was of potential benefit to his own position. Once in England he would effectively have been a foreigner, largely reliant on his estranged mother and in particular on her skills as a tactician and negotiator. It would have been a situation that required total trust and that may as a result have had little appeal.

Emma spent at least eight months fighting her corner in Harthacnut's name, but she could not do so interminably. Towards the latter part of 1036 she apparently looked for salvation from elsewhere, for Harthacnut was by no means the only key to her future as the *de facto* Queen, or at least matriarch, of England. After all, she had other children who had an equal, if not greater, claim to the throne. So, in a startling turn of events, it seems that Emma abruptly began making overtures to the sons she had relinquished nearly twenty years beforehand.

A letter was despatched to Edward and Alfred in Normandy.[9] 'Emma, Queen in name only', the missive starts, sends greetings to her sons. Everyone, it continues formally, mourns the death of the King (which would have been doubtful in the case of Edward and Alfred). And since Emma's own dear sons are with every passing day increasingly deprived of their rightful inheritance she is writing to ask what plans they have been developing. The letter adds cryptically that they must be aware that their delay is playing into the hands of the man who is usurping their position: he has been ceaselessly touring the country and through threats, bribes and prayers, has been cajoling and appealing to the leading men of the nation for their support. But, the letter notes encouragingly, these men would far rather that one of Emma's sons should rule them. She therefore begs one of her sons to come to her privately and very quickly so that she can advise on how the outcome that she so wishes to see can be achieved.

The implication here is that Edward and his younger brother Alfred were both well aware that the instability in England could be usefully exploited. It seems that they had each been intending to make separate bids for the crown, although they were perhaps being dilatory, or at least cautious, in their endeavours. The letter, of course, is urging them on and indiscriminately offering one or other of them endorsement and valuable help from inside the country. Crucially, such assistance is to be forthcoming to whichever of the sons comes with all speed to England.

But it was all a dastardly trap – according to Emma's author. He maintains that the letter was forged by Harold Harefoot and conveyed by 'deceitful' messengers to the exiled princes, who unwittingly received them with honour. The writer claims that this was an 'unrighteous scheme' to lure Emma's innocent sons to England, and into danger.

At a time of very limited literacy it would not have been a difficult task to forge a letter. Scandinavian stories hold that Emma herself had earlier used just such a device to promote Harthacnut's interests in Denmark. Handwriting and general style of correspondence were, of course, of little note because documents were written by clerics. The most obvious guarantee of authenticity was a letter's seal, and since Harold Harefoot had apparently raided Emma's large treasure trove he may well have had just such a personal item of hers in his possession.

But all is not as black and white as it may appear. Emma herself was hardly an artless bystander and she was just as capable of complex plotting as her enemies.

Her author was writing with the considerable benefit of hindsight. Disastrous events were shortly to come, and he was composing the book with these very much in mind: the story of the apparently fraudulent document was a means of absolving the dowager queen of any blame for a crime that was to shock the nation. The letter is the pivotal point in the tale the writer chose to tell about Emma, providing ostensible evidence of Harold Harefoot's underhand methods and utter wickedness. Yet it survives only because it is quoted, purportedly verbatim, in her book. Did the letter ever actually exist? And if it did, was it really a forgery?

It may be that the story told by Emma's author should be taken at face value: perhaps her Norman sons did receive a document devised by Harold Harefoot and because of this were tricked into coming to England. Judging by the reports about the nefarious activities of Aelfgifu of Northampton in Immo's correspondence from the German court, Cnut's first family was adept at such scheming.

Equally, it is possible that the letter was not, in fact, fraudulent and that Edward and Alfred eagerly set out for the Anglo-Saxon kingdom at the genuine behest of their mother. She would subsequently have persuaded her author, man of God though he was, to frame Harold Harefoot as the culprit of a resulting tragedy.

However, a third possibility is that there was no such letter at all.

Emma may well have been in touch with her sons through messengers and possibly through other correspondence, encouraging them to come to England and offering support. Because this culminated in calamity for the dowager queen, she and her author may subsequently have invented a tale to deflect responsibility for the events and also to blacken the name of Harold Harefoot.

Whatever the murky truth, it seems that towards the end of 1036 both Edward and Alfred returned to England. They made their way separately. Edward landed at Southampton, purportedly with about forty ships[10] – which would have been quite some force: even if the vessels were small the crew would have amounted to at least 1,000 men, probably more. He proceeded swiftly to Emma in Winchester.[11] Alfred was not so fortunate. Apparently accompanied by even more troops than his brother, he arrived in Kent. But he was never to meet his mother, nor was he ever to return to Normandy.

CHAPTER ELEVEN

Fall and Rise

It is late autumn in 1036. A large fleet of longships,[1] bristling with shield-bearing soldiers, approaches the shores of Kent. Once the vessels are sufficiently close to the land, groups of warriors disembark into the chilly water, and amid some splashing and muted shouting the ships are dragged towards flat expanses of beach. More warriors spill out and soon the stretches of shingle are crowded with troops hefting the vessels ashore. Some of the soldiers then swiftly fan out, clutching their swords or axes and forming a line of defence. Meanwhile a small party has gathered within the area of armed security. The group stands aside from the activity, evidently engaged in close discussion. These commanders had intended to land further south and closer to Dover[2] but seeing a large and hostile-looking force along the coastline there they had swiftly changed course. Now they need to assess their best route forward over land. Although they had intended to make straight for Winchester, the commanders decide that their safest option is to head for London first. Having escaped a clash with enemy troops who were awaiting their arrival, they realise that more soldiers will be lurking along the roads leading directly to their destination in the south-west. They are anxious to avoid such ambushes.

Leaving a number of their men to guard the beached ships, the foreigners set out,[3] the commanders riding horses that they have transported in the larger vessels, the troops marching behind them. They take with them as many provisions as they can reasonably carry and forage for more supplies as they pass through the countryside, grazing sheep and pigs being rustled and swiftly slaughtered. Where they are able, they commandeer food and lodging from village communities who are brusquely intimidated into providing them with their needs – and put up little resistance.

After several days they have made good progress. They have left Kent and are in an area south of the River Thames and fairly close to London. Suddenly scouts ahead of their party send word back to the commanders, alerting them that a large posse of horseriders is approaching. The foreigners stop abruptly and wait. A thud of hooves and jangle of harnesses is heard in the distance.

The noise also stops. Evidently the other group has come to a halt. This party sends out just one rider. He makes his way towards the group of horsemen, dismounts and bows, kneeling on one leg. One of the commanders, his cloak hitched back to reveal a finely polished sword hilt, steps forward, still mounted.

The foreign soldier, by appearance somewhere in his mid-twenties, is evidently the leader of the force. He is Alfred, son of the late King Aethelred and his Norman queen, the Lady Aelfgifu as she is still called in England. He has a little difficulty in understanding the kneeling messenger: Alfred is slightly unfamiliar with his native language, having left his homeland in hurried exile as a child of less than five years old and having only now returned for the first time. The man before him succeeds in conveying the information that he is an attendant of Earl Godwine, the close ally of Alfred's mother. The Earl, he indicates, is waiting nearby with a large retinue and has come to welcome Alfred and offer him and his men protection.

Accompanied by attendants who can if necessary act as interpreters, Alfred and Godwine ride towards each other and exchange formal greetings. Godwine can now see the extent of Alfred's troops and can size up the operation. Though large, it is insufficient in number for any serious attempt at an invasion: he senses that the men have been rallied principally as a show of strength, and that Alfred is hoping to gain support from at least the southern region of England by presenting himself as a credible figure of power. But is this really a forceful private army or a ragbag collection of slaves and quickly hired help? And how able would the men be if put to the test? Godwine knows that quite apart from posturing as a military leader, Alfred needs at least some soldiers for very practical reasons: he runs a great risk of being attacked or ambushed by Harold Harefoot's men – or indeed other hostile parties.

Alfred, the foreigner, is the more wary of the two men. And Godwine hardly sets him at ease. He presents Alfred with the unwelcome news that his brother, and rival, has already reached England.[4] Edward, he says, has successfully made his way to Winchester with his soldiers, having arrived in Southampton, a port that provides conveniently quick access to the royal base, unlike Alfred's more tangled route. Godwine informs Alfred that Edward has been warmly welcomed by the Lady, his mother, and has been with her for several days. He then tells Alfred that it was a surprise to learn that he, too, was arriving back in his homeland. His mother had wanted one of her sons to come to her from Normandy but had not expected them both. However, she was so heartened to receive communication of Alfred's imminent landing that she asked the Earl himself to seek him out, intercept him on his journey and offer him secure passage. Godwine says that his spies have spent some time searching for Alfred's party, extensive though it is. He had not thought they would venture so close to London – which holds great danger for them. And equally, he did not anticipate that Alfred would come with quite so many men. Edward is supported by Norman troops and Godwine appreciates that Alfred's greater force is unlikely to have come from the same source, so from where has he raised such a large army and acquired the vessels to transport them all to England?

Alfred explains that he has sailed from the province of Boulogne and that from there he has taken the swiftest sea route to his homeland. His mother, he says, may not have informed Earl Godwine about new family connections with Normandy's powerful neighbour. A little over a year ago the Lady's daughter Godgifu lost her husband, the Count of Amiens and the Vexin, but she has recently remarried. Alfred's new brother-in-law is Count Eustace of Boulogne, who has been a great support to him. Eustace has seen fit to support Alfred by supplying him with a good number of ships and men, whose strength and fighting abilities are, he claims, second to none.

Godwine is only marginally impressed, and adamant that in spite of the force Alfred has with him it would be folly to venture anywhere close to London – the town has many hostile troops garrisoned there, men who are staunchly loyal to Harold Harefoot and who by this stage would know of Alfred's moves in their direction. He persuades the Queen's son that the best course of action is to redirect his party on a more southerly route to Winchester, where his mother awaits him. Godwine himself can accompany Alfred there.

Godwine and his men lead Alfred and his army to the small town of Guildford.[5] Here they are to spend the night. Alfred, accompanied by just a few attendants, is taken to lodgings in one of the town houses.[6] His other men, split up into small groups, are given accommodation in the town's great hall and in a number of barns and other outhouses. During the evening Godwine entertains Alfred and his attendants with much food, drink and music. Then they retire, Alfred to his lodgings, Godwine to his separate quarters. They are to reconvene the following morning and proceed on their way to Winchester.

But that night, under the cover of darkness, a large group of sword-clad strangers swarms silently into the town. They know exactly where to go. All of Alfred's splintered army is variously surrounded, surprised from their sleep, and then manacled while their weapons are removed. Alfred himself is woken roughly and under armed guard marched swiftly to an awaiting boat. Under powerless protest he is forced on board and conveyed along the River Wey towards London.

As day breaks over Guildford Alfred's now leaderless soldiers are shoved and kicked from their lodgings, their arms still tightly bound. Like animals, they are roped together and herded to an open space just outside the town. Some of them spit and say that Godwine has treacherously betrayed them. Others look around in vain for help from his troops. There is no sign of the Earl and his retinue. They are either lying low, complicit in the underhand attack, or have made a hasty getaway from the area.

The captors brusquely line up Alfred's soldiers. Every tenth man is pushed and prodded aside, their bindings cut. These individuals are told they will be spared. Most of them have little understanding of the

Anglo-Saxon tongue but a good number of these men from Boulogne can guess at the meaning of what is being said. They have heard of a practice of execution whereby for every nine prisoners killed one is allowed to live. This, though, is known to be a very mixed mercy: those saved will be subsequently sold as slaves and will probably end their lives lashed and burnt out as galley serfs. But before they are taken away to be exchanged for silver coins they are made to watch the slaughter of their fellow warriors.

The rest of Alfred's soldiers are savagely set upon. A few lucky men are fairly swiftly despatched: beheaded with axes or stabbed and then hacked to pieces. But most of the troops have a slower and more tortured ending: their hands and feet are cut off or they are scalped, beaten and left to die. Later that day the people of Guildford venture just outside the town and find the butchered bodies amid great pools of blood. Some of the townspeople, loyal to the Queen, quickly send messengers to Winchester with news of this carnage and of Alfred's abduction.

Meanwhile the Queen's son is taken to London amid much jeering that he has arrived at the city he had intended, foolishly, to visit. But Alfred's captors do not stop there for long. They hurriedly take their boat on and, by way of rivers, make for the remote and marshy reaches of East Anglia. They are aware that by now search parties will have been sent out and that the Queen's men may be on their trail so they move with speed and stealth, their prisoner lying bound and gagged at their feet.

Several days after leaving London they arrive at Ely, an inland island that can be difficult to reach because of the shifting bog and water around it. Alfred, his hands still tied behind his back, is pushed out of the boat as his captors disembark. With much cruel mockery they announce that he is to be tried for crimes against the Anglo-Saxon state. Exhausted by the journey and weakened from lack of food and drink, Alfred has little comprehension of what is happening, and is given no opportunity to speak in his own defence. He is sentenced to be blinded for his sins. His hands are unbound and he is laid spread-eagled on his back with his arms, legs and chest held down by a group of his captors. Then his eyes are brutally cut out.

Leaving Alfred writhing on the shore, his abductors rapidly return to their boat and sail away.

Aware of a distant commotion and of a boat somewhere in the vicinity, the monks at the large monastery of Ely send out lay servants to search the island. A few hours later some of these men find Alfred bleeding profusely and barely conscious. Footprints in the mud around him indicate that the perpetrators of this savagery have departed. With no idea who he is or why he has been mutilated in this manner, the servants gently lift Alfred and carry him back towards the monastery. He is dead on arrival.

The monks lay out the body and pray for the soul of this unknown man, that he may find eternal peace despite his wretched end. Then, amid the chanting of hymns and the utterance of more prayers of penance, they bury the stranger honourably within the confines of their consecrated land.

Shortly afterwards armed men arrive at Ely. They are deferential but their respect is tempered with a sense of urgency: they have much pressing business to discuss. These men tell the monks that they are on the trail of criminals who have captured the son of the dowager Queen, and they ask for information about any untoward activities that those at the monastery might have been told of or even seen themselves. Starkly the truth is pieced together. The monks and the messengers realise with growing horror that the newly interred stranger is none other than the aethling Alfred, appallingly murdered in the prime of his life. He is reburied more fittingly in the south chapel at the west end of the monastery's church.

*   *   *

Who was ultimately responsible for Alfred's death? Emma's author pins the blame firmly on Harold Harefoot, who supposedly had lured both of the Queen's sons to England in the first place. The writer claims that the men who murdered the Prince and slaughtered his troops were 'leagued with the most abominable tyrant Haraldr'. But what of Godwine, who appears to have been with Alfred precisely to protect him against just such an eventuality? The writer gives no indication as to what the Earl and his retinue were up to during the abduction of

Alfred and the massacre of his men, although they can hardly have been unaware of what was happening.

Others are not so silent on this matter. In some versions of the *Anglo-Saxon Chronicles*[7] Godwine himself is held to be the perpetrator of the crime, acting as Harold Harefoot's agent. They even break into alliterative verse about the event. The writers maintain that rather than greeting the Prince on behalf of his mother, Godwine took the Queen's son and his troops into captivity. They allege that it was Godwine's own men who butchered some of the soldiers, sold others as slaves and sent Alfred off to Ely and to his death there, a line of thought also held by later English and Norman chroniclers.

Of course the interpretation of the events rather depends on when the records were written. At the time that Emma's author produced his book Godwine was enormously powerful. It would have been foolhardy in the extreme to implicate him in this controversial episode. The stories told in the *Anglo-Saxon Chronicles*, where Godwine is clearly held guilty, probably originated at a slightly later date. The first version of these events was no doubt written during the period of the Earl's subsequent fall, when many people would have wanted to discredit him as much as possible. Later still, Godwine became a much despised target for the post-Conquest writers, in Normandy as well as England. English chroniclers writing at the turn of the eleventh century would have regarded Godwine and his family as rapacious thugs responsible for creaming off the riches of the country and leading the nation astray. For the Normans of this time, Godwine was infamous principally as the father of Harold (a younger man, not to be confused with Harold Harefoot), who dishonourably seized the throne of England when it should have been inherited by their duke, William.

Whatever the motives behind the various stories of Alfred's death, it is highly likely that Godwine was culpable of at least assisting Harold Harefoot in his plans to murder Emma's son, and he may even have directly orchestrated the deed itself. During the increasingly fraught period when Harthacnut failed to return to England, the alliance between Emma and Godwine appears to have broken down. It seems that once she started to encourage the claims of her two sons from Normandy, he expediently began to support Harold Harefoot's ever more militant bid for the throne, quite possibly without Emma's knowledge and quite probably amid much treachery. The upshot was disaster for Emma.

Her author maintains that the Queen was 'dazed beyond consolation' by the murder of Alfred. It was a crime that shocked the nobility if not the entire nation. But although Emma may have been genuinely distraught about the death of a son she had not seen for more than twenty years, the subsequent ramifications of her position were no doubt of more pressing concern. She was suddenly very much alone, far more isolated and unsupported than she had been just after the death of Cnut, when Harold Harefoot had stripped her of the royal treasure.

On receiving news of Alfred's wretched demise, Edward had rapidly, and wisely, fled, returning to Normandy.[8] Presumably Alfred's remaining troops who were guarding his ships on the Kentish coast also made a hasty exit. Harthacnut, meanwhile, stayed obdurately in Denmark. With no backing from her surviving sons, and amid insinuations that she had been responsible for enticing Alfred to England – and to his death – Emma lost any credibility with those of the aristocracy who had remained faithful to her cause. The writer of her book alludes to her 'uncertainty concerning what remained of her own life' and suggests that some 'odious' and 'spiteful' people maintained that because of the foul and tragic end of her son she should have contemplated death for herself. But that, he says, would have been unorthodox and unworthy. Nevertheless, at a time of deep Christian conviction the veiled suggestion of suicide emphasises how very bleak Emma's outlook was.

And her situation spiralled further downwards. However reluctantly, the nobility now backed Harold Harefoot and he once again laid claim to the whole of England – regardless of the agreement that had been reached at Oxford some months beforehand. No longer was the country to be divided, and no longer was Emma's son Harthacnut to be considered a tenable successor to at least part of his father's kingdom: he had stayed away too long.

Despite her many and varied schemes to retain power, Emma had been completely outmanoeuvred by Harold Harefoot and his mother, Aelfgifu of Northampton. The last anointed Queen of England would now lose most of her property; she certainly could no longer remain at the palace in Winchester where she had been resolutely entrenched for almost a year, and unless she left the Anglo-Saxon kingdom her life may well have been at risk – even if she sought sanctuary in a convent she would still have been a dangerous figure in the ostensibly quiet confines of the church.

It was probably sometime before Harold Harefoot was formally declared king of all the country that Emma departed from England, an exile once again. Under the year 1037, one writer of the *Anglo-Saxon Chronicles* dramatically records that she was 'driven out without any mercy to face the raging winter', which might be overstating the situation but does at least indicate that Emma would have been on her way from Winchester at some stage during the inclement months of January and February. She did not, however, seek sanctuary in her native land as she had done during the height of the Viking invasions back in 1013. It may be that Emma received notification to the effect that she would be unwelcome at the Norman court: Alfred had, after all, been very largely brought up there and his murder would have caused shock waves. Meanwhile Emma was held at least partly responsible and as a result her reputation among her immediate Norman family would have become tarnished. But in any case, Normandy might not have been Emma's destination of choice. Governed by regents on behalf of her great-nephew, the boy duke William, the province had become politically unstable and was therefore not the best place to plan a comeback – for Emma seems to have had no intention of accepting defeat and appears to have regarded her second exile only as a temporary hiatus in her career as Queen, or at least Queen Mother, of England.

It was in Flanders that she sought, and was apparently generously given, refuge. For this she had cause to be grateful for the statesmanship of her second husband. Cnut had established good relations with the Flemish court when he undertook his pilgrimage to Rome and travelled through the thriving province back in 1027. Emma herself also had family connections with Flanders: Count Baldwin V was the stepson of her niece Judith, daughter of Richard II of Normandy. According to Emma's author, Baldwin himself provided the exiled queen with a house in the Flemish city of Bruges, and in a manner fitting her dignity supplied her with 'security' (presumably armed guards) and 'entertainment' (probably attendant ladies and a band of minstrels). But Bruges was by no means just a comfortable hideaway. In the early-eleventh century it was a bustling hub of Continental trade and as a result also saw much political traffic. Here Emma was ideally placed to keep abreast of developments in England and to plan her next moves.

Her first course of action was to summon Edward from Normandy. Clearly, at this stage, she had not given up hope that her surviving son of royal Anglo-Saxon blood could still win the throne of England. At this juncture, Edward's relations with his mother were no doubt tempered with a great deal of caution. But somewhat surprisingly he showed himself not unwilling to hear what she had to say. The author of Emma's book records that after receiving messengers from his mother, Edward mounted his horse and duly rode from Normandy to Flanders. His visit to Emma seems to have been motivated by pity rather than potential gain. Having reached Bruges, he apparently held long discussions with his mother, sympathised with her very sorry predicament – and flatly told her that he was unable to help. Then he remounted his horse and cantered back to distinctly unremarkable prospects in Normandy, the crown of England a roundly rejected objective.

Emma, meanwhile, settled into Bruges and according to her author earned the heartfelt esteem and gratitude of its citizens, conversing pleasantly with the rich and giving generously to the poor. She no doubt also continued her practice of patronising the Church. It was while she was living in Bruges that she would have established connections with the monastery of Saint-Bertin in St Omer. Whether she ever actually visited this city in southern Flanders is not known but she evidently had sufficient contact with the monastic community there to develop a working friendship with one of the monks. She may even have employed this ecclesiastic as her personal priest in her household at

Bruges and might subsequently have taken him back with her to England. He, at any rate, was later to become the author of her book.

But above and beyond her acts of church devotion and charity, Emma was still angling to regain her position in England. With Edward no longer willing to act with and for her, she refocused her efforts and appealed to Harthacnut yet again. This time the messengers she sent to Denmark were successful in their entreaties. Her author, the monk from St Omer, infers that Harthacnut had not already heard about Alfred's murder, which, given the waves of scandal that it had caused, seems unlikely. He reports that when the Danish king received news of his mother's sorrow and of the crime committed against his half-brother he was so shocked his 'ears trembled' with rage. He also, apparently, burned with desire to seek vengeance – but sensibly appreciated that in the first instance he should visit his mother and work out the best course of action with her.

On a more strategic level, Harthacnut had by now subdued Magnus of Norway and felt sufficiently confident to leave Denmark without fear of further incursions from this aggressive neighbour. Indeed the situation was apparently stable enough for him to prepare a great fleet that stood by in readiness for battle beyond Scandinavia. Emma's author reports that Harthacnut cunningly hid the force of ships and men in 'an inlet of the sea' and then set sail for Flanders with just ten ships. This would have been a careful manoeuvre so as to avoid travelling with a large army and thereby sending out signals of imminent invasion.

The monk from St Omer writes that Harthacnut had a rough passage to Bruges. So much so that his ten ships were forced to take shelter from a 'murky tempest'. This was, though, an act of God, who on the night of the storm appeared to Harthacnut in a dream. He told the young Danish king that all would be well: the 'unjust usurper' of England had little longer to live and the kingdom would soon be returned to its rightful inheritor. The next morning the sea's fury had abated and Harthacnut, much encouraged by his holy encounter, continued swiftly to Flanders, his sails bellying in favourable winds.

The author no doubt included this tale as a means of foreshadowing

Harold Harefoot's death – and of implying that it was an act of divine retribution. In reality the abrupt demise of the English monarch was fortuitous, and would have been unexpected on the part of Emma and Harthacnut. Whether or not he was delayed by a terrible storm, the Danish king reached Bruges safely; his mother greeted him with relief and purportedly with much joy after minimal contact over the last fifteen or so years; they began to plan how they could retaliate against the murder of Alfred and also reclaim England; then they received the glad tidings that the throne of the Anglo-Saxon kingdom had become vacant – 'to wit Haraldr was dead'. The Almighty, so it seems, was very much on their side.

Harold Harefoot was officially King of England for about three years. But beyond the fact that he died as a young man (of about twenty-three years old), there is almost no surviving documentation about his rule. During his brief reign, the *Anglo-Saxon Chronicles* chiefly list church business: the death of archbishops and bishops and who is appointed to succeed them. In addition, one chronicler offers information about a skirmish with the Welsh in 1039 and also notes under that year 'Here came a great gale',[9] with no further details.

Just one official document of court business[10] remains from Harold Harefoot's reign, probably written fairly early in the following year. It records that King Harold restored Sandwich to Christ Church in Canterbury, following an argument concerning the port between this establishment and Canterbury's other great religious institution, St Augustine's. The document also states that at the time it was written the King was at Oxford and so severely ill that he had little hope of survival. Harold Harefoot almost undoubtedly died from natural causes – elfshot, literally attacked by elves, is how the Anglo-Saxons frequently diagnosed potentially deadly diseases and viruses. The *Anglo-Saxon Chronicles* report that King Harold 'passed away in Oxford' on 17 March 1040. He was buried at Westminster, the monastic centre on Thorney Island some miles west of London, the choice of interment site probably a reflection of the great support he had enjoyed in that area of the country.

Harold Harefoot is believed to have had one son, Aelfwine, thought to have been illegitimate. Whether there was any attempt by Aelfgifu of Northampton to claim the crown of England on behalf of her grandson is not recorded. Nor is there any further information about what happened to this redoubtable, and now childless, queen mother. She seems to have retired into obscurity, probably to a convent in her native Midlands. She was certainly to trouble Emma no further.

Meanwhile Harthacnut was the uncontested heir to the throne. The leading churchmen and aristocrats acted quickly. The group, which would have included Godwine and his rival Earl Leofric as well as Bishop Lyfing of Worcester and the new Archbishop of Canterbury, Eadsige, appear to have known full well that Harthacnut was at this stage with his mother in Bruges and would have suspected that he was planning an invasion. The *Anglo-Saxon Chronicles* record that 'they [an unspecified party] sent to Bruges for Harthacnut', adding disparagingly that 'it was supposed that they did well'.[11] Emma's author is rather more enthusiastic about the situation: the nobility apparently begged the Danish king to come to England and rejoiced 'in jubilation of every kind' at the prospect of his accession.

Harthacnut and his mother set out, the shores near Bruges 'perturbed by lamentation and groaning' from the good citizens who felt bereft at seeing Emma depart. Accompanied by sixty or so ships – which presumably had sailed swiftly over from Denmark – they arrived at Sandwich, and Harthacnut was swiftly proclaimed king.

One of his first notable acts as king was to seek out the remains of his half-brother Harold Harefoot. According to Florence of Worcester,[12] writing about sixty years later, Harthacnut sent Godwine, the Archbishop of York, 'Throng, his executioner' and many others of 'great rank' to the London area. They apparently exhumed the body of the late king and, as ordered, threw it into the surrounding marshland. They were then commanded to retrieve it and, presumably as a further sign of contempt, dump it unceremoniously in the River Thames. From there, however, it was purportedly rescued by fishermen who are said to have taken Harold Harefoot's by now much mangled corpse to the

Danish community in London who had been so loyal to him and who honourably reburied him in their own cemetery.

The new king was overtly wreaking vengeance for the murder of another half-brother, Alfred, whom he had never met. He was also acting in retaliation for the suffering of his mother, by now firmly restored to a prominent position at court. Most of all, however, Harthacnut was aggressively taunting those who had supported his rival. It was an implicitly violent and tyrannical means of crushing any potential dissent. It did not bode well for the future.

PART IV

QUEEN MOTHER

CHAPTER TWELVE

The Book

The monk's table has been laid out with his writing materials. On one side of a sloping board is an ox horn containing ink. This liquid is a solution of iron salts and oak galls – growths or 'warts' created on twigs and leaves by insect eggs. On the other side of the board is a selection of quills – sharpened swan and goose feathers – and a knife for scouring out mistakes and for re-cutting the quills as and when they become blunt. At the centre of the table, pinned on to the slanting surface, is the monk's parchment.[1] This has been laboriously prepared: lengths of sheep skin were steeped in vats of lime to remove the hair, then stretched while still damp, scraped smooth and sprinkled with chalk that serves as a whitening agent.

The parchment has been trimmed and then cut into double-page sheets of the required dimensions. The monk will be writing a secular document, so his book is to be of reasonably modest size – unlike the large, elaborately illuminated bibles and psalters created for great monasteries, but rather bigger than the miniature copies of the Holy Gospels that some senior ecclesiastics carry with them on their travels. The blank pages of the monk's book have been carefully ruled out: dotted lines have been pricked into the parchment to mark the margins, top and bottom, left and right. The monk has given junior scribes clear instructions as to the measurements. The delineated area that will be filled by the written word is not only proportionately pleasing to the eye, it also leaves scope for explanatory notes, or glosses, to be added later around it. Within the rectangle so defined more dots have been pierced to show where the author should write so as to keep his words in a straight line.

Once he has finished composing his work, the text will be corrected, an exercise that the author will either undertake himself or, preferably, second to another scribe. Smaller errors that he did not rectify while writing his manuscript will be scratched out with a knife, the marks on the parchment filled in with chalk powder. Larger mistakes will be scored through with a quill and ink, and an amendment added above the line or in one of the margins. The manuscript will then be folded into sequential pages that will be sewn together and bound on to wooden boards. Leather thongs will keep the book closed when not in use. The covers and the thongs are not just for show: they will protect the book from damage and, importantly, help stop the parchment from shrinking and rucking. The stretched and treated skins are prone to contract to their former, animal shape.

The author's completed manuscript is to be something of a rough draft. It will be copied by other clerical monks who will reproduce the text in more finely crafted books.[2] Vellum, made from costly calf skin, will be used instead of parchment, and embellishments will be added. Drop capitals at the start of sections and at intermittent paragraph breaks will be decorated with colour, as will the opening lines of the work: red created from lead, green from copper, blue from an extract of the woad plant.

In view of the expense and the craftsmanship required even in preparing the basic materials, it is daunting for any scribe to begin working on a blank page. Doubly so for the monk from St Omer: he has the rare task of creating an original work.

Since being asked to undertake this job, he has spent many hours in discussion with his patron, the Lady Emma whose son Harthancut became King of England in this last year, namely 1040. The manuscript is to be in Latin – the monk from Flanders has little knowledge of how to write in the Anglo-Saxon vernacular, and besides the Lady wishes the work to be recorded in the language of learning. On the face of it, the book is to be an account of recent events in the Anglo-Saxon kingdom: a record of how the Danish kings gloriously took control of the country and the manner in which, after some hardship, King Harthacnut came to rule the realm. The monk has heard many different stories about what happened, and why, but he appreciates full well that it is the Lady's interpretation of these events he needs to write. She is not unfamiliar with the process of presenting facts from a distinctive angle. The monk is aware that as a young girl at the court of her father, Count Richard I of Normandy, his patron was present when the great scribe Dudo, of the monastery of St Quentin, began work on his history about the Norman state – and he has read subsequent copies of this text. He knows that such documents are almost entirely coloured by the motives of those who commission them.

However, there is also a question of the monk's own, more academic, interests. Entirely new works are seldom commissioned and such unusual compositions provide an almost Heaven-sent opportunity for the display of much knowledge. Through his text the monk from St Omer will be able to reveal his Classical learning to the world,[3] or at least to those of his ecclesiastic colleagues who are literate and can appreciate his scholarship. Others will hear his text read out loud and will no doubt be unaware of such subtleties. He is proud of his education in Virgil, Sallust and, to a lesser extent, Lucan. Besides the use of Classical language and Classical allusions, he will as a matter of course incorporate plenty of reference to the Almighty God and to his Son the Saviour. He wants also to include a few passages of rhymed prose in the manner of such recent authors as Dudo.

He will follow an established formula for the book. It is to start with a prologue that will emphasise his concern over the historical accuracy of the work and will also serve as an apology for his shortcomings as an author – a stylistic show of humility. This is to be followed by an Argument, a précis of the main events heavily laced with praise of his patron. The laudatory lines will be included not simply to appeal to her vanity, they will have the important function of making it plain that it is the Lady who has commissioned the manuscript and has directed the work. But the first two sections of the book will in fact be written last of all, after he has finished the main body of the text and is clear about what needs to be summed up and introduced. The principal part of the book will be divided into three sections: Swein Forkbeard's invasion of England; King Cnut's conquest, his marriage to the Lady and his acts of Christian devotion; and the tangled period when the aethling Alfred was murdered, all culminating happily with peace and harmony in the time of King Cnut's son, Harthacnut. But there is also to be a final twist. The King's half-brother Edward has recently arrived at the English court from Normandy. He is apparently to be joint ruler of the realm, and the Lady wishes this singular arrangement to be explained briefly in the very last lines of the book.

In her instructions, the Lady has been very clear about how the story of the Danish kings of England should begin, and she has stipulated which episodes of the period in question she wishes the author to omit and the deeds she wants him to emphasise. The monk from St Omer has made some notes on wax tablets but has mainly committed what his patron has told him to memory, reciting her words over and over in his mind, as he might do when learning a passage of the Holy Scriptures. Long before embarking on the act of writing, he has spent many hours in silent contemplation, thinking through his project: he has decided on how to present the different aspects of the Lady's story; how he will couch his Latin phrases; and how best to please his patron while attempting to keep within the parameters of what he knows to be accurate facts. He will allow himself a small flourish of personal reflection by including his own observations of King Cnut's visit to St Omer – and this eyewitness account will usefully add credibility to his text. He has already composed much of the main body of the manuscript in his head.

He bows his head in prayer. Then he picks up a quill. He slowly dips it in his inkhorn, wipes a dribble of liquid from the nib, and carefully begins to write: '*Regem Danorum Sueinum inquam*'. He dips again: '*ueridica comperi relatione omnium sui temporis regem ferme fortunatissimum extitisse . . .*' (Swein, king of the Danes, was, I declare, as I have ascertained from truthful report, practically the most fortunate of all the kings of his time . . .)[4]

* * *

According to the ecclesiastic from St Omer, the Viking who conquered the Anglo-Saxon kingdom in 1014 had a charmed life in that he was blessed with worldly honour, popularity among the people of his homeland, and enormous might. The Flemish monk was clearly presenting the subjugation of England from a very Danish bias.

He excels with his descriptions of the invading longships – glorious, nimble and very plentiful creations. The prows of Swein Forkbeard's fleet are adorned with gilded lions, dragons, bulls, dolphins and centaurs. Cnut's later force is a terrifying spectacle: 200 ships ablaze with sunlight reflected on gold and silver and filled with the fittest and most ferocious of fighting men. The author claims this army is superlative and that there are no slaves, old men or even those of the lower classes among the warriors. But outstanding though the soldiers are, he makes it plain that they battle against a thoroughly worthy foe – although, of course ultimately Cnut becomes king.

The detail, the choice of words and the rhetoric would have come from the monk of St Omer. But the overall views must have been Emma's. She commissioned the work, she it was who wanted to record events from a particular angle. The book is, of course, extremely politicised and one-sided. It is all the more extraordinary for being so. Among the surviving documents from the period there is nothing like it – orchestrated either by male or female (although Emma's future daughter-in-law, Edith, was later to follow this example and commission a book of her own[5]). Here was a woman using very sophisticated means of flexing political muscle. The resulting text is full of artifice. It is a work of propaganda but remarkably it offers us a close approximation of the voice of an eleventh-century woman.

It also remains a puzzle. What is it really meant to be about? At the start it glorifies Swein Forkbeard and his army yet the patron of this book was herself a victim of his invasion – and for a time suffered deep uncertainty and deprivation as a result. Emma chose to suppress this fact. Indeed she chose to suppress many facts.

Strikingly, her book makes no mention at all of her marriage to Aethelred. Nor does it give any indication that she was ever in England during the Viking attacks. Emma herself does not enter the story until at least halfway through: after Cnut has taken control of the country and is seeking a bride. She is first referred to as a worthy queen, living in Normandy. Of course this is wishful thinking: it is more than likely that Emma was in London at the time, and a captive of Cnut. The King swears an oath that only his son by his new bride will be the rightful heir to England. The author subsequently highlights the happy event of the birth of this child – then rapidly fudges the issue as to what happened to Emma's other sons. The 'two parents', he writes, send their 'other legitimate sons' to Normandy to be brought up there while they keep the heir to the throne in England. That these sons, Edward and Alfred, were from a former marriage is not explained, nor is the fact that they were abandoned.

Other dubious passages and glaring omissions occur after Cnut's death. Quite apart from the issue of the ostensibly forged letter that lured Alfred to his death, no reason is offered as to why Emma's sons in Normandy had a claim to the throne in the first place. Nor is any mention made of Edward's visit to England just prior to Alfred's arrival – a detail given in the works of later Norman and Anglo-Saxon chroniclers. Emma, meanwhile, is portrayed as a passive victim of Harold Harefoot's scheming, although it is highly likely that she was just as dexterous and cunning. Her book in itself is evidence of her political wiliness.

But why was it commissioned? On the face of it, Emma's motives are not entirely clear. The book does not seem, for example, to have been written primarily for posterity – it is far from being a report along the lines of the *Anglo-Saxon Chronicles*. The rights of the Danish line of succession to the throne of England appear to be the chief concern of the author, yet Harthacnut had already become king when the work was written and therefore few contemporaries would have needed to be persuaded into formally accepting his legitimacy. As for Emma herself: she had clearly been through a period of great misfortune but by the time the initial manuscript was produced she was back in a position of much authority and had little opposition to quash. So who was the target audience for this text?

The book seems at first to have had no title – a label of some sort might have given a few indications as to the whys and wherefores of its origination. By the late-medieval period, however, the work was known as *Gesta Cnutonis Regis*, or the 'Deeds of King Cnut', inaccurately so, since scant detail is actually given about the reign of Emma's second husband. The book subsequently acquired the title *Encomium Emmae Reginae*, an only marginally more apposite designation essentially meaning 'a work of high-flown praise for Queen Emma'. Given that Emma becomes a prominent figure only towards the end of the story, this name, too, seems inadequate.

A large and startling clue as to the book's rationale lies in the final two paragraphs of the surviving manuscript from the eleventh century. In a sudden, and radical, turn of events Emma's eldest son Edward is invited over from Normandy to assist his half-brother Harthacnut in governing England. The monk from St Omer writes that once ensconced as king, Harthacnut, out of 'brotherly' love, sends messengers to Edward, asking him to 'hold the kingdom together with himself'. The book ends with Edward happily taking up this offer, and with the mother and her two sons – a type of earthly trinity – sharing the rule of the kingdom.

Emma must have commissioned her work with this situation very much in mind. The intended audience would, then, have been the Anglo-Danish court, many of whom were no doubt bemused at Edward's recent arrival – and probably deeply suspicious that there was trouble brewing as a result. Some of the aristocrats were Danes who had been brought to England by Harthacnut; a few were Normans who had accompanied Edward on his return to the kingdom of his birth; but the majority were Anglo-Saxon and naturalised Scandinavian nobles who had been riven by the recent problems over succession to the throne and amongst whom there would still have been a great deal of bad blood. Acrimony between the parties led by the two great earls, Leofric and Godwine, no doubt continued to be marked.

Most, if not all, of those at court would have been familiar with the realities behind the story told in Emma's book. Indeed most, and probably all, would have been well aware that Emma's first husband was King Aethelred. They would have heard a number of different tales about the plight of Edward and Alfred, and the shocking death of the Queen's younger son. Although Emma's author clearly excluded many facts from the manuscript, those details were already known by the audience. It might be tempting to think of Emma as a power-crazed individual, flagrantly rewriting history and eliminating awkward episodes, yet if her author was writing for well-informed courtiers then the omissions become almost irrelevant. They would have been made because those aspects of the past were not directly pertinent to his patron's underlying concerns.

The most plausible explanation is that Emma's book was intended to present a view of past events in order to shape the future:[6] to bring Edward into play and to reconcile the bitter divisions at court. And, of course, along the way it also provided convenient scope for Emma to explain her own actions in the recent dramas and to be absolved of any blame for Alfred's death.

The book is all the more remarkable for being, at least in part, the work of a woman who would have had little knowledge of the written word. But what of her intended audience – could they read?

A few of Harthacnut's courtiers may have been literate: Godwine's son Harold, for example, is reputed to have owned books about his all-consuming passion of hawking, although whether he was actually able to read them himself is another matter. Certainly the majority of the nobility would not have been able to decipher the ink markings on a page of parchment or vellum. Most of them would, though, have had some knowledge of spoken Latin. This they would have absorbed primarily through church attendance and also through court business, much of which was recorded in the official language of learning. Emma's Latin manuscript was no doubt read out loud to them by monks much practised at such tasks. It would have been a form of mandatory entertainment and the nobility might have fully understood and appreciated the book – or not. There is no surviving evidence as to whether the assembled Anglo-Saxon, Danish and Norman aristocrats regarded the work as a dismal, and scarcely comprehensible, dirge or a riveting sensation. Would they have smiled in pleasure at the author's vivid descriptions of glittering ships, chuckled with glee at the beheading of the terrible turncoat Eadric Streona, and bowed their heads in respect at the death of Edmund Ironside? And would they have been aware of the underlying message of appeasement?

It is tempting to imagine that the book had a conciliatory effect on

Godwine, and that it could have shamed him into an act of atonement. At around the time it was published the Earl very publically made amends with the royal family. Florence of Worcester,[7] writing about sixty years after the event, records that Godwine presented King Harthacnut with a lavish gift: a beautifully crafted ship with a great gilded prow, fully equipped with eighty soldiers. Whether the Earl was to continue paying for these men is not clear, but they certainly arrived generously kitted out. According to Florence, each of the crew bore a coat of mail, a partly gilded helmet, a sword, an axe with gold and silver bindings, a shield with golden studs, and a spear. In addition, all the soldiers were adorned on each arm with golden rings weighing sixteen ounces apiece. Florence reports that on delivering his splendid present, Godwine then swore to the King and to the chief nobles of the land that the blinding of Alfred had not been his 'wish' but that Harold Harefoot 'had ordered him to do what he did'. In other words he was admitting to the murder of the King's half-brother, and through his gift he was seeking honourable redemption. The cost of Godwine's magnificent ship and finely turned-out crew would have been enormous and was, quite probably, the equivalent of the *wergild*, or compensation rate, of a prince.

Emma, meanwhile, tried to turn her son, the dead prince, into a saint. In her book, the author records that after Alfred was buried on the Island of Ely 'many miracles' occurred at his tomb, and the writer comments 'it is justly so: for he was martyred in his innocence' and he goes on to suggest that Alfred should therefore be considered a fitting conduit for the salvation of other innocent people. The Queen Mother supplemented her efforts to elevate her son by presenting splendid gifts to the church at Ely: Emma donated a purple banner (purple being extremely expensive to produce); and she herself reputedly set to with needle and thread and made a number of altar cloths for the monastery at Ely,[8] one of which was extravagantly, and magnificently, covered in gold. But her attempts to create a cult that would result in Alfred being declared a holy martyr did not succeed. Understandably so, for Emma's son had been an unknown foreigner and apart from his miserable murder there was nothing to recommend him either to the church or to the local people of East Anglia. They were not to be persuaded by dislocated claims of miracle cures even if these were on royal authority.

Remorse about Emma's murdered son was no doubt a contributing factor to the abrupt and very acceptable change in Edward's fortunes. But it was only a small one. Emma's book tells us nothing about Harthacnut's rule of England. In the final few lines he arrives, is gloriously received – and then generously invites Edward to share his kingdom. Amen. In reality, there were salutary political reasons as to why a landless exile in Normandy was suddenly offered the golden opportunity to become a quasi, if subordinate, monarch of England alongside his Danish half-brother.

The *Anglo-Saxon Chronicles* offer some explanation. After being accepted as king in 1040, Harthacnut rapidly made himself deeply unpopular through severe levels of taxation. The chronicles record that shortly after he arrived at Sandwich with about sixty ships he promptly demanded large amounts of money for the crews. From the perspective of the Anglo-Saxon freemen and women who were expected to produce the funds, this was wickedly rapacious. Here was an alien Danish warrior who had been graciously given the throne of England but on setting foot in his new kingdom arrogantly started exhorting substantial payments for his own retinue. It was the behaviour of a belligerent conqueror rather than a peaceable king. Moreover, the hefty payments had a knock-on effect on the general economy: the *Anglo-Saxon Chronicles*[9] report that the price of wheat spiralled. But worse was to come.

In May 1041 Harthacnut sent a number of his housecarls across the country on a quest to collect yet more taxes. Resentment at the new king's tyrannical behaviour reached a peak. Two of the housecarls were set upon by an angry rabble and were murdered in the upper room of a tower at Worcester monastery.[10] Some months later Harthacnut retaliated with appalling ferocity raiding, according to the *Anglo-Saxon Chronicles*, the whole of Worcestershire.

Florence of Worcester offers details about the attack on the city of Worcester itself. His monastery had been at the core of the trouble, and here stories about the incident were no doubt still in circulation at the

end of the eleventh century, when he was writing. He maintains that a
very large army marched on the town. The forces included prominent
members of the nobility, Godwine and Leofric among them – and these
aristocrats would each have swelled the troops with their own men.
The soldiers apparently reached Worcester on 12 November and spent
four days ceaselessly burning and looting the city and also setting fire
to the surrounding countryside. In addition, the troops had been hoping
to kill a great many local men but, forewarned about the imminent
arrival of the army, the country folk had fled from their hamlets and
villages while a large number of the townspeople took refuge on an
island in the River Severn. Here they managed to hold out against the
King's forces. After five days the army departed and they returned to
what remained of their smouldering homes.

According to Florence, it was very shortly after this brutal episode
that Edward came to Harthacnut's court. The brothers would never
have met before and would have made a somewhat bizarre pair:
Edward, by now aged a fairly venerable thirty-six, was a very Norman
prince, despite being of Anglo-Saxon stock. Harthacnut, very Danish
and very much a man of the sword, was about thirteen years younger
yet politically he was quite clearly the senior of the two. However,
they had some circumstances in common: neither was married and
they were both to a large extent dependent on their mother for their
positions of power. There can be little doubt that Emma herself was
the principal orchestrator of the strangely conceived arrangement.
The evidence of the few surviving charters[11] from Harthacnut's reign
shows that the elderly Queen Mother held a very prominent position
at court and was a close adviser to her Danish son. After what had
amounted to a rebellion in Worcestershire, however comprehensively
checked, Harthacnut was in all probability persuaded by Emma that
Edward could offer a solution to the increasing unpopularity of the
royal family. By incorporating a brother of true Anglo-Saxon blood
into his regime Harthacnut might reverse his reputation as a violent
despot and show himself to be a leader of honour and generosity.
According to the *Anglo-Saxon Chronicles*[12] Edward's position as junior
king was even inaugurated with a special ceremony. This, though, may

have amounted to little more than the swearing of oaths of mutual friendship and support and is unlikely to have included formal coronation rites.

What role Edward was to have is not clear. It could be that this was simply window dressing and that the Norman prince was to remain little but a stooge. It may be that Harthacnut intended his half-brother (guided by Emma) to act as his regent in England while he returned to Denmark, which by now was threatened once again by Magnus of Norway. But whatever Harthacnut's plan, just a few months later the situation at court changed abruptly. In the early summer of 1042 the King attended the wedding of an Anglo-Danish aristocrat, Tofi the Proud, who had been his father's standard bearer. Tofi's bride, Gytha, was the daughter of one Osgod Clapa, a Scandinavian magnate and former courtier of Cnut who held lands in East Anglia. The celebration for the union of these two great northern families took place in Lambeth, across the Thames from London. It was no doubt a big event, the feasting liberal. Ale, *beor* and wine would have flowed, and great quantities, it seems, were consumed by Harthacnut. While drinking with fellow guests he suddenly collapsed, losing his powers of speech. In all probability this was the onset of a stroke brought about by an excessive intake of alcohol. He died a few days later on Tuesday 8 June, aged about twenty-three years old.

The *Anglo-Saxon Chronicles* comment that 'he never accomplished anything kingly for as long as he ruled'[13] – which was little more than two years. Henry of Huntingdon, writing about eighty years later, is rather kinder and records a popular myth that Harthacnut was, at least, a very generous bon viveur, apparently ordering that the dining tables of his court be 'laid four times a day with royal sumptuousness'.

Harthacnut was buried in the Old Minster at Winchester, alongside his father Cnut. According to a contemporary chronicler, shortly afterwards Emma gave a costly relic to the city's other great church, the New Minster, for the salvation of her son's soul. This gift was the head of St Valentine, then a martyr unconnected with courting couples[14] and thought to have been either a murdered Roman priest or a butchered Bishop of Terni.

With his half-brother interred, Edward, so the *Anglo-Saxon Chronicles* record, was then unanimously elected full King of England. But his accession was by no means a foregone conclusion for there was another strong claimant.

Harthacnut's cousin, Swein, would have been regarded by many as the natural successor to both Denmark and England.[15] The son of Cnut's sister Estrith, Swein had been sent by Harthacnut to defend Denmark against Magnus of Norway, and he was in Scandinavia at the time of his cousin's sudden death. There he quickly positioned himself as King of Denmark and was eventually accepted in 1047. In the richer and more powerful kingdom of England, a number of powerful Anglo-Danish aristocrats lobbied for his cause there.

The crux of the matter was whether the country should continue to be ruled by descendents of Swein Forkbeard, who had, collectively, been in power for a good twenty-five years and who were now led by Swein Estrithson, or whether it was preferable to revert to the ancient royal Anglo-Saxon line, as represented by Emma's son Edward. Most of those in a position of authority in England were at this juncture of mixed Anglo-Saxon and Danish blood and their loyalties would have been divided – if not confused. Edward, son of Aethelred, descendant of Alfred the Great, and a member of the illustrious West Saxon house of Cerdic, had the upper hand in that he was in England and could negotiate on his own behalf. Significantly, he succeeded in winning the support of Godwine – no doubt with promises of great power. Theirs was an unlikely alliance. The Earl not only had a murky reputation for being in part responsible for the death of Edward's brother, he was also a relative of the Danish claimant: his wife, Gytha, was Swein Estrithson's aunt.

Yet it was largely thanks to Godwine that England's senior churchmen and aristocrats were persuaded into accepting Edward as king. He was crowned on the first day of Easter, 3 April 1043. Later to earn the epithet 'The Confessor' because of his ostensible piety, Edward was to be the last Anglo-Saxon monarch of truly royal blood. On his coronation, his mother's reactions to the sudden swings of fortune are unknown. By now a redoubtable fifty-plus, Emma may have been too elderly, and possibly too bereaved at Harthacnut's death, to have played a part in easing her eldest son into power. Was she relieved to remain, in effect, the mother of England, and did she expect to retain a position at court?

CHAPTER THIRTEEN

Disgrace

Since April, when she attended her son's coronation in Winchester, Emma has been increasingly absent from the court as it shifts around the country. She has made the palace at Winchester her base and for the last few months has been permanently in residence there. Many of the nobility understand with some sympathy that she is elderly and that the court's itinerant existence is no longer comfortable for her. They imagine that she simply wants to retire. However, far from it, the Queen Mother has if anything assumed a more powerful position than she would have been accorded at court – she has taken control of the King's treasury, which is housed in Winchester's royal residence.

It is now mid-November, and preparations are underway for the feast of the holy apostle and martyr St Andrew, which takes place at the end of the month. This is a major event across Western Christendom and the celebrations at the great hall of the royal residence will be large and lavish, particularly in view of the fact that the Queen Mother herself will be present. Great sacks of grain from local estates and farms are being conveyed to the city by oxcart. More importantly, deliveries of ale and *beor* have started to arrive – to be kept under guard within the palace grounds. In addition, several barrels of wine have been imported from further afield, to be served only to the noblest of the guests at the banquet. Meanwhile pigs, sheep and cattle are being herded into royal enclosures in preparation for slaughter. The meat left over from the feast will be salted and dried for future consumption.

Amid the bustle of sorting and storing the principal ingredients for the revelry, a horse-borne messenger canters up to the palace gates.[1] He has urgent news for the Lady. Having dismounted and removed his sword, he is escorted inside, shown into an ante-room of the great hall and told to wait. After a short interval the Queen Mother, her elderly face barely visible behind her head robes, is ushered in, with several of her womenfolk in attendance. The stranger, apparently abashed at being in the presence of such a venerable and famous figure, quickly delivers his message. The King, he says abruptly, is on his way to Winchester and will be arriving imminently.

The Lady is taken aback. Why has she had no warning of this happy prospect? How large is her son's party? Are they bringing provisions with them? How long will they expect to stay? The messenger can, or will, provide no answers. He bows and retreats.

Orders are rapidly issued to prepare the palace for the King and his retinue of unknown size and to assemble supplies intended for St Andrew's feast in readiness for the court's requirements. But the Queen Mother's serving people have barely begun their tasks when the thunder of approaching horses can be heard. The palace gates are pulled open and a band of horseriders floods in.

The King has arrived with a relatively small but immensely powerful entourage. In addition to a menacing-looking group of well-armed housecarls, he is accompanied by the most prominent earls of the country: Godwine of Wessex, Leofric of Mercia and Siward of Northumbria. Ignoring the efforts being made to welcome them with ceremonious dignity, the King and his retinue make straight for the great hall. From there they summon the Queen Mother.

The Lady is offered only the most perfunctory of greetings as she and a few of her attendants enter the large chamber. Then a hush descends while she stands before her son and his chief advisers. It is as if she has been put on trial. The King announces sharply that after much delibera-tion with his councillors he himself has seen fit to deliver an important communication to the Queen Mother. He says that it is inappropriate for her to behave as if she were a monarch, or even designated regent, of the kingdom and that she has no authority to be in command of the royal treasury. She must deliver up the keys immediately. In addition, the King declares that he is confiscating many of his mother's estates and will reallocate them however he so pleases. The Lady is told that she can, if she wishes, continue to live at the palace but only in limited quarters where she will be expected to show frugality and to keep the smallest of retinues. However, under the circumstances, she may prefer to remove herself to her own, more modest property in Winchester[2] – given to her many years ago by the King's late father. It is then curtly made plain that she is to have no further involvement at all in the government of King Edward. And, furthermore, she is told that she can expect no help or support from her closest ecclesiastic adviser, Stigand. Her former priest who has risen to the position of Bishop of Elmham in East Anglia is, at this very time, being divested of his office.

Emma does not attempt to question her son's sudden judgement. She is not in a position even to protest, or to ask as to Stigand's alleged misdeeds. The treasury keys are presented to the King and while she and her retainers are left in the custody of the housecarls, Edward and his earls explore the storehouse of royal riches that she has been holding. And what treasures they find. Among the fortune that was amassed by King Cnut, snatched by Harold Harefoot and then reclaimed and added to by King Harthacnut and the Queen Mother herself are goblets of gold encrusted with precious stones; quantities of gold and silver coins; imported silks; beautifully bound and decorated books; and a number of priceless relics. A skull is identified as the head of St Ouen; a bone as part of the arm of St Augustine.[3] King Edward requisitions the former; Earl Leofric, the latter. They take these sacred items as future gifts for churches of their choosing: such donations will usefully cast them as gracious and extremely generous benefactors.

Their business done, Edward and his earls depart as abruptly as they arrived, carrying off some of the royal treasures and leaving several housecarls to guard the rest of the hoard in the storehouse. The Lady and her retainers, meanwhile, are released, deeply shocked and in a state of confusion following the unprecedented actions of the King. Many of the Queen Mother's retinue will no longer be able to remain in her household and will need to attach themselves quickly to other patrons. Those whom the Lady is able to keep in her employment face almost as much uncertainty. Royal though she is, Emma has suddenly become a figure of disgrace. A mighty queen and symbol of survival has been ignominiously reduced.

Emma is, of course, no stranger to misfortune: she has weathered Viking invasions, been widowed twice, twice driven into exile and lost two sons. So far she has managed to triumph over her setbacks and recover from her tragedies. However, to be publicly humiliated and stripped of most of her property by her eldest son seems the cruellest blow of all. An old woman who has until now been able to twist most events to her advantage, she faces a bleak future in the twilight zone of near banishment.

*   *   *

That it took a king and three earls to remove an elderly lady from a position of apparently self-appointed control is either a reflection of how much power Emma still exercised despite her distance from the day-to-day business of court life, or an indication of the animosity in which she was held. Possibly both. Edward undoubtedly felt he had good cause for turning against his mother. He was probably much encouraged by Emma's friend-turned-adversary Godwine, and perhaps to a lesser degree by Leofric and Siward. It was evidently a jaw-dropping act, and was reported with scandalised overtones in the meagre records that survive from the period.

The *Anglo-Saxon Chronicles* give a number of reasons as to why Edward suddenly seized movable wealth and land from the Queen Mother. In one version it is because 'earlier she was very hard on the king her son', ascribing to Edward an understandable and abiding resentment of the way his mother had abandoned him a great many years beforehand. Another chronicler comments that the Lady 'did less for him [Edward] than he wanted before he became king, and also afterwards', suggesting that Emma was not only unsupportive of Edward in earlier years but that she was also churlishly uncooperative after his coronation. However, in addition, some of the chronicles allege that Emma wilfully withheld the royal treasure from the King: 'she had kept it from him too firmly'. Meanwhile one chronicler writes that Emma's ecclesiastic councillor Stigand was punished because he was purportedly the real source of the problem and had been misguiding the Queen Mother all along: he was 'put out of his bishopric and all that he owned was taken into the king's hand, because he was his mother's closest advisor and because she did just as he advised her – so men supposed'.

It would be belittling Emma to suggest that her actions were entirely directed by her former priest. However, it is, of course, perfectly possible that Stigand egged her on in the role she assumed as custodian of the royal coffers. He was a very deft political operator, and Emma's move to assume a position of power even if distanced from the court was shrewd if not ingenious. Yet both bishop and Queen Mother clearly overstepped the mark and their fall was abrupt, severe, and apparently unexpected. It is no coincidence that a large chunk of Emma's property in the very part of the country where Stigand had been bishop was rapidly given by Edward to the church of Bury St Edmunds.

But shocking though it was, the dual disgrace was not enduring. Within a year Stigand was restored as Bishop of Elmham, and continued to enjoy a burgeoning career, later to become both Bishop of Winchester and Archbishop of Canterbury. Emma, meanwhile, must have lobbied hard and inveigled her remaining friends – both ecclesiastic and aristocratic – to plead with the King on her behalf. She duly recovered her dignity and during 1044 appears to have been rehabilitated by Edward. Among the surviving charters that she witnessed that year are records of a grant of land in Witney, Oxfordshire, given by Edward to Aelfwine, Bishop of Winchester, and another grant from the King of fifteen hides in Somerset made over to the Old Minster in Winchester.[4] In both documents Emma, still referred to as Aelfgifu, is listed second only to the monarch. Edward, it seems, had formally forgiven his mother and, judging by the fact that her East Anglian lands were restored, he no doubt returned most of her property to her. But whether the former splendour of Emma's life was fully resumed in 1044 is not known, and nor is the extent of her influence beyond Winchester.

Yet however rapidly she was reinstated, Emma's fall became the stuff of legend. Rumours about her very public disgrace circulated long

after the event and acquired something of a life of their own, particularly in the tales told after the Norman Conquest. William of
Malmesbury,[5] writing towards the end of the eleventh century, reports
that at the start of his reign Edward was regarded as a naïve ruler,
totally in thrall to Godwine and his sons and unaware of increasing
levels of corruption in law courts and monasteries across the country.
William writes that, according to popular stories, Edward's mother,
meanwhile, had transferred her contempt for her first husband to their
son and, worse, rapaciously 'stuffed her money bags with bullion gathered from every source', refusing to give any of it to the poor and
destitute. William himself comments that in his opinion Emma was a
'saintly' woman who gave generously to the churches of Winchester
and other religious houses, but he reports that in folk tales it was not
considered dishonourable when the ostensibly wicked Queen Mother
was stripped of her unjustly hoarded riches so that those in need might
benefit.

William's contemporary, Goscelin of Canterbury,[6] offers a rather
wilder version of Emma's fall from grace. He records that she was
punished under suspicion of an act of gross treason, having allegedly
been supporting a Norwegian campaign to invade England. Ostensibly
she supplied Magnus the Good of Norway with treasure and other
resources so as to help fund an imminent attack – hence the fact that
her riches were taken from her. The theory is unlikely but not completely
beyond the bounds of possibility. It is, at a pinch, conceivable that Emma
was so disaffected by Edward's alliance with Godwine, who was after
all held largely responsible for the murder of one of her children, that
she agreed to act in league with England's Norwegian enemy. Indeed,
until Magnus's death on 25 October 1047, there were many rumours
that he was about to invade – and the *Anglo-Saxon Chronicles* record
that in 1044[7] King Edward set out from Sandwich with thirty-five ships,
which may well have been have been a defensive measure to drive away
a Scandinavian fleet. How, though, Emma herself would actually have
benefited from a liaison with the Norwegian ruler is very much open
to question.

Yet humiliation as punishment for a purported act of betrayal is by no means the end of Goscelin's tale, which becomes ever more colourful. The fallen queen, he claims, was saved through the intercession of St Mildreth, or Mildred. The seventh-century Kentish saint was believed to be especially supportive of widows and had good cause to be grateful to Cnut and Emma. Amid much fanfare, they had orchestrated the removal of Mildreth's body from its initial resting place at Minster in Thanet, where the saint had been a brave, blameless and thoroughly godly abbess, to the church of St Augustine in Canterbury. In recompense St Mildreth was particularly protective of her benefactors. Cnut she had earlier saved from near shipwreck on his return from pilgrimage to Rome.[8] Now Emma needed her help. From beyond her new and much visited shrine at Canterbury St Mildreth ostensibly used her spiritual influence to ensure that the disgraced queen received earthly redemption and guided Edward into restoring his mother to a position of honour.

In a late-twelfth-century account, however, it is St Swithin who is principally credited with rescuing Emma, in thoroughly dramatic circumstances, as relayed by one Richard of the monastery at Devizes. In Richard's tale[9] Edward accuses his mother not of hoarding treasure or of plotting treasonous acts but of sexual misconduct.

Chronologically tangled and factually very garbled, the story seems primarily to have been written to expose the extent of pernicious Norman influence on Edward's reign. Richard records that the King of England summoned a number of high-profile courtiers and clergy from the land of his exile and gave them prominent jobs in his new kingdom. Among the Norman newcomers was the senior ecclesiastic Robert, from the large monastery of Jumièges, who was appointed Bishop of London and then Archbishop of Canterbury. He became a very controversial figure. Under Robert's guidance, Edward strips his mother of all her riches and shuts her away in Wherwell convent.[10] Meanwhile he also confiscates the land and wealth of the Bishop of Winchester, Aelfwine,[11] who is charged with being the Queen Mother's lover. This impeachment would not necessarily have indicated that Emma acquired a reputation for moral degeneracy or indeed sexual prowess: accusations of debauchery between royalty and important members of the clergy were not altogether uncommon[12] as convenient ploys to remove and redirect political power.

In Richard's tale, Emma is mortified at the situation, not so much on her own account as that of the innocent bishop. From her convent-prison she manages to send out letters to several other bishops who she hopes have remained loyal to her. In these missives she swears that she and Aelfwine are guiltless and have never done anything shameful. She says that she is prepared to let God show that they are beyond reproach and asks the bishops to persuade the King that she should undertake a trial by ordeal in front of him at Old Minster in Winchester. She is confident that St Swithin, whose great tomb lies in the church, will guide and protect her.

In the early-medieval period, there were effectively two ways of determining whether an alleged offender was innocent. If the individual's lord or other appointed 'oath-helpers' swore an oath attesting to his or her good character, the accused could thereby be exonerated. Such a pledge was extremely serious and presumably would not be undertaken lightly, although how far this differed from the sworn evidence of actual witnesses is not clear. The other method of judgement was trial by ordeal, the results of which were decided by God. The accused was subjected to an excruciatingly painful exercise and innocence was proven if God saw fit to allow the individual to survive unharmed or to ensure that the resulting wounds healed quickly. The ordeals most often involved fire or water. The accused might be thrown into a deep pond or tank, ordered to lift a large stone out of a vat of boiling water or made to walk a number of paces either clutching a fired iron bar or treading on the scalding substance.

In Richard of Devizes' story, Emma asks to be tried by white-hot metal. Edward hears her request and announces that such an ordeal can take place provided Archbishop Robert agrees[13] – Richard comments that the King is so swayed by the Norman ecclesiastic he would claim black is white if so told by this adviser rather than believe the evidence of his own eyes. The Archbishop expostulates that Emma is a thoroughly evil woman who agreed to the murder of her son Alfred and who has also plotted to poison her other son King Edward, but because she is a queen she has the right to request a trial. She should, he says, be made to take nine steps barefoot on nine white-hot ploughshares – the large cutting blades used for turning over soil. Four steps should be taken on her own behalf, five on the part of Bishop Aelfwine. Should she fail to tread fully on each ploughshare, should she stumble, or should she sustain any injury at all she will be deemed a wicked fornicator.

A day is set for the trial, and news of the impending event quickly spreads across the kingdom. More people gather at Winchester than have ever been seen there before. The bishops make their way to the city; the King arrives; Aelfwine is summoned to attend; the Queen is fetched. The only person missing is Archbishop Robert, who pretends to be ill and slinks off to Dover so that if the judgement fails to show Emma guilty he can make a hasty exit from England.

Richard writes that the night before her ordeal the Queen keeps a vigil beside the tomb of St Swithin at the Old Minster. She falls asleep for a short time and hears the voice of the blessed saint telling her not to be afraid and assuring her that her persecutors will be shamed. The next day the clergy and a great host of people crush into the church. The King himself sits apart on a raised platform. Emma is brought before him and publically proclaims her innocence of any crimes against him and against Alfred, and denies the charge of sinful acts with Bishop Aelfwine. Meanwhile nine white-hot ploughshares are placed in a line along the nave of the church. After a short blessing the Queen's shoes are removed and her outer robes divested. Then, flanked by two bishops who display far more apprehension than she does, Emma is led to her ordeal.

Against a noisy and mournful backdrop of public weeping and urgent supplications to St Swithin to protect the Queen, Emma calmly walks down the nave of the church, treading firmly on each ploughshare. But she does not see the blades nor does she feel the heat. She reaches the church doors and, sensing that she is being taken outside by the two accompanying bishops, she asks when her trial will begin. Amazed, they tell her to look back and see that her ordeal is over. She turns around – and realises that a miracle has been performed: St Swithin has saved her.

Richard recounts that Emma is then led to the King, now lying prostrate on the ground. She shows him her feet, marvellously unharmed, and he begs her forgiveness. The Queen, however, refuses to grant Edward pardon until he has rectified matters with Bishop Aelfwine. This he duly does. Then both Emma and the bishop are honourably given back all their property. In gratitude for the miracle in turn they each give nine manors – that Richard does not name – to St Swithin, which in effect means that they donate these estates to the Old Minster. Archbishop Robert, meanwhile, flees from the country, never to return.

Richard's story is, of course, thoroughly apocryphal. There is no evidence that Emma was ever tried for any crimes, and there are several very glaring inaccuracies in the tale: it was Stigand not Aelfwine who was close to Emma (the confusion probably arising because Stigand later became Bishop of Winchester); it was Edith, Emma's daughter-in-law, who was later sent to the convent of Wherwell; and, probably most significant of all, Robert of Jumièges did not, in fact, arrive in England until 1044, the year after Emma's disgrace. Yet the story does show that, long after her death, Emma had become absorbed into folklore. Domineering yet devout, she evidently fired the popular imagination. However, she was not the only eleventh-century noblewoman to do so. One of Emma's direct contemporaries may have been just as strong-willed: she inspired another colourful legend, laced with its own risqué element.

In the year of Emma's disgrace the foundations were, quite literally, laid for a myth that was to be far more enduring than any story about the Norman queen. Sometime during 1043[14] Earl Leofric and his wife funded the establishment of a monastery at Coventry, and so started a personal connection with the town. Leofric had risen to power under Cnut, who had appointed him Earl of Mercia; he had later supported Harold Harefoot's claim to the throne but had then made himself amenable to King Harthacnut; along with Godwine he was now one of King Edward's chief advisers. Emma would have known him and his wife Godgifu, or Godiva, for a great many years.

Stories about Godgifu must have been in circulation for a good century and a half before the first known account of her actions was published. The author was Roger of Wendover,[15] writing at about the same time as Richard of Devizes. Heavy taxation forms the political backdrop to his tale: *Danegeld*, the nationwide defence tariff instigated by Aethelred back in 1012, continued to be exacted until 1051. On top of this there would have been other royal levies, although in view of the fact that Harthacnut had made himself deeply unpopular through his steep financial demands, Edward may have been wary about imposing too many tolls on his subjects.

Nevertheless, in addition there appear to have been a growing number of local taxes that were bitterly resented. Such, it seems, was the case in Coventry, which fell under the jurisdiction of Earl Leofric. According to Roger, Leofric's wife Godgifu was a woman of great Christian charity. She was deeply concerned for the people of the town where she had become a great patron and she begged her husband to release them from their oppressive financial burdens. But, Roger comments, Leofric merely scoffed at her, remarking that she was foolish for making an appeal that would be greatly to his disadvantage and he tried to forbid her from raising the issue ever again. Yet Godgifu was determined to pursue the matter and so exasperated her husband with her constant pleadings that he made an outrageous stipulation: if she would mount her horse and ride naked from one end of Coventry's market to the other he would grant her request. So, writes Roger, Godgifu loosened her hair, which then covered her undressed body like a veil, and accompanied by two 'knights' set off on horseback through the market 'without being seen, except her fair legs'. On her return, her astonished husband had no honourable option but to rescind the taxes, a deed that Roger claims Leofric confirmed by charter, although no such document now exists.

Later embellishments were added to this myth: notably a request by Godgifu that all the people of Coventry should remain indoors during her ride; and a seventeenth-century addition of a voyeur, Peeping Tom, who is variously struck blind or dies after stealing a look.

Whatever the truth behind the evolving story of the Lady Godgifu, the flesh-and-blood woman is known to have had an extremely long and affluent life. She survived her husband by at least ten years and died well into her sixties, possibly even in her seventies, sometime after the Norman Conquest. *Domesday Book*, William the Conqueror's tax survey of 1086, records, probably posthumously, that in her own right Godgifu owned large amounts of land in Leicestershire, Nottinghamshire and Warwickshire.

Rich as Godgifu and her husband were, their wealth was barely on a level with that of England's other great noble family, the Godwines. Leofric and Godwine had been in power for roughly the same period, had backed different political candidates during the crisis of 1036, and were no doubt arch rivals at Edward's court. Godwine's supremacy, however, was very publicly confirmed on 23 January 1045 when the King married one of his daughters.

During the many years of his exile in Normandy, Edward had been unable to marry, or at least to marry nobly, because without land and without significant riches he had nothing to offer. In 1045 he was aged about forty, well past his prime and extremely old to be taking a wife for the very first time. He would hardly have been considered a bride-groom of obvious vigour by his new spouse, Edith, who was at least fifteen years his junior. She was one of nine or so children who were born to Godwine and his Danish wife Gytha between about 1020 and 1035. Partly brought up at the enclosed royal convent at Wilton, Edith had some formal education and, according to the book she herself later commissioned,[16] she 'diligently' read religious and secular books and 'excelled' in the art of writing prose and verse. In the two years between Edward's coronation and her marriage to the new king her family had placed themselves centre-stage at the royal court and had become ever more powerful: in 1043 her eldest brother Swein was given an earldom made up of shires in Somerset, Berkshire, Oxfordshire and Herefordshire; in 1044 her next brother Harold was created Earl of East Anglia. The following year Edith herself was fully consecrated as Queen of England.

Emma must have been appalled. Edward had formed bonds of kinship with the man who had as good as murdered his brother. Worse, from a personal perspective, was the very existence of a daughter-in-law – the crowned consort of her son. Limited though her involvement in Edward's regime may have been, Emma would now be superseded as queen by Godwine's daughter. She had become an almost powerless figure of the past.

There would have been little option but for the Queen Mother to retire gracefully. She may, however, have witnessed a final charter after Edward's wedding. A document dated 1 August 1045[17] confirms privileges conferred by the King on the abbey of Westminster, a church Edward was later gloriously and famously to revamp. It is a dubious record and may well have been forged after the Norman Conquest, but the list of witnesses is thought to have been copied from an earlier, authentic charter. 'Aelfgifu Emma, mother of the king' is ranked immediately after the monarch; Edith, the King's consort, is placed just below this redoubtable woman.

Thereafter Emma's name disappears from the remaining records of court business, and Emma herself presumably retreated from public life. She may have elected to live quietly in Winchester, either at the palace or on the small manor she owned in the city. There is no evidence to suggest that she ever formally withdrew to a convent, the conventional retirement of a great many widows, but during her dotage she may have toured some of the many religious establishments that she had so flamboyantly patronised. She clearly retained an active interest in Christian business on the Continent for she is known to have helped fund the building of the church of Saint-Hilaire in Poitiers, which was inaugurated in 1049.

During 1050, Emma would have heard, doubtless with some satisfaction, of a growing rift between Godwine and the King. It was then that Edward appointed Robert of Jumièges as Archbishop of Canterbury and in doing so affronted his father-in-law, whose ecclesiastic kinsman Aethelric was widely considered the candidate of choice for this senior church office. The following year relations between Edward and Godwine collapsed completely.

The breakdown between the King and his most powerful earl occurred in the autumn of 1051 and began with a visit to England by

Eustace of Boulogne. He had married Emma's daughter Godgifu in about 1036 but she may have fairly recently died for in 1049 Eustace took a new wife, Ida of Bouillon. The reason for his trip to England is not recorded: the *Anglo-Saxon Chronicles* elliptically state that he arrived, spoke with the King 'about what he wanted' and then 'turned homeward'.[18] Eustace may have come to discuss issues of succession with Edward who, after more than five years of marriage, remained childless. At the same time, he may also have paid his respects to his former mother-in-law. Such matters were probably unrecorded because they paled into insignificance by comparison to the national crisis that was sparked during the return leg of Eustace's journey.

The Count of Boulogne and his men reached Canterbury, in Godwine's territory of Wessex, where they had a meal. They proceeded on to Dover, planning to spend the night there before sailing home across the Channel. Either they were anticipating problems or were intending to create trouble: the *Anglo-Saxon Chronicles* comment that they put on their coats of mail before arriving in the town. While looking for accommodation at Dover they fell into an argument with a disobliging householder and wounded him. In retaliation he killed one of Eustace's men and a full-blown fight ensued. It was a bloody business. The fatalities numbered twenty townspeople and nineteen of the Count's party. Eustace and his remaining men fled. They returned to the King and complained about the savagery. Edward then ordered Godwine to punish the folk of Dover but the Earl refused to show any hostility to his own people. In an attempt to resolve an increasingly ugly situation, a meeting of the King's *witan* was then called in Gloucestershire. But by now the antagonism had spiralled out of control. Godwine's most prominent political rivals Leofric and Siward arrived to support Edward with well-armed troops while the Godwine family called up their own men. Outright civil war seemed a distinct possibility so the meeting was adjourned and postponed. Twelve days later, on 21 September, the King and his council gathered in London to meet the Godwines. The upshot was that almost the entire clan – Godwine and his wife Gytha, and his sons Swein, Harold, Tostig, Gyrth and Leofwine – were outlawed. Meanwhile Godwine's daughter Edith, the consecrated Queen of England who had so far failed to produce an heir to the throne, was rejected by the King and sent away to the convent of Wherwell.

In just one version of the *Anglo-Saxon Chronicles*[19] a brief record states that shortly after this 'Earl' William arrived from 'beyond the sea' – in other words, Normandy – with a large troop of Frenchmen. He was apparently received by the King, and then departed. Such a visit would have been extremely significant but since it is not mentioned anywhere else in either English or Norman documents, there is some doubt as to whether it actually took place. It is tempting, though, to think that William came to discuss issues of inheritance and during the trip called on his great-aunt Emma.

At the time, she may have felt triumphant at the downfall of the great Godwine family. To her this must have been tantamount to divine justice: retribution, at last, for the death of Alfred. Within less than a year the Godwines were, in fact, to be pardoned[20] and reinstated while their principal enemies, including Archbishop Robert, were banished. Leofric, Siward and Bishop Stigand had tactically counselled the King that he had little option in this matter if he wanted to keep the kingdom united and avert the possibility of internal warfare. Stigand subsequently profited hugely from the advice and succeeded Robert as Archbishop of Canterbury.

The Queen Mother, however, did not live long enough to know of this or of the Godwines' recovery. She died on 6 March 1052, aged nearly seventy, a very old lady indeed. Despite the ongoing dramas about the Godwines that were being recorded in England at the time, Emma merited a final mention in the *Anglo-Saxon Chronicles*. 'Here in this year passed away Aelfgifu Emma, mother of King Edward and of King Harthacnut.' It was not exactly a fitting tribute for the woman who had survived so much, had triumphed against enormous odds and had exerted a staggering amount of power and influence over the nation. Death, however, is not entirely the end of Emma's story.

Epilogue

Emma was buried in the Old Minster at Winchester. It must have been in a spirit of generosity that Edward allowed his mother to be interred there, alongside her second husband Cnut, rather than with his father Aethelred at the church of St Paul in London. The Old Minster, however, was not her final resting place.

In 1093 the building was demolished to make room for a Norman cathedral that had been under construction beside it (and practically on top of it) for the last thirteen years. Sometime beforehand, the remains of the great and the good were exhumed from the Anglo-Saxon minster and transferred to the new church. Royalty and bishops are believed to have been reburied around St Swithin's shrine, rebuilt behind the high altar. Among them were the bodies of Emma, Cnut and also Stigand, who died in 1072. During the Reformation many of the Anglo-Saxon notables, along with several later regal and ecclesiastic corpses, were again dug up and the bones placed in mortuary chests. Somewhat unfortunately, Cnut and Emma were made to form a foursome by sharing a box with Bishop Aelfwine and also Rufus, son of William the Conqueror and one of England's most unpopular monarchs (he was the king who, to the relief of many, died in 1100 after being shot, reputedly with a single arrow, while out hunting). The mortuary chests remained undisturbed for about a century. But during the Civil War of 1642–6 Winchester's great church was vandalised by Parliamentarian troops: its famous library was badly damaged and many of its tombs, statues and stained-glass windows were desecrated. According to *Mercurius Rusticus*, the newsbook of the Royalists, Cromwell's soldiers smashed those windows they were unable to reach with the butts of their muskets by chucking at them the bones of kings, queens and bishops. In other words the mortuary caskets were raided for useful ammunition. The contents were then left strewn around the Cathedral amidst shards of glass. It would have been an impossible task subsequently to identify all the bones. These were returned *ad hoc* to the chests, which were subsequently placed at the top of the screen around the choir, where they remain. One box bears a Latin label in sixteenth-century hand claiming that therein are Kings Cnut and Rufus, Queen Emma and Bishop Aelfwine. In reality, however, Emma's remains lie spread about in this and other boxes, jumbled among the bones of her aforesaid companions as well as her close friend Stigand, King Egbert of the seventh century, King Cynegils of the sixth, and several others.

Elsewhere in Winchester it is remarkable that more than 950 years after her death there is still some evidence of the life of this formidable queen. On the city's busy High Street a restaurant occupies Godbegot House, a later medieval building that was constructed on the site of Emma's manor house and that still bears its name. It was part of the estate that she was given by Aethelred in 1012. This lay within the north side of the city walls near the market place and encompassed a church dedicated to St Peter. A surviving charter[1] from 1012 states that the Queen is free to dispose of the estate however she wishes, and that its inhabitants are to be exempt from any obligations to the King – which would have included taxes as well as the repair of bridges and military service. Emma's will does not survive but she is believed to have bequeathed the property, along with a small estate at Hayling Island in Hampshire, to the Old Minster,[2] one of her attendants, Wulfweard White, being given a life-interest in five hides of the latter. Astonishingly, the Godbegot estate retained its privileges for just a shade off 530 years. It remained independent of the jurisdiction of the King, and indeed the city mayor, until just after the Reformation: a court roll of Henry VIII rescinded its rights in 1541.[3]

Intriguing though the survival of Emma's more manifest effects may be, her intangible legacy is of far greater significance. It was through her that a new and enduring dynasty was founded in England. In her lifetime Emma had tried to push the role of Queen Mother, but after her death it was as an aunt that she became a more potent figure, and it was this kinship that effectively legitimised the takeover of a foreign invader.

Her own children did not supply any lasting heirs to the crown. Emma was predeceased by at least two of her five offspring. Alfred and Harthacnut had both been unmarried, and had both died without issue. In addition, it is likely that Godgifu, her daughter by Aethelred, died before she did. Godgifu, however, did have children: with her first husband, the Count of Amiens and the Vexin, she is known to have raised at least two sons; she seems to have been less productive with her second husband, Eustace of Boulogne, by whom she appears to have had just one daughter. Meanwhile Gunnhild, Emma's daughter by Cnut, had either died or was in religious retreat at the time of her mother's funeral. By then, Gunnhild's only child, Beatrice, may have become an ordained nun at the convent of Quedlinburg in Germany. Most importantly, however, Edward was childless. This situation was later ascribed to his godliness – after the Norman Conquest stories were to circulate that due to religious scruples he never consummated his marriage.

At the time of his mother's death, the King of England was about forty-seven years old and by that stage, and age, he seems to have had little expectation of fathering any children. His seven years of marriage had not produced any male heirs – or even daughters – and he had in any case banished his wife. He may even have considered divorcing her. Although Edith was later reinstated at court, her failure to provide any successors to the throne may have become an embarrassment. By the mid-1050s Edward had started to flirt with a number of potential successors. It was a means of flexing much diplomatic and political muscle.

He may have dangled the possibility of attaining the crown at his nephews, Godgifu's sons. They were his closest blood relations. In particular, Ralf of Mantes seems to have been especially favoured: he may have first arrived in England in 1041 as part of Edward's original entourage, and he appears to have been created Earl of Hereford in 1050. But neither he nor his elder brother Walter survived Edward. Walter died, childless, in 1064; Ralf in 1057, his son Harold becoming a ward of the royal court. By that juncture, though, Emma's one known great-grandson would have been well down the list of the King's possible beneficiaries. Edward had made overtures to far grander candidates, and he was profligate with his promises.

According to the German chronicler Adam of Bremen,[4] Cnut's nephew Swein of Denmark was recognised as Edward's heir. In the 1050s and 1060s Scandinavian ambitions for the English throne were by no means an issue of the past and this ostensible agreement was said to have been part of an Anglo-Danish alliance against Norwegian aggression. It is, however, extremely unlikely that the arrangement would have been formally ratified by the King of England, and even if a pledge was ever made in all seriousness it was by no means exclusive.

Norman chroniclers maintain that Edward felt beholden to the court of his exile. They claim that as a result Duke William, the son of Emma's nephew Robert, became the acknowledged heir to the King of England. The most detailed of the reports comes from William of Poitiers.[5] He alleges that binding oaths were duly sworn to this effect in England by Leofric, Siward and Stigand, that the arrangement was brokered by Archbishop Robert, and that Godwine's young son Wulfnoth and his grandson Hakon were then given as hostages to Duke William – surety of the King's good intentions. If this were indeed the case, the pledge must have been made before the end of 1052, the year in which Archbishop Robert was banished from England. It is also likely that the hapless Godwine hostages were offered at a time when most of the rest of their family were in exile – and when there would be little objection to Wulfnoth and Hakon being shipped over to Normandy. This would date the arrangement more narrowly to between 1051 and 1052, lending some credence to the story that William visited his elder cousin Edward at that stage. Emma would still have been alive then and it is appealing to imagine that shortly before she died the old queen had some influence over the promise of succession to one of her Norman kinsmen.

For all the Norman writers' claims, however, Edward evidently did not consider himself committed to William. Just a couple of years later

he started actively seeking out another of his relatives, long overlooked yet with as much claim to the throne as he had – possibly
more. For about thirty-five years the royal court in Hungary had been
providing an honourable place of exile for the only other surviving
descendants of Aethelred from the male line. Edward's elder half-
brother, Edmund Ironside, who had briefly been king of half of England
and had been murdered in 1016, had fathered two sons both of whom
had been hurriedly sent away from England when Cnut was declared
king. One boy had died soon afterwards, the other was brought up
among the entourage of the Magyar king, Stephen I. As a former exile
himself, Edward may have felt some sympathy for this nephew. But
although a refugee for most of his life, the Prince – also called Edward
– had been treated well in Hungary and despite his lack of wealth
had married into the royal family there. By the time his uncle started
to make formal enquiries about him he had produced three children:
two girls and a boy, Edgar. In 1057 it seems that the entire family
came to England on the King's invitation. Edward 'the Exile', however,
never met his uncle: he died shortly after arrival and was buried with
due ceremony at St Paul's in London. His children were quickly
absorbed into the English court. In particular, the young Edgar, little
more than five years old on his father's death, was nurtured by both
King Edward and Queen Edith.

But for all that Edward lined up nominees for the throne, he failed
to provide any confirmation as to who was the heir apparent. Meanwhile,
the Godwine family was becoming ever more powerful despite the period
of their disgrace.

The Earl himself, however, died in the year after his return to court.
According to William of Malmesbury,[6] God finally punished him for his
complicity in Alfred's death. He was, William writes, dining with the
King one day when the murdered prince's name came up in conversa-
tion. Godwine apparently announced that he was innocent of any
involvement in Alfred's death and proclaimed that God would prevent
him from swallowing if his words were not true. He choked and died.
In less gossipy versions of his death he seems to have suffered a stroke.
The *Anglo-Saxon Chronicles*[7] record that on the second day of Easter,

1053, he was being entertained by the King at Winchester when he was suddenly rendered both paralysed and speechless. He did not recover and three days later 'gave up his life'. Edward appointed his son Harold to succeed him as Earl of Wessex.

Harold Godwineson flourished. As an active military commander he brought north Wales more or less under English control; as a landowner he amassed a fortune and became the richest person in the country after the monarch; and as an administrator he appears to have taken over much of the management of England. He was in effect Edward's regent. Meanwhile his brothers also prospered: Gyrth in East Anglia; Leofwine in the south-east; Tostig in the north – where he was created Earl of Northumbria in 1055. By the 1060s much of the kingdom was therefore collectively under the Godwines' immediate authority. However, due to heavy local taxes and a number of scandalous murders Tostig became much hated by the Northumbrians. In 1065 they rose against him – and Harold, rather than supporting his brother, persuaded the King to back the rebels. Tostig then fled to Flanders.

The following year, on 5 January, Edward died. He was an old man of about sixty-one and had been King of England for nearly twenty-four years. He was buried at Westminster Abbey, the church he had magnificently refounded on Thorney Island a few miles from London. It had been consecrated only the previous December. His patronage there was to have impressive dividends. It was largely thanks to the monks of Westminster, and to a lesser extent to a book[8] about his life commissioned by his wife Edith, that Edward earned a reputation for unswerving piety and holiness. Stories of miracles were recorded – amazing cures that purportedly took place not only at his tomb but also during his lifetime – and a cult rapidly grew. Ironically this was precisely the outcome his mother had tried to achieve for his murdered brother through her own patronage and publication. Emma's endeavours to create circumstances whereby Alfred would be sanctified had not been successful. But the spiritual champions of her eldest son were more effective, and nearly a century after Edward's death their objective was achieved. In 1161 Pope Alexander III officially declared Edward a saint and 'confessor' – the term essentially defining a fervent Christian who has not suffered martyrdom but has nevertheless led an outstandingly godly life.

In reality, Edward does not appear to have been exceptionally devout, and contemporary documents contain little to suggest that his demonstrations of Christian reverence extended much beyond the foundation of Westminster Abbey. But he seems to have been considered a thoroughly decent, clean-living king, and by comparison to his predecessor Harthacnut he must have been seen as a model of moderation. In the *Anglo-Saxon Chronicles* Edward's life is commemorated in a traditionally alliterative poem[9] in which he is described as 'good in virtues, pure and mild'. Perhaps too 'mild': despite his many and varied propositions to appoint a successor who was either a relative or of international political standing – and in the case of Duke William of Normandy, both – it seems that at the last moment he allowed himself to be swayed by his in-laws, the Godwine family. Reputedly, with his last breath he bequeathed the kingdom to his wife's brother Harold Godwineson, who was among the many people hovering around his deathbed.

Harold was crowned the next day. The ceremony, at Westminster Abbey, took place with unseemly speed straight after Edward's funeral – there can barely have been a pause between the two services. The *Anglo-Saxon Chronicles*[10] state with precision that he held the throne for forty weeks and one day. He appears to have encountered no opposition within the country but his brief reign was, of course, dominated by war.

That April a 'haired star', Halley's Comet, was seen in the night sky.[11] It was an ominous portent. In May Harold's exiled brother Tostig started to ravage the English coast, probably with Flemish mercenaries and presumably in an attempt to force the new king to restore his Northumbrian earldom. The outlaw then teamed up with the Norwegian king, Harold Hardrada (or 'Hard Ruler'), and with a combined fleet of more than 300 ships attacked the north-east of the country. With Harold and his troops in the south, the Norwegian and Flemish forces captured York, from where their commanders made plans to conquer the entire kingdom. The new king of England, however, rapidly made his way north and on 25 September launched an assault on the invaders. The battle took place at Stamford Bridge, about eight miles east of York. Tostig and Harold Hardrada were killed and their surviving troops fled.

So ended the very last Viking incursion of England. But in the meantime a belligerent Duke William, accompanied by a very large Norman army, was well on his way to the Sussex coast. Harold raced back south – a journey thought to have been undertaken in just five days. He heroically managed to muster a big force, and he famously confronted the Normans at the Senlac ridge near Pevensey on the morning of Saturday, 14 October. By the end of the day he, along with a great many Anglo-Saxon nobles and *ceorls*, was dead.

Harold's preoccupation with the Battle of Stamford Bridge and his geographical distance from the landing of the Normans were, clearly, contributing factors in his defeat by Emma's great-nephew. In addition, Norman cavalry gave the invaders a big advantage over the English forces: Anglo-Saxon nobles may have ridden to war but they did not use their valuable mounts on the battlefield. The Bayeux Tapestry, that glorious piece of Norman propaganda, shows how William's cavalry soldiers brought their horses across the Channel crammed, astonishingly, into their boats – longships not dissimilar to those of the flotilla in which Emma had originally arrived in England some sixty-four years before.

Aged thirty-nine, her great-nephew was crowned King of England on Christmas Day, 1066. He ruled the country for twenty-one years, ruthlessly crushing any opposition and peppering the country with stone castles that were symbols of his might and authority. He is held responsible for changing the language by bringing over large numbers of Norman governors, and he radically altered the social fabric of the nation by imposing a Norman type of feudalism. If he had peaceably inherited the kingdom would his reign have been so oppressive? On the other hand, if Harold had not procured the throne on Edward the Confessor's last gasp, would William necessarily have been the accepted heir of the Anglo-Saxon kingdom? Such questions are tantalising but, of course, unanswerable.

William, Duke of Normandy and King of England, died in Rouen on 9 September 1087. Among the colourful tales about his burial at the

Church of St Stephen in Caen is a story[12] that he was so corpulent his bowels burst as he was being squeezed into his sarcophagus. After this ignominious exit he was succeeded in Normandy by his eldest son Robert. England he bequeathed to his third son, William Rufus, who was succeeded by his brother Henry who, after a period of civil war, was succeeded by his grandson, another Henry, who was succeeded by his son Richard . . . so Emma's bloodline continued.

CHRONOLOGY

	Emma's life	England	Western Europe	Rest of World
880s			Rollo the Viking reaches northern France. He is later ceded territory here, which becomes known as Normandy	Vikings in Russia: Kiev becomes the capital of a state that extends from the Gulf of Finland almost to the Black Sea
		King Alfred of Wessex makes a treaty with Guthrum, leader of the Viking forces in the east of the country		
				Maori civilisation begins in New Zealand
978		Aethelred II crowned King of England		World's first novelist, Murasaki Shikibu, born in Japan (her book, *The Tale of Genji*, is written before 1026)
980s	Emma born towards the end of the decade	Second wave of Viking attacks starts	Hugh Capet becomes King of France	Viking voyagers reach Labrador, Canada
1002	Emma marries Aethelred	Massacre of the Danes	Brian Boroimhe recognised as high king of Ireland	Toltecs take over Mayan city of Chichen Itza in the Yucatan Peninsula
1005	Possible date of birth of Emma's son Edward	Famine throughout the country	Scottish chieftain Maelbeth, or Macbeth, born	

	Emma's life	England	Western Europe	Rest of World
1006–13	A daughter, Godgifu, and another son, Alfred, are born			
1013	Exile in Normandy	Swein Forkbeard conquers the country		
1017	Emma marries Cnut	The Viking invader Cnut crowned King of England	Cnut becomes King of Denmark	Byzantine emperor Basil II crushes the Bulgarians
1020s	Emma's son Harthacnut and daughter Gunnhild born	King Cnut visits Rome	Cnut becomes King of Norway Roger, Norman conqueror of Sicily, born (in 1061 he captures Messina from Muslim rulers)	Airlangga recognised as overlord of Java
1035		King Cnut dies on 12 November	Duke Robert I of Normandy dies on pilgrimage to Jerusalem	
1036	Attempts to claim the throne on behalf of her son Harthacnut	Emma's son Alfred murdered	Henry III King of Germany	

	Emma's life	England	Western Europe	Rest of World
1037	Exile in Bruges	Harold Harefoot declared king	Spanish warrior El Cid born	
1040	Returns to England	Harthacnut becomes king		Turkish Seljuk dynasty conquers most of Iran and Iraq
1042	Emma's book completed	King Harthacnut dies – Emma's son Edward is accorded the crown	Peter the Hermit, apostle of the First Crusade, born in Amiens	
1052	Emma dies in her late sixties (possible even seventy)	Exiled Godwine family reinstated		

Notes

PROLOGUE

1. See Campbell, Introduction to *Encomium Emmae Reginae* (Cambridge, 1998).
2. *An Atlas of Anglo-Saxon England*, D. Hill.
3. A. Hagen, *A Second Handbook of Anglo-Saxon Food and Drink* (Norfolk, 1995).
4. A. Werner, *The Changing Shape of Londoners from Prehistoric Times to the Present Day* (London, 1998).

CHAPTER ONE

1. The scene is based on the magnificent description of longships in Emma's manuscript *Encomium Emmae Reginae*, on records of near-contemporary royal weddings in Europe, and on images from the Bayeux Tapestry.
2. In his *Gesta Normannorum* Dudo skirts this issue and simply alludes to Poppa as the mother of Rollo's son William. There is no mention of the nature of this relationship, although the implication is that Poppa is simply a concubine. William of Jumieges adds the legitimising element in his *Gesta Normannorum Ducum*, and he identifies Poppa as the daughter of a distinguished man called Berengar. It is while on a rampage around Bayeux that Rollo takes up with her and shortly afterwards is 'bound' to her in accordance with these unspecified Danish customs.
3. Dudo was clearly flattering Gunnor, while also emphasising her Danish origins.
4. Dudo's *Gesta Normannorum* ends with the death of Richard I and the florid lamentations of his people.
5. Elisabeth van Houts makes this suggestion in 'Countess Gunnor of Normandy' (*Collegium Medievale 12*, 1999): it is known that Gunnor's brother Herfast, who served, possibly as a steward, at Richard II's court, held land in the Cotentin.
6. This tale is told by Robert of Torigni, a monk of Le Bec writing in the twelfth century. He revised earlier Norman histories and added details that he gleaned from descendants of Gunnor.
7. Translated by C. J. McDonough in *Warner of Rouen* (PIMS, 1995).
8. *Anglo-Saxon Chronicles* Peterborough manuscript (E) (London, 2001).

CHAPTER TWO

1. The by-law is mentioned in a grant of land in Canterbury, dated 888, although, given that the bishop elect of Sherborne is a witness, this may be a mistake for 868.
2. Canterbury Cathedral was, however, badly damaged by a fire in 1067 and subsequently rebuilt in the new, Norman style.
3. Written and illustrated between 820 and 840, the *Utrecht Psalter* is one of the finest examples of the style of art that developed during the period of the Carolingian empire.
4. 'Old English Riddles' from the *Exeter Book*, translated and edited by Michael Alexander (London, 1980).
5. Ibid.
6. But not rabbits: these were introduced by the Normans as a useful source of protein after 1066.
7. Eric Bloodaxe, the last Scandinavian king of York, was ousted and killed in 954.
8. The earliest surviving reference to 'the Danelaw' as an entity is in Aethelred's law codes of 1008.
9. *Anglo-Saxon Chronicles* Peterborough manuscript (E).
10. See P. Stafford, *Queen Emma & Queen Edith* (Oxford, 1997), p.216, and S. Keynes's *The Diplomas of King Aethelred the Unready* (Cambridge, 1980), pp.257–9 and 132–4.
11. Liturgy for a marriage service in use from the eleventh–sixteenth century. From the *Sarum Missal*, translated by Frederick E. Warren (London, 1911). See *Women's Lives in Medieval Europe* edited by Emilie Amt (Oxford, 1993), p.83. The topic is also discussed in Stafford, *Queen Emma & Queen Edith*, p.68.
12. According to the Venerable Bede in *Historia Ecclesiastica*, St Augustine arrived from Rome to convert the people of Kent in 597. About forty years later the Irish Church sent missionaries from Iona to convert the people of Northumbria.
13. Aelfric's *Lives of Saints Book I*, no. 17, De Auguris. See also B. Griffiths, *Aspects of Anglo-Saxon Magic* (Norfolk, 1996).
14. No. 37 in A. J. Robertson (ed.) *Anglo-Saxon Charters* (Cambridge, 1939).
15. Translated in *Councils & Synods 871–1204* D. Whitelock, M. Brett, C. N. L. Brooke ed. (Oxford, 1981).
16. *Anglo-Saxon Chronicles* Peterborough manuscript (E).
17. A translation of the letter is published in *English Historical Documents I* D. Whitelock ed. (Oxford, 1979).
18. The first three properties are listed in G. Gaimar's *L'Estoire des Engleis*. The *Anglo-Saxon Chronicles* tell us that Exeter was managed by Emma's reeve, or sheriff. See also Stafford *Queen Emma & Queen Edith*, p.128–30.
19. The 'Frideswide' charter detailed in Chapter Three.
20. Will of Wynflaed, *Anglo-Saxon Prose* M. Swanton ed. (London, 1993).
21. See D. Banham, Monasteriales Indicia (Norfolk, 1991).
22. Stafford, *Queen Emma & Queen Edith*, p.162.

23. A. Hagen, *A Second Handbook of Anglo-Saxon Food & Drink, Production and Distribution*, p.144.
24. Ibid., p.101.
25. Ibid., p.220.
26. R. Lavelle *Aethelred II* (Stroud, 2002), p.7.
27. As translated by Seamus Heaney (London, 1999).
28. During a banquet for Beowulf a minstrel sings the sad saga of Hildeburgh, a Danish princess married off to her family's enemy with tragic results. Later in the poem, Beowulf himself voices his doubts over the forthcoming marriage of the Danish king's daughter to a neighbouring ruler with a bloodthirsty grudge. The spear, Beowulf comments, is 'prompt to retaliate . . . no matter how admirable the bride may be' (translation by Seamus Heaney).

CHAPTER THREE

1. In Old English, *seo hlaefdige*, or the lady, is literally the bread server, while *hlaef*, or lord, means bread.
2. Equally, it might have been that Emma's predecessor was also required to assume the name of Aethelred's sainted grandmother.
3. For more on Aethelred's *witan* see Keynes *Diplomas*.
4. Holding two sees simultaneously was technically not permitted. But Wulfstan II, like his two predecessors, became Bishop of both York and of Worcester as a kind of double act. It was probable that the sees were originally united on the grounds that Northumbria had been ravaged by the Danes and the possession of the southern bishopric was necessary to maintain the northern one. However, in 1016 another Bishop of Worcester was appointed, probably acting under the auspices of Wulfstan.
5. *Anglo-Saxon Chronicles* Peterborough manuscript (E).
6. In *The Chronicle attributed to John of Wallingford* R. Vaughan ed., (London, 1958).
7. J. Campbell, in *The Anglo-Saxons* (London, 1991), suggests she may have been put on one side on the grounds that her marriage to Edgar was incestuous.
8. William of Malmesbury *De Gestis Regum*.
9. *English Historical Documents I*.
10. Henry of Huntingdon writes that she stabbed him with a dagger as she was giving him a cup to drink; Florence of Worcester maintains that Edward was unjustly murdered by his own men at the command of his stepmother, Queen Aelfthryth. Roger of Wendover asserts that Edward's stepmother 'allured him with her caresses, and kissing him offered him a cup, and as the king eagerly quaffed it, he was stabbed with a dagger by one of her attendants'.
11. *Passio Sancti Edwardi* see C. Fell, *Woman in Anglo-Saxon England* (London, 1984).
12. Abingdon manuscript (C).
13. Peterborough manuscript (E).
14. The Frideswide Charter, *English Historical Documents I*.

15. Lavelle, p.98
16. *English Historical Documents I.*

CHAPTER FOUR

1. 'Exeter was broken down through the French churl Hugh whom the Lady had set as her reeve.' *Anglo-Saxon Chronicles* Peterborough manuscript (E). This is the first known use of the word churl as a disparaging expression. Hugh is referred to as a count in later chronicles describing this event. There is no surviving information as to what happened to him: he might have fled, he may, however, have been killed by angry Devonians.

2. Gunnhild is not mentioned in the *Anglo-Saxon Chronicles*; the story comes from William of Malmesbury writing in the 1120s.

3. This description of Swein's fleet comes from the *Anglo-Saxon Chronicles* Peterborough manuscript (E).

4. Details of the document, known as 'Northumbrian Priests' or 'Law of the North People' are given in F. Stenton, *Anglo-Saxon England* (Oxford, 1998) pp.508–9.

5. From Alfred's introduction to his Anglo-Saxon translation of Boethius's Latin *Consolation of Philosophy*. Although probably not original with Alfred, it is in an addition to his translation that the notion of three estates that, respectively, pray, fight, and work surfaces for the first time. Alfred comments on the 'tools' by which a king reigns: '. . . he must have prayer-men and army-men and workmen (*gebedmen, fyrdmen, weorcmen*) . . . without these tools no king can exhibit his craft.'

6. D. Whitelock, *The Beginnings of English Society* (London, 1952), p.108.

7. Translated in *Councils & Synods AD 871–1204.*

8. Peterborough manuscript (E).

9. According to the Jomsviking saga.

10. S911, considered authentic.

11. S. Crawford, *Childhood in Anglo-Saxon England* (Stroud, 1999).

12. *Leechdoms, Wortcunning and Starcraft of Early England* vol. I, collected and edited by Revd Oswald Cockayne (London, 1864).

13. Ibid., Vol. III.

14. Ibid., Vol. I.

15. *Gesta Regum Anglorum.*

16. Roger of Wendover's *Flowers of History*, translated by J. A. Giles (London, 1849).

17. Florence of Worcester died in 1118 and his original chronicle was produced, edited and expanded by another monk, John of Worcester. How far John would have altered Florence's comments is a matter of some debate.

18. *Anglo-Saxon Chronicles* Peterborough manuscript (E).

19. Ibid.

20. *Councils & Synods 871–1204.*

21. Peterborough manuscript (E).

22. *The Chronicle of John of Worcester*, edited by R. R. Darlington and F. McGurk (Oxford, 1995).
23. *Anglo-Saxon Chronicles* Peterborough manuscript (E).
24. There are a few doubts as to the authenticity of the charter S925 granting Emma this land; however, a later writ of Edward the Confessor does confirm that the property belonged to her.

CHAPTER FIVE

1. 'And a great part of his [Swein Forkbeard's] people was drowned in the Thames, because they did not look out for any bridge' smirk the *Anglo-Saxon Chronicles* Peterborough manuscript (E).
2. According to William of Jumièges in *Gesta Normannorum Ducum*.
3. Ibid. William of Jumièges is the only source of this instance of Richard II's rapacious double dealing.
4. From Adam of Bremen's geographically astute if sanctimonious *History of the Archbishops of Hamburg-Bremen*, translated by Francis J. Tschan (Columbia, 2002).
5. William of Malmesbury, Roger of Wendover and Florence of Worcester are among those providing jubilant versions of this story of Swein's death.
6. *Anglo-Saxon Chronicles* Peterborough manuscript (E).
7. The story was first written down by Snorri Sturluson in the early-thirteenth century in *St Olaf's Saga*.
8. *Anglo-Saxon Chronicles* Peterborough manuscript (E).
9. Swanton, *Anglo-Saxon Prose*.
10. This version of events from Emma's author may be chronologically incorrect: Thorkell may not have reconciled himself with Cnut until after Aethelred's death (See Keynes in the Introduction to the 1998 reprint of *Encomium Emmae Reginae*).
11. A similar story is told in both the *Anglo-Saxon Chronicles* and Emma's book, *Encomium Emmae Reginae*; however, in Emma's version Edmund himself does not confront Cnut but sends messengers instead.
12. *The Chronicle of Henry of Huntingdon*, translated and edited by Thomas Forester (London, 1853).
13. Roger of Wendover's *Flowers of History*.

CHAPTER SIX

1. No figures are directly given as to London's population in the eleventh century – even *Domesday Book* (of 1086) omits the city. However, from archaeological evidence and tangential references in surviving documents it is estimated that Londoners numbered some 10,000 by the 1080s. Working backwards from this, a population of 8,000 seems feasible for the year 1017.
2. Until surprisingly recently the site of Lundenwic evaded archaeologists;

however, in 1988 excavations began to reveal traces of a settlement around
The Strand, Trafalgar Square and Covent Garden.

3. The creation of this cunning bypass is recorded in the *Anglo-Saxon Chronicles*
Peterborough manuscript (E).

4. No documentary evidence survives as to where Emma was at this stage. It is
likely, however, that she was with the King when he died in London – and was
subsequently trapped in the city.

5. Florence of Worcester (*Chronicon ex Chronicis*) maintains that Cnut's troops periodically left the siege of London to do battle elsewhere. However, it is likely that
at least some of the Danish force would have continued to guard and harass the
city.

6. Peterborough manuscript (E).

7. *Gesta Normannorum Ducum.*

8. Stafford, *Queen Emma and Queen Edith*, p.230.

9. S997a.

10. P. Dronke, *Poetic Individuality in the Middle Ages – New Departures in Poetry
1000–1150* (London, 1986).

11. E. van Houts, 'Countess Gunnor of Normandy' (*Collegium Medievale* 12, 1999).

12. *Encomium Emmae Reginae* p.33.

13. An extract of the *Chronicle of Thietmar of Merseburg* is printed in *English
Historical Documents I.*

14. *The Chronicle of Henry of Huntingdon.*

15. The Tower of London was the creation of William the Conqueror.

16. According to William of Malmesbury (*Gesta Regum Anglorum*), Eadwig was not
murdered in exile but later returned to England and was killed when he
attempted to rally a force against Cnut.

17. *L'Estorie des Engleis.*

18. See Stafford, *Queen Emma and Queen Edith*, p.175.

CHAPTER SEVEN

1. *Anglo-Saxon Chronicles* Worcester manuscript (D). The Peterborough manuscript (E) also mentions the occasion – simply reporting, 'And at Oxford Danes
and English were agreed'.

2. Swanton, *Anglo-Saxon Prose.*

3. R. K. Gordon ed. *Anglo-Saxon Poetry*, (London, 1954).

4. Charter S950 – where Lyfing is referred to by his other name, Aelfstan.

5. *Councils and Synods 871–1204.*

6. *History of the Archbishops of Hamburg–Bremen.*

7. *Anglo-Saxon Chronicles* Canterbury manuscript (F).

8. *Councils and Synods 871–1204.*

9. *English Historical Documents I.*

10. The exact dates of birth are not known. It is evident in the *Anglo-Saxon
Chronicles* that Harthacnut was a child or baby in 1023. Gunnhild's childhood
is more difficult to trace but it is known that she was married in 1036 – when

she may have been fourteen or older, and therefore born in 1022 or before.

11. Adam of Bremen's *Gesta* – see Lawson p.114.

12. This may be a gloss for Emma, however. See Stafford p.233 note 105 and M.K. Lawson *Cnut: The Danes in the Early Eleventh Century* (London, 1995), p.132.

13. *Councils and Synods 871–1204.*

CHAPTER EIGHT

1. The scene is based on a description of the translation of Aelfheah's body to Canterbury in the D manuscript (Worcester) of the *Anglo-Saxon Chronicles*, which lists the Bishops of Wells and Winchester as well as the Archbishop of Canterbury as being present. In addition special mention is made of Emma's attendance with Harthacnut. Although the occasion was witnessed by 'earls and very many, ordained and lay' there is no specific mention that either Godwine or Leofric were there – but given that there would have been a three-line whip for Cnut's close advisers to take an active part in the proceedings it seems more than likely that these councillors were also present. Lawson suggests, however, that Cnut remained in London and did not attend the final rites although Osbern (see below) has him steering the boat that carried the archbishop's relics to Rochester.

2. Further details about the removal of Aelfheah to Canterbury are recorded by the monk Osbern, writing just after the Norman Conquest, who claims that one of his sources – a monk named Godric – was an eyewitness to the events. It is from Osbern that details about Viking plans to throw Aelfheah's body in the Thames and about Cnut's soldiers being sent to protect the Canterbury monks are drawn. See D. Rollason, *Saints and Relics in Anglo-Saxon England* (Manchester, 1986) and N. Brooks, *The Early History of the Church of Canterbury* (Leicester, 1984).

3. According to the *Anglo-Saxon Chronicles* Winchester manuscript (A) this grant was not made until 1031, but given that the timing of events during Cnut's rule becomes confused in the chronicles it is probably more accurate to link the gift with other bounty bestowed on Christ Church in 1023.

4. Although this was apparently not the only occasion when Cnut gave away a crown. Goscelin in his *Translation of St Mildreth* claims that at Winchester one Easter Cnut refused to wear his crown and placed it instead on a crucifix, saying this was a more worthy place for it. See Rollason p.163.

5. Peterborough manuscript (E).

6. Lawson, p.93.

7. Abingdon manuscript (C).

8. Campbell, pp.84–5.

9. In England, the laws of both Aethelred and Cnut make it plain that a boy becomes responsible for paying compensation at this age.

10. Lawson, p.93.

11. *Flowers of History.*

12. In *Gesta Regum Anglorum.*

13. Which they date, probably erroneously, as 1031 – it is unlikely although not impossible that Cnut made two trips to Rome.
14. *Anglo-Saxon Chronicles* Peterborough manuscript (E).
15. Snorri Sturluson, 'St Olaf's Saga' in *Heimskringla, History of the Kings of Norway,* Lee M. Hollander (Texas, 1964), p. 447.
16. *History of the Archbishops of Hamburg–Bremen.*
17. In 1030, see the *Anglo-Saxon Chronicles* Peterborough manuscript (E).

CHAPTER NINE

1. This account for the most part remains faithful to the story of St Bartholomew's arm in Eadmer's *History of Recent Events in England.* There are, though, three additional suggestions. Firstly that the Bishop of Benevento periodically despatched his booty back to Apulia – it is unlikely that he would have been encumbered by obvious wealth. Secondly that Stigand was directly involved in the Bishop's negotiations with Emma: Eadmer makes no mention of him, but as Emma's priest at the time he was a probable conduit. Thirdly that the relics of St Swithin and St Wilfrid were placed on the altar of Christ Church: Eadmer writes that the bishop swore over other saints' relics, and in an account he also wrote about Christ Church Canterbury he specifically details St Swithin's and St Wilfrid's remains as belonging to the Cathedral.
2. T. A. Heslop, 'The production of de luxe manuscripts and the patronage of King Cnut and Queen Emma', *Anglo-Saxon England 19* (Cambridge, 1990).
3. In his *Gesta Pontificum Anglorum.* See also Heslop.
4. In *Chronicon monasterii de Abingdon* ed. J. Stevenson. See also Heslop.
5. Heslop.
6. Ibid.
7. Revelation ch. 20, vv. 12 and 15.
8. P. Nightingale, *The Ora, the Mark, and the Mancus: Weight-Standards and the Coinage in Eleventh-Century England* Numismatic Chronicle 144, 1984; and also Lawson, pp. 196–202.
9. IV Aethelstan 6.2, as cited in *The Blackwell Encyclopaedia of Anglo-Saxon England.*
10. The imperial image, however, is not unique to Cnut: issues of coins in the reigns of both Edgar and Aethelred II show the King's head similarly decorated.
11. This theory is brilliantly expounded by Keynes in 'The Aethlings in Normandy', Anglo Norman Studies, Vol. 13, 1991.
12. In *Gesta Normannorum Ducum.*
13. According to Roger of Wendover in *Flowers of History.*
14. According to Goscelin's *Life of St Wulfsige* – see Stafford, p.144.
15. S975 – probably authentic.
16. Lawson, p.113.
17. Peterborough manuscript (E).
18. *The Chronicle of Henry of Huntingdon.*

CHAPTER TEN

1. The fragment of an early-eleventh-century frieze was found during excavations of Winchester by Martin Biddle in the 1960s. This is thought to have been part of a narrative sequence illustrating the Volsunga saga and dating from Cnut's reign. It is now in Winchester's City Museum.
2. *Anglo-Saxon Chronicles* Worcester manuscript (D).
3. *Chronicon ex Chronicis.*
4. Peterborough manuscript (E).
5. Keynes introduction to 1995 reprint of *Encomium Emmae Reginae.*
6. *Gesta Regum Anglorum.*
7. Stafford, p.240.
8. Barlow, *The Godwins* (London, 2002).
9. Keynes introduction to 1995 reprint of *Encomium Emmae Reginae.*
10. According to William of Jumièges in *Gesta Normannorum Ducum.*
11. Florence of Worcester (*Chronicon ex Chronicis*). William of Jumièges (*Gesta Normannorum Ducum*), however, maintains that on landing Edward was almost immediately confronted by a hostile force, that he triumphed but then returned to his ships and sailed back to Normandy.

CHAPTER ELEVEN

1. The author of *Encomium Emmae Reginae* claims that Alfred arrived with just a few men. However, William of Jumièges (*Gesta Normannorum Ducum*) claims that he was accompanied by a very large military force.
2. William of Jumièges (ibid.) maintains Alfred crossed from Wisant to Dover. But in *Encomium Emmae Reginae* he does not reach his proposed landing site because of enemy troops who have gathered there.
3. Details between Alfred's arrival in England and his interception by Godwine are not given. The following passages are the most likely course of events.
4. See ch. 10 note 11 with regard to Edward's ostensible visit to England.
5. It is conceivable that Alfred could have dragged some of his ships overland and then sailed up inland rivers to Guildford. Lying on the Wey, the town would have had reasonable river access. William of Malmesbury (*Gesta Regum Anglorum*), however, claims that Alfred was taken to Gillingham in Kent.
6. The details about the division of Alfred and his men, and the subsequent executions are given in *Encomium Emmae Reginae*, which also offers the story that Alfred was blinded at Ely.
7. Abingdon manuscript (C) and Worcester manuscript (D).
8. According to Florence of Worcester (*Chronicon ex Chronicis*).
9. Abingdon manuscript (C).
10. S1467.
11. Abingdon manuscript (C).
12. *Chronicon ex Chronicis.*

CHAPTER TWELVE

1. The monk might have been writing on vellum, but given that this was the first draft of a manuscript it seem likely that the cheaper alternative of parchment was used.
2. Only one eleventh-century manuscript of Emma's book survives. However, three much later copies also exist: a seventeenth-century manuscript in the National Library of Wales; a seventeenth/eighteenth-century partial transcription in the British Library; and a sixteenth-century copy in the Bibliothèque Nationale de France.
3. In his introduction to the 1949 publication of *Encomium Emmae Reginae*, Alistair Campbell provides impressive detail about 'The Learning and Latinity of the Encomiast' – included on pp.cv–cxxii of the 1998 reprint.
4. Edited and translated by Campbell, *Encomium Emmae Reginae* (1998 reprint), p.9.
5. *Vita Aedwardi* – or The Life of Edward.
6. For more details of various theories about the purpose of *Encomium Emmae Reginae* see Keynes introduction to the 1998 reprint pp.lxvi–lxxi and Stafford *Queen Emma and Queen Edith* pp.28–40.
7. In *Chronicon ex Chronicis*.
8. See Heslop, *Deluxe Manuscripts*.
9. Peterborough manuscript (E).
10. The Abingdon (C) and Worcester manuscripts of the *Anglo-Saxon Chronicles* provide basic information that Worcestershire was raided because of the death of two housecarls. Florence of Worcester adds the detail that they were killed in the monastery at Worcester.
11. S994 and S997 are believed to be authentic.
12. Abingdon manuscript (C) and Worcester manuscript (D).
13. Winchester manuscript (A).
14. According to the *Oxford Dictionary of Saints*, p.475.
15. Barlow, *Edward the Confessor* (Hale, 1997), pp.55–60.

CHAPTER THIRTEEN

1. The *Anglo-Saxon Chronicles* imply that Emma was completely taken by surprise; however, it is likely that there would have been a small advance party to make preparations for the King's arrival.
2. The 'Godbegot' estate given to Emma in 1012.
3. St Ouen's head was later given to Westminster Abbey, St Augustine's arm to the monastery at Coventry. See Heslop *Deluxe Manuscripts*.
4. S1001 and S1006 respectively, both deemed authentic.
5. *Gesta Regum Anglorum*.
6. Translation of St Augustine, see Stafford *Queen Emma and Queen Edith*, p.249.
7. Abingdon manuscript (C).
8. This was part of a deal: Cnut agreed to the translation of St Mildreth to

Canterbury once he had safely returned from Rome. On the return leg of his trip his ship floundered and St Mildreth apparently saved the day. Goscelin also ascribes this miracle to St Augustine. See Lawson, p.102.

9. *Annals of Winchester.*

10. Richard confuses Emma's disgrace with the later banishment of her daughter-in-law Edith, who was sent away to the convent at Wherwell.

11. Aelfwine was in office 1032–47 (died August 1047).

12. Stafford cites the case of the French Queen Emma who was accused of an adulterous liaison with the Bishop of Laon, Adalbero, in the 980s. See *Queen Emma and Queen Edith*, p.250.

13. Robert was not, in fact, appointed either Bishop of London or Archbishop of Canterbury until after Emma's fall: he was in office in London from 1044–51 and subsequently at Canterbury between March 1051 and September 1052, when he was expelled.

14. S1000 of dubious authenticity but probably based on an earlier charter of the 1040s.

15. *Flowers of History.*

16. *Vita Aedwardi.*

17. S1011. The actual manuscript is spurious but the document is thought to have been based on a charter drawn up in 1045.

18. Peterborough manuscript (E).

19. Worcester manuscript (D).

20. In *Chronicon ex Chronicis* Florence of Worcester maintains that Godwine's eldest son Swein did not return. The Abingdon manuscript (C) of the *Anglo-Saxon Chronicles* states that he died that year on pilgrimage to Jerusalem.

EPILOGUE

1. S925.

2. See *Anglo-Saxon Writs* in which 111 is a confirmation by Edward the Confessor, made after his mother's death, of her bequest to the Old Minster. The part relating to her Winchester property is considered authentic, but the additional clause relating to Hayling Island is suspect.

3. Ibid.

4. In his *History of the Archbishops of Hamburg–Bremen.*

5. In *Gesta Gvillelmi.*

6. In *Gesta Regum Anglorum.*

7. Abingdon manuscript (C).

8. *The Life of King Edward who rests at Westminster.*

9. This appears in both the Abingdon manuscript (C) and the Worcester manuscript (D).

10. Winchester manuscript (A).

11. *Anglo-Saxon Chronicles*, Abingdon manuscript (C) and Worcester manuscript (D).

12. This appears in *De Obitu Willelmi* by an anonymous monk of Caen.

Select Bibliography

PRIMARY SOURCES

Encomium Emmae Reginae, edited by Alistair Campbell with a supplementary introduction by Simon Keynes (Cambridge: Cambridge University Press, 1998).

The *Anglo-Saxon Chronicles*, translated and edited by Michael Swanton (London: J. M. Dent, a division of the Orion Publishing Group, 2001).

Councils & Synods 871–1204, edited by D. Whitelock, M. Brett and C. N. L. Brooke (Oxford: Clarendon, 1981):

Early-eleventh century. A tract on the terms of betrothal (Be Wifmannes Bedweddunge). Aelfric's pastoral letter for Wulfsige III, Bishop of Sherborne c.995.

King Aethelred's Laws Issued at King's Enham c.1008.

1009 The Edict when the Great Army came to England.

1019 Letter from King Cnut to the People of England.

Writ from Wulfstan, Archbishop of York, to King Cnut and Queen Aelfgifu.

Selection from the laws of Cnut.

Anglo-Saxon Charters, edited by A. J. Robertson (Cambridge: Cambridge University Press, 1939).

Anglo-Saxon Writs, F. E. Harmer (Manchester: Manchester University Press, 1952).

Charters of St Augustine's Abbey, Canterbury and Minster in Thanet, edited by S. E. Kelly (Oxford: OUP, 1995).

English Historical Documents I, edited by Dorothy Whitelock (Routledge: London, 1979):

Letter of Pope John XV to all the faithful, concerning the reconciliation of Ethelred, King of England, and Richard, Duke of Normandy (991).

Letter of Fulbert, Bishop of Chartres, to King Cnut.

Renewal by King Ethelred for the monastery of St Frieswide, Oxford, of a privilege for their lands at Winchendon, Buckinghamshire and Whitehill, Cowley and Cutslow, Oxfordshire after their church and deeds had been burnt down during the massacre of the Danes (7 December 1004).

SECONDARY SOURCES

Histories – English

Bede's Ecclesiastical History of the English People, edited by Bertram Colgrave and P. A. B. Mynors (Oxford OUP, 1969).

The Chronicle of Henry of Huntingdon. The history of England, from the Invasion of Julius Caesar to the accession of Henry II, translated and edited by Thomas Forester, London 1853.

Eadmer's History of Recent Events in England (Historia Novorum in Anglia), translated by Geoffrey Bosanquet (London: Cresset, 1964).

The Chronicle of John of Worcester, edited by R. R. Darlington and P. McGurk. Translated by Jennifer Bray and P. McGurk (Oxford: Clarendon, 1995).

The History of the English Kings (Gesta Regum Anglorum), William of Malmesbury, edited and translated by R. A. B. Mynors, R. M. Thomson and M. Winterbottom (Oxford: Oxford Medieval Texts, 1998).

Roger of Wendover's Flowers of History: The History of England from the descent of the Saxons to AD1235, translated by J. A. Giles, London 1849.

The Life of King Edward who rests at Westminster, attributed to a monk of Saint-

Bertin, edited and translated by Frank Barlow (Oxford: Clarendon, 1992).

'Annales Monasterii de Wintonia', in *Annales Monastici Vol. II*, attributed to Richard of Devizes (London: Rolls Series, 1865).

Aelfric's Lives of Saints Book I, edited by Walter W. Skeat, Early English Text Society 1890.

The Chronicle attributed to John of Wallingford, edited by R. Vaughan, Camden Miscellany XXI (Camden: 1958).

Domesday Book – A Complete Translation (Alecto Historical Editions) (London: Penguin, 2003).

Histories – Norman

L'Estorie des Engleis by Geoffrey Gaimar, edited and translated by Sir Thomas Duffus Hardy and Charles Trice Martin, Chronicles & Memorials of Great Britain and Ireland 1889.

Gesta Normannorum Ducum of William Jumièges, Orderic Vitalis and Robert of Torigni, edited and translated by Elisabeth M. M. C. van Houts (Oxford: Clarendon, 1992).

The Ecclesiastical History of Orderic Vitalis, edited and translated by Marjorie C. Hibnall (Oxford: Clarendon, 1968).

William of Poitier's Gesta Guillelmi – The Deeds of William, edited and translated by R.H.C. Davis and Marjorie Chibnall (Oxford: Clarendon Press, 1998).

History of the Normans (Gesta Normannorum), Dudo of St Quentin, translated by Eric Christiansen (Suffolk: Boydell, 1988).

Rodulfus Glaber (first half of the eleventh century). Text and translation: *Rodulfi Glabri Historiarum Libri Quinque*, edited by J. France (Oxford: Clarendon, 1989).

De Obitu Willelmi by an anonymous monk of Caen. See English Historical Documents II 1042–1189, edited by D. C. Douglas and G. W. Greenaway, 2nd ed. (Routledge: London, 1981).

Histories – Scandinavian and German

History of the Archbishops of Hamburg–Bremen, Adam of Bremen, translated with an introduction and notes by Francis J. Tschan. 2002 edition updated by Timothy Reuter (Columbia: Columbia University Press, 2002).

Chronicle of Thietmar of Merseburg, English Historical Documents I, Dorothy Whitelock, London 1979.

'Saint Olaf's saga'. In *Heimskringla, History of the Kings of Norway*, by Snorri Sturluson. Translated by Lee M. Hollander, Texas 1964.

Jómsvíkinga Saga: the Saga of the Jomsvikings, edited and translated by N. F. Blake (1962).

SECONDARY SOURCES – OTHER

Alexander, Michael, trans., 'Old English Riddles', from the *Exeter Book* (London: Anvil Press, 1980).

Amt Emilie, ed., *Women's Lives in Medieval Europe* (Oxford: Routledge, 1993).

Banham, D., *Monasteriales Indicia: The Anglo-Saxon Monastic Sign Language* (Norfolk: Anglo-Saxon Books, 1991).

Barlow, F., *The Norman Conquest and Beyond* (London: Hambledon, 1983).

—*The Godwins* (London: Pearson Education, 2002).

—*Edward the Confessor* (Yale: Yale University Press, 1997).

Brooke, C., *Europe in the Central Middle Ages, 962–1154* (London: Longmans, 1964).

Brooks, N., *The Early History of the Church of Canterbury* (Leicester: Leicester University Press, 1984).

Brown, M., *Anglo-Saxon Manuscripts* (London: British Library, 1991).

Campbell, J., ed., *The Anglo-Saxons* (London: Penguin, 1991).

Campbell, J., *Some Agents and Agencies of the Late Anglo-Saxon State in Domesday Studies*: Papers read at the Novocentenary Conference of the Royal Historical Society and the Institute of British Geographers, Winchester 1986, edited by J. C. Holt (Suffolk: Boydell, 1987).

Cockayne, Oswald (Revd), ed., *Leechdoms, Wortcunning and Starcraft of Early England* (London: Rolls Series, 1864).

Crawford, S., *Childhood in Anglo-Saxon England* (Stroud: Sutton, 1999).

Dronke, P., *Poetic Individuality in the Middle Ages: New Departures in Poetry 1000–1150* (London: University of London Committee for Medieval Studies, 1986).

Farmer, D. H., *Oxford Dictionary of Saints* (Oxford: OUP, 1978).

Fell, C., *Women in Anglo-Saxon England* (London: British Museum, 1984).

Finberg, H. R. R., *The Formation of England 550–1042* (London: Granada, 1974).

Fletcher, R., *Bloodfeud, Murder and Revenge in Anglo-Saxon England* (London: Allen Lane, 2002).

Gordon, R. K., edited and translated, *Anglo-Saxon Poetry* (London: J. M. Dent, a division of the Orion Publishing Group, 1954).

Griffiths, B., *Aspects of Anglo-Saxon Magic* (Norfolk: Anglo-Saxon Books, 1996).

Hadley, D. M., *The Northern Danelaw* (Leicester: Leicester University Press, 2000).

Hagen, A., *A Handbook of Anglo-Saxon Food, Processing and Consumption* (Norfolk: Anglo-Saxon Books, 1992).

—*A Second Handbook of Anglo-Saxon Food and Drink, Production and Distribution* (Norfolk: Anglo-Saxon Books, 1995).

Heaney, S., trans., *Beowulf* (London: Faber & Faber, 1999).

Heslop, T. A., *The production of de luxe manuscripts and the patronage of King Cnut and Queen Emma*, Anglo-Saxon England 19 (Cambridge: Cambridge University Press, 1990).

Hill, D., *An Atlas of Anglo-Saxon England* (Oxford: Blackwell, 1981).

Hollis S., *Anglo-Saxon Women and the Church* (Suffolk: Boydell, 1992).

Hooper, N., 'The Housecarls in England in the Eleventh Century' in *Anglo Norman Studies VII* (Suffolk: Boydell Press, 1985).

John, E., *The Encomium Emmae Reginae: A Riddle and a Solution* (Manchester: The John Rylands University Library of Manchester Vol. 63, Autumn 1980).

Jones, G., *A History of the Vikings* (Oxford: OUP, 1968).

Kanner, B., ed., 'The Women of England from Anglo-Saxon times to the present', Mansell 1980 (An Introduction to Women in Anglo-Saxon Society by Sheila C. Dietrich; Land charters and the legal position of Anglo-Saxon women by Marc A. Meyer).

Keen, L., ed., *Studies in the Early History of Shaftesbury Abbey*, (Dorset County Council 1999).

Keynes, S., 'The Aethlings in Normandy' in *Anglo Norman Studies*, Vol. 13, (Suffolk: Boydell, 1991, pp.173–205).

—'Anglo-Saxon Kingship' (Kent: *History Today*, Jan. 1985, Vol. 35).

—*The Diplomas of King Aethelred the Unready 978–1016* (Cambridge: Cambridge University Press, 1980).

Keynes, Simon and Lapidge Michael, *Asser's Life of King Alfred and other contemporary sources*. Translated with an introduction and notes (London: Penguin, 1983).

Lacey, R., and Danziger D., *The Year 1000* (London: Abacus, 1999).

Lapidge, Michael, Blair, John, Keynes, Simon and Scragg, Donald eds., *The Blackwell Encyclopaedia of Anglo-Saxon England* (Oxford: Blackwell, 2001).

Larson, L. M., 'The king's household before the Norman Conquest' (Wisconsin: Bulletin of the University of Wisconsin, 1902).

Lavelle, R., *Aethelred II, King of the English 978–1016* (Stroud: Tempus, 2002).

Lawson, M. K., *Cnut: The Danes in England in the Early Eleventh Century* (London: Longman, 1995).

Loyn, H. R., *The Vikings in Britain* (London: Batsford, 1977).

—*The Governance of Anglo-Saxon England 500–1087* (London: Edward Arnold, 1985).

McDonough, C. J. ed., *Warner of Rouen* (PIMS, 1995).

Nightingale P., 'The Ora, the Mark, and the Mancus: Weight-Standards and the Coinage in Eleventh-Century England', *Numismatic Chronicle 144*, 1984.

Owen-Crocker Gale, R., *Dress in Anglo-Saxon England* (Manchester: Manchester University Press, 1986).

Page, R. I., *Life in Anglo-Saxon England* (London: Batsford, 1970).

Pelteret, D. A. E., *Slavery in Early Mediaeval England* (Suffolk: Boydell, 1995).

Petersson, H. B. A., *Anglo-Saxon Currency: King Edgar's Reform to the Norman Conquest*, Lund 1969.

Richard, J. D., *Viking Age England* (London: Batsford/English Heritage, 1991).

Rollason, D., *Saints and Relics in Anglo-Saxon England* (London: Blackwell, 1989).

—*The Mildrith Legend, A Study in Early Medieval Hagiography in England* (Leicester: Leicester University Press, 1982).

Rosedahl, E., trans. Margeson, Susan M. and William, Kirsten, *The Vikings* (London: Penguin, 1998).

Sawyer, P., ed. *Anglo-Saxon Charters: An annotated list and bibliography* (London: London Royal Historical Society, 1968).

Searle, E., 'Emma the Conqueror' in *Studies in Medieval History* ed., Harper-Bill, C. (Suffolk: Boydell, 1989).

—*Predatory Kinship and the Creation of Norman Power 840–1066* (California: University of California Press, 1988).

Sox, D., *Relics and Shrines* (Sydney: George Allen & Unwin, 1985).

Stafford, P., *Queens, Concubines and Dowagers: the King's Wife in the Early Middle Ages:* (Athens GA, 1983).

—*Queen Emma and Queen Edith. Queenship and Women's Power in Eleventh-Century England* (Oxford: Blackwell, 1997).

—'The Portrayal of Royal Women in England, Mid-Tenth to Mid-Twelfth Centuries', in *Medieval Queenship*, ed. Parsons, J. C. (London: Sutton, 1994).

Stenton, Sir F., *Anglo-Saxon England* (Oxford: OUP, 1998).

Swanton M., ed. and trans., *Anglo-Saxon Prose* (London: J. M. Dent, a division of the Orion Publishing Group, 1993).

van Houts, E., *Countess Gunnor of Normandy*, Collegium Medievale 12, 1999.

Werner, A., ed. *London Bodies: The Changing Shape of Londoners from Prehistoric Times to the Present Day* (London: Museum of London, 1998).

Whitelock, D., *The Beginnings of English Society* (London: Penguin, 1952).

Wilson, D. M., *The Bayeux Tapestry* (London: Thames & Hudson, 1985).

Yorke, B., *Kings and Kingdoms of Early Anglo-Saxon England* (London: Seaby, 1990).

WEBSITES

http://www.ucalgary.ca/UofC/eduweb
Look under Eng1401 for courses and texts in Anglo-Saxon.

http://www.trin.cam.ac.uk/sdk13/chartwww/eSawyer.99/eSawyer2.html
Online version of the revised edition of Sawyer's Anglo-Saxon Charters.

http://psalter.library.uu.nl/
Illustrations and information on the *Utrecht Psalter.*

http://www.hillside.co.uk/arch/cathedral/nave.html
Canterbury Cathedral archaeological work.

http://www.domesdaybook.net
Domesday Book.

http://www.trin.cam.ac.uk/sdk13
Homepage of Professor S. D. Keynes, for links to other sites about Anglo-Saxon England.

Acknowledgements

The process of immersing myself in eleventh-century England has been by no means a solitary occupation. My very respectful thanks to Dr Debby Banham, whose course in Anglo-Saxon Society at Birkbeck College was an inspiration. I am also extremely grateful to Kevin Blockley for invaluable archaeological insights; Dr Michelle Brown at the British Library for advice on manuscripts; John Clark at the Museum of London for help over early eleventh-century London; and Frances Stradling for her Latin expertise. In addition I owe a big debt of gratitude to the staff at the British Library, the Roskilde Viking Ship Museum and the Copenhagen National Museum. Huge thanks also go to my editor Rosemary Davidson and to Mary Davis and Mary Tomlinson at Bloomsbury, as well as to my agent David Miller. Friends and family have been vital: the book took shape largely due to the support and help of Gina Cowen, Frances Cripwell, Cal Bailey, David Bowen, Peter Durrant, Joanna Head, Mairi Fraser, Kristina Ferris, Sarah Miller, Roger Mills, Roderick O'Brien, Nicholas Palmer, Cleo Paskal, Sarah Spankie, Catherine Stebbings, Jonathan Stebbings and Pol Thasiding. Most of all, Miranda Chalk and Sally Palmer were unstinting with their time, patience and encouragement while reading and commenting on the work as it progressed. I can't thank you both enough.

Index

A NOTE ON THE TYPE

The text of this book is set in Linotype Goudy Old Style. It was designed by Frederic Goudy (1865–1947), an American designer whose types were very popular during his lifetime, and particularly fashionable in the 1940s. He was also a craftsman who cut the metal patterns for his type designs, engraved matrices and cast type.

The design for Goudy Old Style is based on Goudy Roman, with which it shares a 'hand-wrought' appearance and asymmetrical serifs, but unlike Goudy Roman its capitals are modelled on Renaissance lettering.

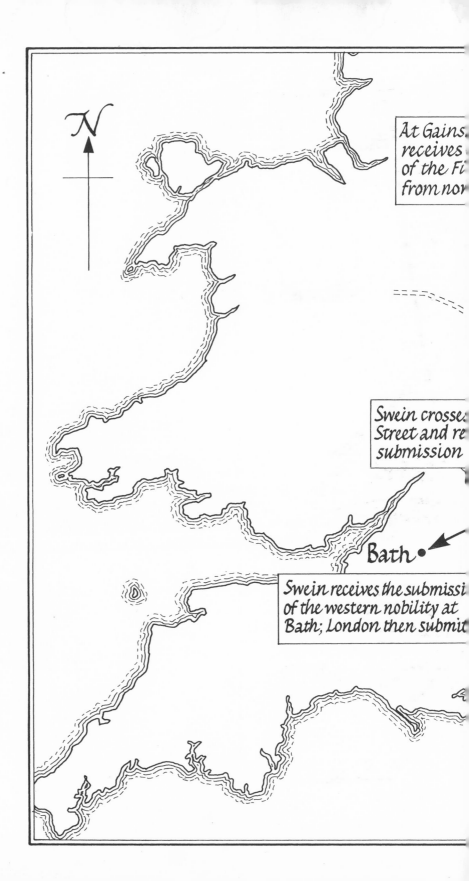

At Gains[...]
receives [...]
of the Fi[...]
from nor[...]

Swein crosse[...]
Street and re[...]
submission [...]

Swein receives the submissi[...]
of the western nobility at
Bath; London then submit[...]

Bath •